Feminist Scholarship

Feminist Scholarship

Kindling in the Groves of Academe

Ellen Carol DuBois
Gail Paradise Kelly
Elizabeth Lapovsky Kennedy
Carolyn W. Korsmeyer
Lillian S. Robinson

University of Illinois Press

Urbana and Chicago

Illini Books edition, 1987

© 1985 by the Board of Trustees of the University of Illinois
Manufactured in the United States of America
P 5 4 3 2

This book is printed on acid-free paper.

Library of Congress Cataloging in Publication Data

Main entry under title:

Feminist scholarship.
  Bibliography: p.
  Includes index.
    1. Women's studies—United States. 2. Inter-
disciplinary approach to knowledge. 3. Interdisciplinary
approach in education. I. DuBois, Ellen Carol,
1947–
HQ1181.U5F46 1985   305.4'07'073   84-2589
ISBN 0-252-01464-2 (alk. paper)

Contents

Preface

The project that was to become this book began one afternoon in 1977 at a symposium at the State University of New York at Buffalo entitled "Feminism: Its Impact on the Disciplines." We participants were five feminist scholars, at that time all faculty members at the University, and, although we were not all attached to Buffalo's Women's Studies College, we had cooperated for several years to build that program. By the mid-1970s academic scholarship on women was no longer an experimental endeavor, we reasoned, and it was time to begin assessing the results of several years of feminist research.

Feminist scholarship was and is usually surveyed by asking what we have learned about women from the various academic fields: history, psychology, anthropology, and so on—important questions that must remain central as our understanding of women's lives develops. In addition to these issues we were interested in the converse: what can we learn from scholarship on women about the scholarly disciplines? Have they altered in any important ways in response to the challenges mounted by the new scholarship on women? In our symposium we posed this question, and all of us spoke briefly about our fields: history, philosophy, literature, anthropology, and education. The audience was receptive, and we decided to pursue the topic in an extended fashion by writing a book.

The key decision we made was to write the book jointly rather than assign each of us to write a discrete section on her own field. One of the striking features of feminist research is the commitment of scholars from different disciplines to bring their work together into a body of research that addresses the complex reality of women's experience and situation, and we wanted our book to reflect this interdisciplinary goal and to investigate the degree to which it has been achieved. In addition, we were interested in comparing, contrasting, and juxtaposing the research on women that arises from different disciplines to get a sense of common – and conflicting – intellectual developments. To do this, we had to take on the difficult task of writing the book together, learning to cross the surprisingly deep chasms that separate our disciplines. This attempt led us to a new respect for the structure and the tenacity of the disciplinary divisions, as well as to an appreciation of the integrative and interdisciplinary impulse of women's studies. As our work progressed, we became more and more interested in this dual character of feminist scholarship – its simultaneous formation out of disciplinary frameworks and out of political, transdisciplinary interests in the issues of women's liberation. Attention to this phenomenon and its multiple varieties is a continuous theme in our book.

Our intellectual decision about the appropriate format for the book committed us to working collectively, a goal and value frequently expressed by the feminist movement. It must be admitted that we did not envision the full implications of such a process at the beginning, and the experience of writing collectively over the past years has dramatized for us certain aspects of the usual conduct of scholarship. Scholarship is ordinarily an individualized endeavor, especially in the fields treated here. The academic frameworks for recognition, reward, and promotion presuppose this, but, even more important, so do our own habits of thought and work. The contradiction between the tradition of individual scholarship and our working together was frequently highlighted by colleagues who would remark (with sarcasm and amazement) that we all still talk to one another after working on the book for more than five years – as if this itself were the most significant of our accomplishments.

For all of us the most exciting part of writing was the early period of discussion, which explored and developed a conceptual framework that would contain and reveal the feminist scholarship of our different fields. Our material was at first tantalizingly resistant to synthesis, and our grasp of the potential of feminist scholarship has been indelibly shaped by the unraveling of disagreements that stemmed from our different disciplinary orientations and ideological perspectives. Our debates were often painful, and they certainly rarely conformed to the simplified notion of sisterhood, which emphasizes comfort and support over debate and disagreement. The book took an unexpectedly long time from its inception to publication. We suspect that the process of collectivity is partly responsible for this. All drafting and re-drafting required meetings and discussion and circulation of texts, in addition to time spent in research and writing. Our method of writing attempted to take into account the vitality of our individual contributions as well as the need to create a text which went beyond those. After initial discussion of a chapter, one or two people were assigned to draft it, after receiving contributions from everyone. Redrafts were done in the same way and were rotated, so that all chapters were drafted and redrafted by at least three people, often more. The end result is a book in which all of us can recognize some of our ideas or our contribution to the development of ideas, but the individual voices have been submerged into the collective. The lack of experience with assessing or appreciating this kind of scholarship no doubt contributes to a certain residual discomfort with the process, even though collectivity was our acknowledged goal.

However, the greatest difficulty we faced was practical: our different work schedules. Jobs, grants, leaves of absence, commitments to other projects found us with different writing priorities, to say nothing of finding us in different parts of the world when work on this book needed to proceed. A project this long in the making is rarely accomplished through the expenditure of wholly equal energies. In our case Kennedy and Korsmeyer were the two who made this book a priority in their professional lives over the years, providing the conditions—the vision of the whole, continuity, attention to detail—that allowed us to finish the project. For a time we toyed with the idea of acknowledging them as "primary authors"; however, the book itself reflects a combination and distillation of all five sets of ideas, of conceptual frameworks, and of prose. The alphabetical listing, therefore, was chosen as the most appropriate and accurate way to attribute authorship.

This book has been a long time in the making—we began it in 1977—and many people have supported and helped us in the process. We want to thank Mary Ballou, Margaret Strobel, Ellen Ross, Mary Vetterling-Braggin, Jean Anyon, and Iris Young for their helpful comments on the manuscript. Carolyn Elliott, Angela Keil, Zoe Zacharek, and Lois Weis also read and commented on various sections of this material. Versions of this work have been presented to several groups, the members of which also contributed their observations and criticisms: the Buffalo Women's Scholars Group and the National Women's Studies Association, in particular. We would also like to thank Sherri Darrow, Robert Dischner, MaryAnne Dorgan, Randy Hollister, Marge Cramer and Terry Blasko for research assistance, and members of the Society for Women in Philosophy for making their materials available. The State University of New York at Buffalo Graduate School funded a portion of this project, and the Department of Social, Historical and Philosophical Foundations of Education, especially its chair, Philip Altbach, were extremely generous with its resources. We want to thank Eileen Raines for typing the manuscript and Dian Jensen for other technical services. Finally, we are grateful to our editors at the University of Illinois Press, Carole S. Appel and Susan L. Patterson, for their support and help.

On a more personal level, we are grateful to David, David, Bobbi, and David for their support and love during the long and sometimes trying years of this project. We also want to thank five children, Jennifer, Elizabeth, Isak, Christopher, and Jonathan.

Introduction

The subject of this book is feminist scholarship and its development within and outside the academic disciplines. Our goal is to understand how feminist scholarship both challenges and is shaped by disciplinary inquiry; to present its emergence as a body of research in its own right; to assess its promise for influencing the future conduct of academic research; and finally to explore the implications of all of this for the nature of feminist scholarship.

The work we explore in this book is relatively new, having its source in the general ferment of the 1960s and early 1970s. That period was one of social and political change in the United States and in many other parts of the world. The continuing movement for civil rights among black Americans, protest against the war in Southeast Asia, the women's liberation movement, and somewhat later the gay movement were principal events that called into question the authority and many of the accepted values of American social institutions. Since a significant segment of the participants in these movements were students and faculty at universities, the educational establishment itself was especially subject to scrutiny and challenge, and the political excitement that marked American campuses in that period had an impact on the direction and methods of intellectual inquiry.[1] There

---

1. For some discussion of the role of scholars and their disciplines in the Vietnam era, see Noam Chomsky, *American Power and the New Mandarins* (New York: Pantheon–Random House, 1969) and the essays in *The Dissenting Academy*, ed. Theodore Roszak (New York: Pantheon–Random House, 1968). Within the disciplines, dissenting research was published in collections like those in Pantheon's series of "anti-texts," e.g.: *Towards a New Past*, ed. Barton J. Bernstein (New York: Pantheon–Random House, 1968); *Reinventing Anthropology*, ed. Dell Hymes (New York: Pantheon–Random House, 1969); and *The Politics of Literature*, ed. Louis Kampf and Paul Lauter (New York: Pantheon–Random House, 1972).

1

were charges that scientific and technological research ultimately served the military rather than the progress of human knowledge, and scholarship in the social sciences and humanities was criticized for its neglect of urgent social issues, the working class, minority groups, and—of most importance for our present study—women.

The criticisms of the American university that emerged from the feminist movement of the late 1960s and 1970s were directed at both the structure of educational institutions and the conduct and content of scholarly research. University administrations and faculties, and in some fields student bodies as well, were increasingly recognized as places that excluded women, and as a part of their struggle for equal opportunity women demanded an end to overt and covert discriminatory practices. When it came to the research conducted within the academy, the assessments and challenges of feminists became more complex, varying with the subjects and methods of each field. It was a uniform complaint, however, that as a subject for research women were being neglected, overlooked, or distorted by existing scholarship. From this criticism flowed a body of new research about, and mostly by, women in a wide range of disciplines. From this criticism also arose a struggle to restructure the academic establishment in ways that more readily permitted the study of women. Women's studies programs were started in many colleges and universities, separate programs where the distorting lenses of traditional study might be corrected.

Thus feminist scholarship was born of a social movement and received into the preestablished structure of the academic disciplines. To capture the essential duality of feminist scholarship—that it is rooted simultaneously in the disciplinary structures of contemporary intellectual inquiry and in a social movement—is one of the purposes of this book. The feminist movement raises basic questions about women and society that transcend the disciplines and deeply affect feminist scholars. But given the organization of knowledge in the present-day university, the majority of professionally trained scholars proceed from the methods and assumptions of a particular discipline. This double root is the source of the content and the form of feminist scholarship, of its unity, and of its diversity, and even disparateness. In this study we explore a series of relationships that we believe obtain between "the academy" and "feminist scholarship": that between the goals of feminist scholars to formulate a complete body of research about women and the methodological perspectives of each discipline; between scholarship on women guided by disciplinary and nondisciplinary political frameworks; and

2

between the writings of academic and nonacademic feminists. These relationships are complex and often fraught with tension, but they are an essential part of the creation and development of feminist scholarship.

Some of this tension derives from the peculiar position of women in the university. Many feminist academics are also active in the women's movement and conceive of their scholarship as a part of that activity. Thus a source of mutual antagonism is the negative stance that institutions of higher education tend to take toward research that candidly serves political or social ends. That most academic fields have been and still remain almost entirely controlled by men is related to this tension. As the women's liberation movement arose and consciousness of women's secondary status in society spread, many women in the academy became acutely aware that they constituted a small minority in their professions and that, by and large, they occupied positions of lesser rank and influence than their male colleagues. With the growing recognition that inequality between the sexes was both unjust and remediable, women academics—faculty members, graduate students, and those without institutional affiliation—began to group together to share experiences, combat their isolation, and remedy their professional situations.[2] Feminist subgroups within national academic organizations were formed to exert pressure on governing boards, convention program committees, and the like to include more women in the activities sponsored within the professions. In the process, these feminist groups fostered critical perspectives on the scholarship conducted within their disciplines and became places from which challenges to the treatment of women as subjects for research were launched.[3] Thus within particular academic professions there arose dialogue, and often heated debate, over the character of disciplinary inquiry.

2. One of the first groups organized within a discipline was conceived at the annual meeting of the Modern Language Association in 1968, when a resolution was passed calling for the establishment of a Commission on the Status of Women in the Profession. Similar groups were established in the American Philosophical Association, the American Historical Association, the American Anthropological Association, and the American Educational Research Association. These special interest groups have engaged in such activities as surveying their professions for discriminatory practices, providing literature and practical support for combating such discrimination, nominating women for important committees or offices within the national organizations, placing women on panels at meetings, and lobbying for childcare facilities at conventions.

3. Some of these organizations, such as the Society for Women in Philosophy and the Coordinating Committee for Women in the Historical Profession, have established a network

However, perhaps the most complex source of tension between feminist scholarship and the academy stems from feminist scholarship itself, particularly that branch associated with "women's studies." In the United States at least, the creation of women's studies programs was an important aspect of the women's liberation movement. Many feminists active in women's liberation in the late 1960s were also active in the student movements, and the drive toward creating women's studies programs was primarily student led. The critical perspective that would later lead scholars to challenge disciplinary research methods began in criticism and rejection of the standard classroom curriculum, where the neglect of women was suddenly obvious.

Of most significance as background for our study is the conception of an alternative way to learn about women that attended the move to establish women's studies programs. In most instances their creation involved a criticism of the traditional organization of knowledge by discipline. No discipline treated women adequately, it was argued, and, further, women's lives and all that affects them could not be contained within the confines of any single field. Thus women's studies programs were from the outset conceived as "interdisciplinary," as programs for study where the boundaries that separate disciplines might be broken down, fostering a broader and more complete approach to the understanding of women.[4] Similar thinking contributed to the later formation of a number of journals devoted expressly to

---

of regional suborganizations as well. The meetings of these groups provide an ongoing forum for the development of feminist thinking.

The Berkshire Conference of Women Historians, begun over fifty years ago by women historians who felt excluded from the "Gentlemen's Profession," has also become very important to feminist scholars. Before the 1970s the conference provided an opportunity for women historians to meet together and to form what in today's parlance are called "networks," but until recently it paid no particular attention to the historical study of women. In 1973 the organization arranged what was to be a "one-shot" conference on women's history. The response was so great that the Berkshire Conference of Women's History has become a regular feature of the organization and its most important service to academia. By 1981, when the fifth conference was held, it was the third largest regularly scheduled gathering of the historical profession in the United States.

4. As early as 1973 there were already approximately 5,000 courses on women offered in American institutions of higher education. No one has undertaken a formal count since then, but Florence Howe estimates that the number of courses on women taught in 1980 exceeded 20,000 nationally. And as of 1980 there were about 350 women's studies programs at colleges and universities in the United States. See Florence Howe, "Women and the Power of Education," *American Association for Higher Education Bulletin* 33 (1981), 13–14.

publishing work on women. Multidisciplinary journals such as *Signs, Feminist Studies*, and *Women's Studies* have been milestones in the development of feminist scholarship.[5] In many cases this interdisciplinary conception was an implicit criticism of the whole structure of higher education itself. The women's movement gave rise to many of the landmark works of feminist scholarship, and studies produced outside the academy continue to be an important source of feminist research. Such work challenges the academy and its pretense to monopoly over scholarly endeavors.

Yet, while women's studies has often seen itself in opposition to the academic establishment and to the organization of knowledge by discipline, it also builds upon those disciplines, being as much shaped by them as by the transdisciplinary political interests of feminism. Its dual nature is reflected in the offerings of women's studies programs, which typically include both courses from single disciplines and courses that assume a topical, interdisciplinary approach. Similarly, women's studies journals publish research from disciplinary as well as interdisciplinary perspectives.

The existence of programs for the study of women and journals for the publication of such research is evidence of some of the changes within the academy wrought by the feminist movement. But has the general conduct of disciplinary scholarship itself similarly changed? The answer to this question is of far-reaching importance but considerably less easy to detect. Comprehending the significance of feminist scholarship, however, requires understanding not only the development of that research but also its impact for the disciplines that contribute to its growth. Therefore, the latter part of this study investigates the response of the disciplines to the rise of feminist research.

In this book we approach our subject from a perspective that tries to balance the double, often conflicting impetus behind feminist scholarship. On the one hand, our task is ambitious in that we try to explore the duality of feminist scholarship, and as such we present it both as disciplinary

---

5. In addition to multidisciplinary journals such as these—and *Frontiers, Women's Studies International Quarterly*, and *Sinister Wisdom*—there are also new journals for the study of women within disciplines including: *Psychology of Women, Women in History, Tulsa Studies in Women's Literature, Women and Literature*, and the recently founded philosophy journal, *Hypatia*.

There are also national multi-disciplinary organizations. The most comprehensive, the National Women's Studies Association, was founded in 1977. Since then its national meetings have drawn between 1,000 and 2,000 participants who are active both in women's studies and in particular disciplines.

research and as a body of scholarship that arises in response to a new set of questions. On the other hand, this book is modest in attempt, making no claims to new research or theory. Our innovation is in the stance we take: comparing feminist scholarship as it arises within five representative disciplines and exploring the unifiable feminist work that clusters around subjects that arise out of the concerns of the women's liberation movement. Our joint presentation of disciplinary research and of the integration of scholarship framed by feminist political concepts distinguishes this book from others, for most books that attempt to survey feminist scholarship do so discipline by discipline without attempting analysis or comparison within the whole.[6] We believe that the view from any one discipline cannot capture the dual nature of feminist scholarship, and indeed that a series of such views suggests a unity of research focus and method that is misleading. This is a point that is amplified in the concluding chapter.

To conduct this study we examine the ways that scholarship arising out of the concerns of the women's liberation movement developed in five distinct disciplinary settings: anthropology, education, history, literature, and philosophy. These five, of course, do not begin to cover the range of disciplines that now house a significant body of scholarship on women. But they do afford sufficient diversity to permit a representative view of how feminist perspectives develop within disciplines and of areas where women's scholarship does and does not permeate disciplinary boundaries. Anthropology comes from the social sciences, as do some of the subfields of education, an umbrella discipline that draws heavily from psychology and sociology. Literature and philosophy represent the humanities. History can be classified as either, sharing some characteristics with the social sciences and others with the humanities. The purviews and methods of these fields also provide variety: the empirical studies of anthropology, education, and history; the textual analysis of literature and philosophy; and the comparative perspectives of anthropology and education. They range from the abstract and theoretical to the applied and practical, the latter being particularly true of the practitioner field of education. And in terms of the

6. See, for example, *The Prism of Sex*, ed. Julia A. Sherman and Evelyn Torton Beck (Madison: University of Wisconsin Press, 1977); *Men's Studies Modified: The Impact of Feminism on the Academic Disciplines*, ed. Dale Spender (Oxford: Pergamon Press, 1981); *A Feminist Perspective in the Academy: The Difference It Makes*, ed. Elizabeth Langland and Walter Gove (Chicago: University of Chicago Press, 1983).

historical development of academic fields, these disciplines range from the oldest—philosophy—to one of the newest—education.

The feminist scholarship we consider here is limited to that produced by scholars in North America, principally in the United States, or by those in other English-speaking countries who have been major influences on U.S. scholars. There are, of course, important international currents in feminist scholarship, some of which we treat here, but there are also distinctive national differences. From the point of view of this book, some of the most important of those differences have to do with the particular institutional contexts in which feminist scholarship in the United States develops. In this country feminist scholarship has developed largely within the universities, linked both to traditional departments and to independent women's studies programs. As we have suggested, the tension between these two locales is one of the aspects of the field that most interests us. Although this book does not pretend to represent the international corpus of new scholarship on women, we hope that the form of our presentation will be useful for the study of other feminist work.

A consideration of the complex roots of feminist scholarship is the context for understanding the nature of feminist scholarship itself, and that is another general goal of this study. The reader will have noticed that we have been using terms such as "feminist research" and "scholarship on women" interchangeably. Clearly the two are not synonymous, for there is work on women that is sexist or even misogynist as well. Nonetheless the looseness of the terminology we adopt is intentional, for we generally found that the concepts guiding feminist work vary so importantly from subject to subject that there is no useful way to use the term in a restricted sense while discussing scholarship as a whole. This conclusion is one that emerges at several points throughout the book, and it is summed up in the final chapter. Rather than postponing the subject entirely, however, let us mention some of the thinking that led us to this inclusive concept of feminist research.

At the outset of our project we were interested in making a distinction between "feminist scholarship"—that is scholarship with a recognizably feminist analytical perspective on the oppression and liberation of women—and work "just on the subject of women." One of our underlying goals was to defend the intellectual integrity of the former, which we believed was often suspect in academia because of its explicitly political character. It was not our concern to engage in the debate on the impossibility of value-free scholarship, a debate that extends far beyond feminist scholarship and has been fully explored by others.[7] However, we believed—we still believe—that the connection to a political movement is the lifeblood of feminist scholarship, not its tragic flaw, and we wanted to demonstrate this by example. Yet when we tried to apply political criteria to scholarship on women, we found it impossible to make the distinction we were seeking. Part of the problem obviously lay in the differences among our disciplines. For instance, definitions that emphasized contemporary political issues, such as equality and abortion rights, were somewhat helpful in distinguishing feminist from nonfeminist work in education and philosophy, but useless in literature. The problem with translating a set of political injunctions into a set of scholarly criteria is that the result is a definition of feminism as an ideal type, in comparison to which almost all scholarship falls short, if only because of limitations of subject matter. Eventually we came to understand that there were many feminist perspectives among scholars, none of which we wished to exclude and that at this stage in the growth of the field, even work "just on women," if it tells us something we did not know before, can be seen as feminist, if that term is broadly conceived.

The problems with feminist versus nonfeminist as a typology for contemporary scholarship on women led us to reconceptualize feminism less as a subcategory of research on women than as the context within which virtually all scholarship on women is currently being developed. An apt illustration of this point is afforded by the field of anthropology, in which there has been a marked increase recently in studies of birthing practices. By and large this research describes social arrangements and attitudes, midwifery practices, and so on without employing any analytical perspective on the role or status of women in society. Lacking this, research on birthing might be classified as work that is "just about women" but not discernibly feminist. However, from a broader point of view it is evident that such descriptive work is accelerated by the explicitly feminist critiques of a

---

7. For a collection of essays on prefeminist criticisms of the idea of value-free scholarship, see *Dissenting Academy*, ed. Roszak. Feminist criticisms of the notion of "objective" scholarship are numerous; see, for instance, Charlotte Bunch, Jane Flax, and Jo Freeman, "Feminism and Education," *Quest* 5 (1979), and Francine D. Blau, "On the Role of Values in Feminist Scholarship," *Signs* 6 (1981).

discipline, which make possible better studies of the lives of women as a result of the challenges they pose to the methodology of a field. Furthermore, one of the principal goals of feminism is a better understanding of women's realities, and the distinctively feminist perspectives that criticize the disciplines for their exclusion of women are complemented by many studies that in isolation—and only in isolation—appear to be work on the subject of women without connection to feminist scholarship.

In fact, the feminist movement has so heightened the political atmosphere surrounding "the woman question" that all recent scholarship on the topic reflects the movement's existence in some way. Indeed, the only categorization that was even marginally useful was the distinction between feminist work, considered in the most inclusive way, and antifeminist work. By antifeminist work we meant the body of scholarship, surprisingly small in comparison to the sentiments it represents, that explicitly sets itself in opposition to the contemporary feminist movement, either by rejecting the notion that women are oppressed (or discriminated against or exploited) or by taking an antifeminist position on a particular issue about which the movement is engaged. Even this scholarship, of course, is profoundly shaped by the questions feminism poses.

This study of feminist scholarship or of the scholarship on women that has grown so remarkably over the last one and one-half decades falls into three distinct parts. Part I, "The View from the Disciplines," takes as its starting point our five fields and examines how feminist perspectives emerged and then developed in each. Chapter 1 considers the way that feminist challenges were first leveled at prevailing disciplinary traditions, and Chapter 2 presents the different ways scholarship in these five fields developed from those challenges. In Part I we consider how work that is recognizably disciplinary is similar to and different from work in other fields; how research traditions have shaped its growth; and how this growth has suggested different analytical and political perspectives on the study of women.

Part II, "Oppression and Liberation: Feminist Questions as Guides for Research," presents work on women from a variety of fields that is unified by the fact that the subjects addressed have their genesis in the concerns of the women's liberation movement and do not readily fall within the purview of any particular discipline. It is this section in particular that explores the integrative goals of feminist scholarship and the surmounting of disciplinary restrictions to extend our knowledge about oppression and the conditions for liberation. Chapter 3 presents research on the dimensions of women's oppression. The concept of oppression is one that comes from the movement without a comfortable home in any of the disciplines, and attention to it has generated provocative and groundbreaking research. Chapter 4 is also organized around a movement concern—how to remedy the oppression of women. It brings disciplinary and interdisciplinary scholarship to bear on discussions of equality, modernization, and socialism, all of which have been the subject of prefeminist research, although with little attention paid to women. Here we suggest the outlines of how much feminist scholarship can contribute to new and fuller perspectives on social change. These new categories of study stemming from the women's movement unify research even when that research is still noticeably disciplinary in methodology. To cast the book's organization in terms of the dual character of feminist scholarship: Part I focuses upon the shape of feminist work imparted by the disciplines of origin; Part II presents its roots in the larger feminist movement and the permeation of disciplinary boundaries through shared research concepts.

The original challenges posed by feminists called into question some of the basic paradigms and assumptions of each intellectual tradition, but have the disciplines responded to these challenges? In Part III, "The Response of the Disciplines," we conduct a study of scholarly journals to see if these established "gatekeepers" of the disciplines have reflected the changes in the larger scholarly world. While this study supplements the discussions of chapters 1 and 2, it also demonstrates the complexities mentioned earlier in formulating a definition of feminist scholarship. By taking a comparative approach to this subject, we demonstrate that working criteria for the measurement of change in scholarship must be carefully formulated in the context of particular disciplines to be usable and informative. This joint approach also permits speculation about the future impact of feminist scholarship.

This discussion clears the way for a summary view of the nature of feminist scholarship, for a cumulative assessment of the growth of this research, and for a critical conclusion about the position of feminist scholarship in the disciplines and the goal of interdisciplinary research. These are the subjects of the Conclusion.

In conducting this project we selected certain questions and topics to pursue and set others aside. For example, our approach to feminist scholarship is wholly limited to the scholarly products themselves, for we do not investigate the writers and their histories, their academic positions, and the implications of their chosen fields of study for their careers. Study of such topics is beyond the scope of our task, though it surely would be interesting. Nor do we claim in any of our discussions to provide an exhaustive review of the relevant scholarship, which would, in any case, be beyond the capacities of any one book. Rather, we have chosen specific examples that we feel highlight the importance of feminist scholarship and provide a useful framework for understanding its development, breadth, and potential.

We hope that this book will be of special interest to a variety of audiences. The presentations of chapters 1 through 4 speak particularly to students in advanced women's studies courses. We hope that the perspective taken throughout the book, the analyses of Chapter 5, and the Conclusion should also be of interest to scholars working on the subject of women in any field. And, finally, we trust that this book will stimulate scholars not yet working on these subjects to begin to incorporate into their own work some of the insights and implications of feminist scholarship.

I

The View from the Disciplines

1

Feminism Arises in the Disciplines

Over the last decade and a half a distinct body of scholarship on women has arisen in almost every academic field. In chapters 1 and 2 we consider the development of this work with reference to five particular disciplines: anthropology, history, literature, philosophy, and education. The first task that faced feminist scholars was the identification of pervasive male bias that was discovered to be deeply imbedded in disciplines, and indeed this still stands as one of their most significant accomplishments. This chapter considers how this common project was carried out in different disciplines and tries to convey a sense of its iconoclasm, enthusiasm, and promise for future scholarship.

By the late 1960s the women's liberation movement was growing rapidly and gaining widespread support as more and more women became aware of their secondary social status and its implications. A newly coined term, "sexism," was suddenly seen as the key to understanding nearly every aspect of women's lives. Employment practices, sexual and family relationships, cultural attitudes and beliefs, patterns of education and training, and the psychological attitudes of women themselves all became illuminated as elements of a social system in which women were considered inferior.

When feminists within academic institutions directed their attention to the scholarship conducted within their fields of study, they found an intellectual mirror of sexism in society: as subjects for scholarly research women were given little attention or ignored altogether and, where they were studied, they were often portrayed in a distorted or stereotyped manner. Moreover, it was discovered, this intellectual reflection of social prejudice was far from inconsequential. It provided continuing ideological support for conditions and policies oppressive to women; certain stereotypes and misapprehensions could even be used to justify women's marginal status in the academic world itself. "In spite of a century of sporadic hue and cry about women's rights and in spite of our rhetoric about the equality of women, women remain a passive majority of second class citizens," pioneer feminist educator Florence Howe wrote in 1969. "Our education is chiefly to blame . . . that education reflects the values of our society . . . generally the purpose of those responsible for the education of women has been to perpetuate that subordinate state."[1]

The first phase that initiated the new scholarship on women thus was the identification of implicit male bias in existing scholarship and the discovery of how it leads to the omission or distortion of the study of women. Such bias might be imbedded in assumptions about what subjects are worthy of study, in methods of data collection, or in the conceptualization of questions guiding research. The efforts to reveal masculine bias warping scholarly inquiry were, at a general level, part of a single, overarching feminist intellectual impulse in which scholars coming out of a variety of different disciplines saw themselves sharing a common goal as a part of the women's movement. Their early critiques of the academy often share a sense of betrayal, reflected in a tone of rage or irony, and a consequent brutal thoroughness in their survey of a discipline's shortcomings.

That this new scholarship on women grew out of an active social movement distinguished it from the noteworthy but scattered studies of women produced in the hiatus between the recent feminist movement and that of the early twentieth century. Women's liberation sparked a new appreciation for previous scholarship on women and brought older studies into new prominence. In fact, several important works on the study of women and gender appeared in anthropology from the 1930s through the 1950s, the best known being Margaret Mead's *Sex and Temperament in Three Primitive Societies* (1935) and *Male and Female* (1953).[2] These works were particularly

1. Howe, "The Education of Women," in *And Jill Came Tumbling After: Sexism in American Education*, ed. Judith Stacey, Susan Béreaud, and Joan Daniels (New York: Dell, 1974), 65.

2. Mead, *Sex and Temperament in Three Primitive Societies* (New York: Dell, 1963; orig. pub. 1935), and her *Male and Female* (New York: Morrow, 1953). See also Ruth Landes, *The Ojibwa Woman* (New York: Norton, 1971; orig. pub. 1938), and her *City of Women* (New York: Macmillan, 1957); Sylvia Leith-Ross, *African Women: A Study of the Ibo of Nigeria* (London: Faber, 1939); Phyllis Kaberry, *Aboriginal Woman: Sacred and Profane* (London: Routledge, 1939); and her *Women of the Grassfields* (London: H.M. Stationery

exciting to the new generation of feminists because they presented full documentation of women's life experiences and, particularly in the case of Mead, investigated the plasticity of gender roles. Throughout the 1930s and 1940s historian Mary Beard explored the varieties of women's activities in the past and the ways in which women were a "force in history."[3] In 1959 Eleanor Flexner published *A Century of Struggle*, opening up the history of feminism itself to scholarly investigation.[4] Contemporary scholars also revived interest in theoretical studies such as Simone de Beauvoir's *The Second Sex* (1949),[5] which investigated women's condition from a range of intellectual perspectives—psychological, historical, sociological, economic, biological, and literary—synthesizing them into an existentialist analysis of women's social condition and consciousness. In literature British feminist Virginia Woolf's *A Room of One's Own* (1929) illuminated the problem of women writing fiction by considering the social, economic, and historical barriers imposed by society.[6]

Appearing in the years between the two feminist movements, these works were responsible for keeping a certain level of intellectual curiosity about women alive in difficult times. They harked back to the first feminist struggle while anticipating issues of the second, but, in the absence of a movement applying and extending a more general dialogue, they did not coalesce into a definable intellectual current. Indeed, the influence and intellectual authority of scholars writing from a feminist perspective and of women scholars as a group declined over the years, reaching a low point in the 1950s. By the late 1960s, as feminism was reviving inside and outside the academy, the work of earlier feminist scholars had either been pushed to the background of their respective disciplines or disappeared from respectable intellectual discourse altogether. With the advent of women's

Office, 1952); Audrey Richards, *Chisingu: A Girl's Initiation Ceremony among the Bemba of Northern Rhodesia* (New York: Grove Press, 1956).

3. Beard, *Woman as Force in History: A Study in Tradition and Realities* (New York: Macmillan, 1946). See also Julia Spruill, *Women's Life and Work in the Southern Colonies* (Chapel Hill: University of North Carolina Press, 1928); Elisabeth Dexter, *Colonial Women of Affairs: Women in Business and the Professions in America before 1776* (Boston: Houghton Mifflin, 1931).

4. Flexner, *A Century of Struggle: The Woman's Rights Movement in the United States* (Cambridge, Mass.: Harvard University Press, 1959).

5. de Beauvoir, *The Second Sex*, trans. and ed. H. M. Parshley (New York: Knopf, 1953; orig. pub. Paris, 1949).

6. Woolf, *A Room of One's Own* (New York: Harcourt, Brace, 1929).

liberation academic feminists realized their need to understand why the disciplines had so little to say about women, what was so problematic about the intellectual methods the disciplines embodied, and why earlier studies of women had not become established as a part of continuing scholarly traditions.

These initial critiques called into question basic assumptions of research and insisted that the disciplines fundamentally alter their purviews to study women – their lives, their works, their concerns. Yet even as feminists stood together in their repudiation of past scholarship, they were doing so from different points of departure, criticizing various forms of intellectual blindness and developing their ideas in distinct scholarly directions. Criticism of male bias developed differently in fields where women previously had been included as subjects for research, in contrast to those where women had rarely, if ever, been mentioned. Challenges to the methods of disciplines that conduct empirical research differed importantly from parallel critiques of nonempirical scholarship. Thus, from the general indictment of male bias there emerged original feminist perspectives on the methods and assumptions of each discipline, not only as it treats or mistreats women but also as that affects everything it studies.

Feminist Critiques: Their Development in Five Fields

The initial feminist criticisms of history and anthropology paralleled each other closely, despite the different methods and traditions of the fields. Both disciplines undertake the study of people and societies, whether contemporary and familiar or distant in time, place, and culture. Feminists turned the observation that research assumptions influence conclusions to their own purposes: if the questions guiding research are designed so that only male activities can provide the answers, then it is difficult if not impossible to obtain an adequate picture of women's role in society, the ways women live and think, and their contributions to history and culture. A complementary and perhaps more obvious erasure of sex bias is required, moreover, so that where women do figure as subjects for scholarly inquiry, their actions will not be interpreted in a stereotyped manner. Once biased assumptions are challenged, new questions and answers arise; and they, in their turn, create the conditions for a radical restructuring of research frameworks so that women are not continually pushed to the margins of academic inquiry.

History is one of the clearest examples of a field in which the initial explosion of feminist energies produced a scathing critique of disciplinary traditions. "Most historians, no matter what their subject, have neglected the history of women's lives," a representative feminist indictment began.[7] Feminists pointed out that there is a bias against women implicit in the events usually considered worthy of historical attention, those from which all other changes are understood to follow: wars and diplomacy, politics and law. The almost total omission of women from traditional historical writing flowed quite naturally from the discipline's characteristic focus on these public activities. The "private" sphere of family and community life, within which most women in the past have lived their lives, has not been a concern of academic historians until recently. Feminists also observed a type of individualist bias at the heart of the discipline that further encouraged the exclusion of women. Historians have long tended to focus on powerful individuals, invariably white men, whose actions were believed to set in motion historical forces and to be responsible for historical change. So long as historians held to such a framework, the masses of women, "who had neither political nor economic nor military power, . . . who accomplished nothing and left no records besides," remained historically mute.[8]

In many subtle ways historians' analytical concepts and frameworks have taken the male experience as the norm for humanity. In an influential article Joan Kelly-Gadol demonstrated how this was the case in one of the discipline's most basic categories of analysis, periodization. She observed, first, that wars, political events, and transitions in rulers have been the traditional markers for conventional periodization; second, that changes in men's status have been the criteria by which periods are differentiated; and, third, that it is assumed—incorrectly, she demonstrated—that women's status changed in the same directions and to the same degree as men's.[9] For instance, the Renaissance and the American Revolution have both been

7. Linda Gordon et al., "A Review of Sexism in American Historical Writing," *Women's Studies* 1 (1972), 133–58. Also see Ruth Rosen, "Sexism in History, or Writing Women's History Is a Tricky Business," *Journal of Marriage and the Family* 33 (1971), 541–44.

8. Linda Gordon, *Towards a Radical Feminist History* (Pittsburgh: Know Press: n.d.).

9. Kelly-Gadol, "The Social Relation of the Sexes: Methodological Implications of Women's History," *Signs* 1 (1976), 809–24.

understood as periods of positive development in human history; yet there is considerable evidence that, in contrast to men, women's status declined in these periods.[10] For history to become truly receptive to the breadth of women's historical experiences, it may take a willingness to mark periods by different kinds of changes, for instance, in reproduction and fertility, rather than in empire and economy.

What little historical work did consider women was itself flawed by these same male-biased categories. A few individual women who achieved public prominence—Jane Addams, for instance, or Eleanor Roosevelt—appeared in historical writings, but, as long as their achievements were not set in the context of other women's lives, their inclusion did nothing to remedy the historical exclusion of women as a group. The only place where women's collective presence appeared was in the history of women's rights, but this was because it fit existing, narrowly construed standards of political activity.[11] Feminist scholars demonstrated that those women grudgingly admitted into the purview of history were frequently subjected to sexist evaluations. This criticism was particularly directed at the handful of male historians who wrote about women's history in the 1950s and early 1960s, before any appreciable numbers of women began to enter the field and write the history of their own sex.[12] Frequently, in the writings of these men, women were judged by some invidious criterion, such as whether or not they were sufficiently "feminine," in a way that had no parallel in the historical treatment of men and reflected no critical awareness of where or how such evaluative criteria had come into being.

Given these criticisms, the growth of a new social historical approach within the discipline seemed to auger well for the history of women. This development had its roots in postwar European and English intellectual developments, but appeared in the United States in the context of the political and cultural liberalism of the 1960s. Social history signaled a turn from wars and politics to a concern with family and community life,

10. Kelly-Gadol's own research was on the Renaissance. On the American Revolution, from the perspective of women's position, see Linda Kerber, *Women of the Republic: Intellect and Ideology in Revolutionary America* (Chapel Hill: University of North Carolina Press, 1980), and Mary Beth Norton, *Liberty's Daughters: The Revolutionary Experience of American Women, 1750–1800* (Boston: Little, Brown, 1980).

11. Ann D. Gordon, Mari Jo Buhle, and Nancy Schrom Dye, *Women in American Society: An Historical Contribution* (Somerville, Mass.: New England Free Press, n.d.).

12. Gordon et al., "Review of Sexism."

demography and culture. Social historians consider how the "articulate few who appear to 'make history' interact with the rest of the people."[13] Indeed, if history's focus on the powerful and the public sphere was all there was to feminists' criticisms of the discipline, women's history might well have lost its distinctiveness and disappeared into social history. That this did not occur indicates the strength of male bias, which had a decided impact on the shape social history took. In particular, the way that social historians addressed the family had contradictory implications for women's history. While their focus on domesticity, children, and sexuality suggested a much greater openness to women's traditional concerns, women themselves were identified with the family in a way that totally ignored their independent existence and hid the conflicts they had in and with the family institution. While the social history of the family has "provided us with a wealth of information about the kin-related experiences of millions of otherwise invisible women," wrote Ellen Ross, "it makes assumptions which obscure rather than uncover the actual historical experiences of women as well as the forces determining the limits of their lives."[14]

In anthropology feminist writings raised questions about male bias both in the theory of human societies and in the way that women have been perceived by anthropologists studying particular cultures. Sally Slocum's "Woman the Gatherer: Male Bias in Anthropology" was the earliest explicit critique of the habit of taking male character and experience as the norm. Although she focused on the particular question of human evolution, her goal was to reveal the subtle and deep effects of male bias on general theories of human society and to indicate how feminists might counter this. She wrote: "Though male bias could be shown in other areas, hominid evolution is particularly convenient for my purpose because it involves speculations and inferences from a rather small amount of data. In such a case, hidden assumptions and premises that lie behind the speculations and inferences are more easily demonstrated. Male bias exists not only in the ways in which the scanty data are interpreted, but in the very language used."[15]

13. Carol Amyx, "Sexism in American Historiography," unpublished paper, 1969.

14. Ross, "Women and Family," *Feminist Studies* 5 (1979), 182.

15. Slocum, "Woman the Gatherer: Male Bias in Anthropology," in *Toward an Anthropology of Women*, ed. Rayna R. Reiter (New York: Monthly Review Press, 1975), 38. This article initially appeared under the name Sally Linton in the first version of Sue Ellen Jacobs's collection, *Women in Perspective: A Guide to Cross-Cultural Studies* (Urbana: University of Illinois, Department of Urban and Regional Planning, 1971). It was originally presented at

Slocum maintained that the evidence does not support the traditional anthropological theory that male hunting activity, which requires increased cooperation and tool-making, was the significant factor in the development of human communicative and organizational skills. In this theory women waited idly at home for the men to return with dinner; isolated by their domestic roles, they contributed little to human evolution. Slocum argued that this theory arbitrarily defines activity among men as the only form of social behavior worth considering. The view that "man the hunter" was the critical factor in human evolution simply ignores the cooperative activities of women and thus probably provides a distorted view of early hominid life.

Slocum attempted to right the imbalance caused by this androcentric view by speculating about women's social contributions. She began to formulate a theory of evolution that includes women's activities in gathering, childbearing, and childrearing. Drawing on existing knowledge of primates and of hunting and gathering societies, she pointed out that it is highly unlikely that at any point in human evolution women stayed at home waiting, and far more likely that they were always active, especially as food-gatherers. She also observed that gathering is a cooperative activity that develops communicative and organizational skills in the process of foraging and sharing. In fact, the increasing dependency of children on their mothers, which characterizes human evolution, makes it probable that the first developed forms of sharing were between mother and child. Similarly, the demands of gathering suggest that containers for carrying food and slings for carrying children were among the earliest human inventions. With this feminist perspective, she made a strong case that men's big-game hunting was not the key factor in human evolution, but rather grew out of cooperative patterns already developed from women's gathering activities.

The basic elements of Slocum's criticisms of male bias as it has affected the study of human evolution may be applied to all the major subfields of anthropology—physical anthropology, archeology, linguistics, and social and cultural anthropology. The social power of men is such that their perspectives mold the research questions asked about men and women alike, distorting the anthropological study, not only of women but also of human society in general. However, male bias does not always manifest itself in

the Symposium on the Anthropology of Knowledge, held during the 60th Annual Meeting of the American Anthropological Association, San Diego, Calif., 1970.

the same way. In the area Slocum chose to study, the theory of human evolution, women had been virtually ignored and the question of female evolution reduced to marginal absurdity as a result of these assumptions. In other subfields of anthropology women had not been overlooked in the same way or to the same degree, yet serious distortion was still present. Of the four highly diverse subfields of anthropology, this book is most concerned with social and cultural anthropology. Women have always been included in scholarship within this area. The structural functionalist approach, which guides a significant portion of the research, assumes that a society functions like an organic structure, each part of which makes a contribution to the whole. From this perspective women and their social activities are impossible to ignore completely. Similarly, the anthropological study of kinship systems necessarily considers the subject of women, central as they are to family life and human reproduction.

Therefore, there was early agreement among feminist scholars in social and cultural anthropology that male-biased categories operate not so much to omit women from consideration as to trivialize and misrepresent them. "Too often . . . women are presented ethnographically in a curiously impersonal dehumanizing way—as shadows moving in and out of engrossing activities of men or as objects to be manipulated by their men folk."[16] Feminist scholars identified many forms of misrepresentation. Often Western stereotypes are simply extended to other cultures, so that women are portrayed "as passive sex objects, as devoted mothers, and as dutiful wives".[17] In addition, the concepts used by anthropologists to discuss culture, though supposedly neutral, implicitly devalue women's contribution. As one feminist observed, "What women do is perceived as household work and what they talk about is called gossip, while men's work is viewed as the economic base of society and their information seen as important social information."[18] These ways of studying and presenting women used an analytic framework that views women's activities in relation to standards developed for men rather than considering them in their own right. It also evaluates women's roles in terms appropriate to men's roles rather than understanding that women's and men's activities might not be comparable.

16. Betty Chiñas, *The Isthmus Zapotecs: Women's Role in Cultural Context* (New York: Holt, Rinehart and Winston, 1973), 1.

17. Michelle Zimbalist Rosaldo and Louise Lamphere, "Introduction," to their *Woman, Culture and Society* (Stanford: Stanford University Press, 1974), 1.

18. Rayna R. Reiter, "Introduction," to her *Toward an Anthropology of Women*, 12.

An even more basic manifestation of this trivialization of women has been the traditional anthropological practice of generalizing about women on the basis of information gathered from men. Relying on male informants was so common that in 1963 Denise Paulme in her introduction to *Women of Tropical Africa* distinguished the essays as representing a "new approach" because they were based on women talking about their own lives.[19] Subsequent feminist scholars picked up this approach and connected the egregious error of using men as the main source of data on women to a more general system of thinking which takes male experience as the norm for human beings.

Another basic manifestation of bias early identified by feminist scholars is anthropology's underlying assumption that biology determines sex roles and woman's secondary status. The tenacity with which anthropology has held on to biological explanations of gender was noted to be quite remarkable, given its general predisposition for cultural and social explanations. As Rayna Reiter points out: "Anthropology has developed a theoretical perspective that separates biology from culture in the investigation of race; it has the potential to make the same discrimination with regard to gender. When investigating other issues, anthropologists rarely make the mistake of reading automatically from a presumed biological base to the superstructure built upon it—yet in analyzing gender, they do exactly this."[20]

Although the concept of male bias was new to anthropology, the concept of bias itself certainly was not. Anthropology had long been aware of cultural bias, or what it calls ethnocentrism—the habit of perceiving and judging another culture in terms of one's own—and included in its professional training ways to counter such bias. Feminist scholars suggested that androcentrism needed to be recognized as a parallel phenomenon to ethnocentrism—and similarly corrected. Ruby Rohrlich-Leavitt, Barbara Sykes, and Elizabeth Weatherford explored the ways that androcentrism influenced the field research by comparing the work of male and female researchers on the Australian aborigines. Whereas Slocum contended that there is no difference between the studies of male and female anthropologists because

19. Paulme, "Introduction" to her *Women of Tropical Africa* (London: Routledge and Kegan Paul, 1963), 1.
20. Reiter, "Introduction," 14.

both are trained in the same assumptions, Leavitt, Sykes, and Weatherford sought to demonstrate that in field research there have been important differences. They showed that male anthropologists have tended to portray the sexes as unequal, to present aboriginal women as passive and insignificant, and to treat the men as brutal and domineering. They have also projected onto aboriginal society the Western notion that physiological differences determine all sex roles. Leavitt, Sykes, and Weatherford argued that women researchers are more likely to "show us men and women living together in equal partnership, the rights, self-respect and the dignity of the members of both sexes being guaranteed."[21] They contended that the differing perspectives of male and female ethnographers on the position of women in aboriginal groups lead to radically different views of the organization of the entire society.

This was a dramatic claim, and it raised difficult questions about the role of women scholars in remedying male bias in anthropology, as well as about the relation between women as the object of scholarship and women as the scholars themselves. Although this link has not yet been fully explored, it remains an important undercurrent as feminists examine and criticize current methods and existing scholarship.

Unlike certain other disciplines, the field of education never avoided gender categories in any area of research, from methods of instruction and the nature of the learner to the thornier issue of what the schools ought to teach. The problem for feminists in education was thus not so much to make women a central concern of research as it was to question previous research on sex differences in educational abilities and outcomes that have prevailed in the discipline, its research, and its translation into school practice. This last factor suggests a significant distinction between education and the four other disciplines considered here: education has a double character, as both a research area and a field for determining policy, the immediate intent of which is to put research findings into practice in the schools. Hence, when feminist consciousness began to arise among

21. Rohrlich-Leavitt, Sykes, and Weatherford, "Aboriginal Woman: Male and Female Anthropological Perspectives," in *Toward an Anthropology of Women*, ed. Reiter, 123–24. Many of the articles in this collection, as well as those in *Woman, Culture and Society*, ed. Rosaldo and Lamphere, provided supplementary feminist critiques of anthropology. For a more recent and comprehensive critique, see Karen Sacks, *Sisters and Wives: The Past and Future of Sexual Equality* (Westport, Conn.: Greenwood Press, 1979).

educationists, it directed critical attention not only to the scholarship in the field but also to its concrete effects on students in the classroom.

Long before educaton became a specialized field, much had already been written about the pedagogic value of female virtue and the desirability of having women teachers working in the primary grades.[22] Nineteenth-century educators presumed that girls and boys were different in their mental capacities and therefore in the way they absorbed knowledge, as well as in their prospective roles in society, for which the schools ought to prepare them. Once established as an academic discipline, educational research continued to center much of its attention on gender. Educators argued on the basis of intellectual measurement and achievement tests that women learn differently (and for the most part less) than men and, therefore, need a special curriculum that does not endanger their health, that suits them for their position in society, and that makes the educational enterprise more efficient. Current literature on learning indicates that girls outscore boys on standardized achievement tests until tenth grade, at which point boys begin to equal girls' scores in reading and to surpass them in math and science; by twelfth grade boys outscore girls. The conventional explanations for these patterns still rely on biological factors.[23] Girls' aptitudes develop earlier and then stop around puberty (the first menstrual flow apparently constituting an effective brain drain), whereas those aptitudes continue to develop for boys.

Modern feminist critiques of this position had an unexpected precursor. Early critics of the notion of "natural" sex differences in learning attacked the schools' treatment of boys, not girls. In *The Feminized Male* Patricia Cayo Sexton explained the test results in terms of the educational system's "cheating boys"[24] by not meeting their distinctly male educational needs. She and others argued that schools run predominantly by female teachers

22. See David B. Tyack, *The One Best System: A History of American Urban Education* (Cambridge, Mass.: Harvard University Press, 1974), and Edward H. Clarke, *Women in Education: Or a Fair Chance for the Girls* (Boston: James R. Osgood, 1873).

23. See, for example, Eleanor E. Maccoby and Carolyn N. Jacklin, *The Psychology of Sex Differences* (Stanford: Stanford University Press, 1974); Jeremy D. Finn, "Sex Differences in Educational Outcomes: A Cross-National Study," *Sex Roles* 6 (1980), 9–26.

24. Sexton, *The Feminized Male: Classrooms, White Collars, and the Decline of Manliness* (New York: Random House, 1969). See also J. R. Ellis and J. L. Peterson, "Effects of Same Sex Class Organization on Junior High School Students' Academic Achievement, Self Discipline, Self Concept, Sex Role Identification, and Attitude Towards School," *Journal of Educational Research* 64 (1971), 455–546.

discourage the development and expression of "natural masculine behavior," identified as aggressiveness and a tendency to physical activity, and that boys so constrained are less able to absorb their lessons. (No explanation was put forward as to why, by age sixteen, boys' natural abilities are apparently no longer being repressed.) Although this critique is hardly feminist, it turned attention away from the individual student and biological explanations for gender differences in educational outcomes to the institution, to the failures of education itself, and hence to the potential for changing those structures.

The feminist scholarship questioning gender-related educational research began for the most part outside of faculties of education; it first emerged in sister disciplines like psychology and sociology, both of which also make gender categories important to their research methods. Probably most influential was Naomi Weisstein's "'*Kinder, Kuche, Kirche*' as Scientific Law: Psychology Constructs the Female," written in 1969.[25] Although Weisstein did not specially discuss schooling, her work had broad implications for educational studies. She raised the possibility that the sex differences researchers found in achievement, which form the basis of both school practices and continuing academic investigation, have their genesis not in physiology or the peculiar characteristics of females but in scholars' prejudices regarding women and in the social institutions from which such sexism grows.

Even though Matina Horner wrote as a social psychologist, she helped to set off a new wave of scholarship in education with her article "Toward an Understanding of Achievement-Related Conflicts in Women."[26] Horner acknowledged and accepted the long-standing body of research on sex differences in achievement (as Weisstein did not) and sought to explain them in terms of psychological conflicts women experience between excelling in school or work and living up to internalized social expectations that they not succeed. Horner admitted that these expectations are transmitted in part by the schools, yet she focused on women's own ambivalence about success to explain their lack of achievement.

In the field of education itself one of the first studies to criticize gender research and its use in the schools was Myra Sadker's and Nancy Frazier's

25. Weisstein, "'*Kinder, Kuche, Kirche*' as Scientific Law: Psychology Constructs the Female," in *Sisterhood Is Powerful*, ed. Robin Morgan (New York: Random House, 1970), 205–20.

26. Horner, "Toward an Understanding of Achievement-Related Conflicts in Women," *Journal of Social Issues* 28 (1972), 157–75.

1973 study, *Sexism in School and Society.*[27] Seeking the causes of the decline
in female achievement in what happens to girls in the educational system,
they analyzed the social organization of the school—curricula, textbooks,
counseling and guidance programs, teacher expectations, and teacher-
student interactions—as well as outright sex discrimination.

A more far-reaching methodological challenge came from sociologist
Arlie Hochschild, who suggested that sex differences in test scores are the
invention of scholars who chose to stress gender over other categories in
analyzing their data.[28] Her criticism, which parallels one made by black
scholars regarding supposed race differences in achievement, centers on the
fact that researchers have chosen to study the variance in scores by sex
rather than by individual. She maintained that individual variance might in
fact be greater than variance by gender and that the apparent inferiority of
women as a group is an artifact of the method of analyzing the data. While
other feminists challenged the sexist explanations offered for the observed
differences in achievement, Hochschild denied that sex is a significant category in achievement differences. The differences in these approaches constitute a theoretical debate among feminists in education. However, the
two approaches—to analyze sex differences where research indicates they
exist and not to invoke them artificially as explanations where they do not—
are closely related, complementary halves of a single feminist perspective
on male bias in educational scholarship.

The three fields discussed thus far—anthropology, history, and education—all involve empirical research in one way or another. In each case
feminists are particularly concerned with the gathering of information and
the accurate assessment of factual evidence regarding women. The empirical element is diminished in the disciplines of philosophy and literature,
where texts and conceptual formulations constitute primary subjects, and
this contrast was manifest in the initial critiques feminists brought to these
fields of study.

When intellectual interest in feminism began to spread in universities and
professional organizations, women in philosophy found themselves confronting a discipline that presented itself as sex-neutral or sex-disinterested.
The questions traditionally broached in philosophical inquiry, whether in

27. Frazier and Sadker, *Sexism in School and Society* (New York: Harper and Row, 1973).
28. Hochschild, "A Review of Sex Role Research," in *Changing Women in a Changing
Society*, ed. Joan Huber (Chicago: University of Chicago Press, 1973), 249–67.

metaphysics, ethics, epistemology, political theory, or any of the other specialities of the field, tend to be abstract and general, exploring such concepts as reality, knowledge, good and evil, the state. Since philosophy purports to be a search for universal truths unhampered by such incidental matters as sex differences, this discipline seemed at first to provide few footholds from which the study of women or the growth of feminist perspectives could begin. But once feminists began to explore how philosophy could be the locus for feminist inquiry or could be employed in the investigation of women's lives, the illusion of sex neutrality and irrelevance to particular women's issues rapidly began to be dispelled. The initial work in philosophy moved in two directions: Some scholarship addressed the assumptions of the discipline itself, including the assumption of neutrality, and began to reveal male biases deeply hidden in the methods and substance of traditional philosophical theory. Other work began to create a place for the study of subjects of particular relevance to women by turning the normative fields of ethics and social philosophy away from more abstract metatheory and toward the application of ideas to particular social problems. Just as women's history both spurred and was fostered by social history, so feminist philosophy has been part of a larger resurgence of interest in applied social philosophy. Thus the growth of philosophical studies of women's issues has taken place alongside studies of such topics as civil rights and liberties, the problems of minorities, and public legislation for social change.[29]

Perhaps the most obvious place for a feminist philosopher to begin was with the observations about women in the influential classics of the field. For, despite the overall presumption of neutrality, numerous philosophers from ancient through modern times have seen fit to remark upon the alleged differences between men and women. Until the advent of feminist investigation, these comments generally had been considered incidental to the substance of the theories in which they appear—mere asides, insignificant to the conceptual frameworks that define the body of thought as a whole. In looking over the history of philosophy, feminists began not merely to document sexist ideas but also to present provocative and controversial

---

29. Just one manifestation of the interest in the application of philosophy to contemporary social issues was the founding in 1971 of the journal *Philosophy and Public Affairs*. See also the early review of the literature on women and philosophy by Christine Pierce, *Signs* 1 (Winter 1975), 487–503.

arguments that the views on women of individual thinkers are not incidental but central to their theories; at times even undermining their claims for universal relevance.

In one of the first of such analyses, Christine Garside examined Aristotle and Søren Kierkegaard, comparing what each says about women to what each believes are the attributes of the good person.[30] She observed that Aristotle's ethics, a theory ordinarily presumed to prescribe a path to virtue for "man the rational animal," in fact contains qualifications that imply that women cannot attain the same level of goodness as men. The virtuous person, for Aristotle, is he who develops practical wisdom, whose reason governs the other faculties. Just as in the soul there is a fitting hierarchy among the faculties, so too in society the rational part is fit to rule over the irrational, and those members of society in whom the irrational soul dominates are children, slaves, and women. Although members of these groups can attain a measure of virtue according to their capacities, those capacities are different and cannot equal the level of virtue attainable by the more rational male. Furthermore, Garside argued, this view is not readily correctible within the boundaries of Aristotle's theory, which is pervaded by a hierarchical framework. Garside concluded with the controversial claim that the feminist challenge that can be raised against Aristotle has implications for the position of women as philosophers vis à vis the whole intellectual tradition: "For women there is a dilemma which arises in the study of certain influential philosophers. A woman cannot, qua human being, appropriate their work, as it turns out in many ways to be a study of man."[31]

30. Garside, "Can a Woman Be Good in the Same Way as a Man?" *Dialogue* 10 (1971), 534–44. Feminist analyses of Aristotle continue in such works as Lynda Lange, "Woman Is Not a Rational Animal: On Aristotle's Biology of Reproduction," and Elizabeth V. Spelman, "Aristotle and the Politicization of the Soul," both in *Discovering Reality: Feminist Perspectives on Epistemology, Metaphysics, Methodology, and Philosophy of Science* ed. Sandra Harding and Merril B. Hintikka (Boston: D. Reidel, 1983), 1–15, 17–30, respectively.

31. Garside, "Can a Woman Be Good," 544. This is an example of an early statement, provocative and polemical, and it characterizes the ambivalence felt by many feminists about their academic traditions. In a later essay, however, Nannerl O. Keohane reflects upon this problem and formulates it in a way that does not pose the same dilemma: "How can feminist philosophers best take up their places in a dialogue with the great figures of the past? . . . Our task is to use this occasion for critical discussion, as the great authors of the past have always done in arguing with their predecessors, to refashion the enduring elements of the tradition in a way that makes them serve new purposes." See her "Feminist Scholarship and Human Nature," *Ethics* 93 (1982), 105–6.

Thus in philosophy, as in anthropology, the role of the female scholar herself demands examination because of the masculine orientation that characterizes the field of study.

In a subsequent article Carol C. Gould confronted the claims of philosophy to be sex-neutral.[32] She argued that the assumption that abstract universality is the criterion for philosophical relevance is itself value-laden and obscures the degree to which these "universals" reflect historically specific interests and the perspectives of particular social groups. Thus she argued that theories about universal, "essentially human" traits are about traits that have come to be associated with the male; accordingly, the attribution to women of "feminine" traits results in their exclusion from the essentially human. She wrote: "In the historical cases we have examined, we find the projection of a specific and historically contingent form—male domination and the subordination of women—as a universal and unchanging one; and as a result, the projection of those characteristics which have priority in such a social form as the essential and dominant features of human nature itself."[33] This was a theme that ran through many of the early feminist writings and developed into fuller perspectives as feminist philosophy grew. Repeatedly a theory of human nature was found to be a theory of the male in disguise, which explicitly or inadvertently conceives of the female as a deviation from the norm and excludes her from full participation in all that is considered human.[34] In these observations one can also see the germ of

32. Gould, "The Woman Question: Philosophy of Liberation and the Liberation of Philosophy," *Philosophical Forum* 5 (1973–74), 5–44. This journal issue was later published as a book, *Women and Philosophy: Toward a Theory of Liberation*, ed. Carol Gould and Marx Wartofsky (New York: G. P. Putnam's Sons, 1976).

33. Gould, "The Woman Question," 24. Or, as another feminist commentator put it, "If the function of being rational in its fullest sense is a human capacity, then the ultimate appeal in the claim that women are inferior is the denial that women are human." Rosemary Agonito, "The Concept of Inferiority: When Women are Men," *Journal of Social Philosophy* 8 (1977), 12.

34. This sort of observation has been made in numerous contexts. See, for example, Hilda Hein, "Woman—A Philosophical Analysis," *Holy Cross Quarterly* (1981), 18–23, which has been excerpted in *Philosophy of Woman: Classical to Current Concepts*, ed. Mary B. Mahowald (Indianapolis: Hackett, 1978), 250–61; Christine Pierce, "Natural Law, Language and Women," in *Woman in Sexist Society*, ed. Vivian Gornick and Barbara K. Moran (New York: Basic Books, 1971), an expanded revision of which was printed in *Sex Equality*, ed. Jane English (Englewood Cliffs, N.J.: Prentice-Hall, 1977), 130–42. Also see Marilyn Frye's comments on "phallism" in "Male Chauvinism—A Conceptual Analysis," in *Philosophy and Sex*, ed. Robert Baker and Frederick Elliston (Buffalo: Prometheus Books, 1975), 65–79.

other, later work. The discovery of a division of male and female in traditional concepts of man foreshadowed a variety of critical explorations of "dualistic" thinking generally that have had an impact on ideas in political theory, ethics, epistemology, and metaphysics, as we shall see in subsequent chapters.

In effect, many of the changes that feminism brought about implied a rejection of the view that philosophical issues should be ideally only of an abstract and universal nature. Analytical critiques of the philosophical tradition had their counterpart in work that applied philosophical inquiry to issues of immediate importance to women. A good deal of the scholarship on women in philosophy came about as feminists broadened the scope of ethics and political theory to include issues of specific concern to women and to the women's liberation movement. Sometimes this occurred through the application of traditional philosophical concepts to subjects particularly pertinent to women. The pressure of contemporary politics helped to expand standard, general philosophical issues such as equality and justice to include questions of affirmative action and preferential treatment. Not historically a part of social philosophy, these topical problems were brought into philosophical discussion because they imply particular and controversial methods of hastening the goal of sex equality.

In other cases concerns arising out of the women's movement and women's experience themselves emerged as matters of philosophical significance. There was, for instance, a veritable explosion of work on the subject of abortion in the 1970s. Since abortion raises questions about life, freedom, and human value, this subject entered an established dialogue concerning identity of persons and the scope of rights fairly readily. Other concerns that have moved from contemporary feminism into philosophical discourse include marriage, love, sexual relationships, mothering, rape, and pornography—an expanding list of subjects that previously would have been wildly idiosyncratic topics for philosophical scholarship, if indeed they were treated at all. Political theory has become an especially rich field for feminist research, as philosophers have joined the feminist movement's quest for an understanding of oppression and liberation. In the process theories of feminism itself have been brought into the purview of the discipline.[35]

35. For a selection of early work on these topics, see *The Monist*, special issue on women's liberation, 57 (Jan. 1973); *Philosophical Forum*, special double issue on women and philosophy, 5 (Fall-Winter 1973–74); *Philosophy and Public Affairs* and *Analysis*, 1971 and

Literary studies, like philosophy, have a double focus. On the one hand, there is a generally accepted body of texts that constitutes the object of scholarly and critical inquiry; on the other, there is a set of theories about literature itself, what it is and how to approach it, as well as about human nature and experience that literature documents and illuminates. Feminist criticism started from the realization that both the established canon and the prevailing literary view of humanity reflect the same confusion between the "masculine" and the "human" that was being discovered in other fields.

At the end of the 1960s the canon of literary masterpieces was, with a few significant exceptions, a masculine preserve. Since the literary canon is an informal institution, whose specific inclusions, exclusions, deletions, and exceptions are nowhere codified, one important test of its male bias is the list of important writers whose work is regularly presented in the classroom. In 1971 Elaine Showalter surveyed freshman anthologies, as well as upper-division syllabi in English courses.[36] She noted that at the first-year level many courses are organized around issues or themes, introducing literary texts as a succession of different perspectives on supposedly universal subjects. In the anthologies that serve such courses, however, the archetypal questions facing modern man turn out to be those confronted and written about only by modern males. At the more advanced level courses are likelier to center on periods or genres, and literary worth is the presumed criterion for inclusion. Once again, however, Showalter found whole literary forms and periods—centuries and sets of centuries—in which not a single female author is represented. Even the expected tokens often fail to materialize in their expected slots on reading lists. Showalter called into question the values that have managed to identify so few women writers as major and relegated so many to lesser status or to total obscurity.

The more recent feminist criticism that we examine in the next chapter builds upon initial critiques like this one. For it was in reaction to the overwhelmingly male bias of the traditional canon and the critical standards that

onward; *Philosophy and Sex*, ed. Baker and Elliston. Also see two more recent anthologies, *Feminism and Philosophy*, ed. Mary Vetterling-Braggin, Frederick Elliston, and Jane English (Totowa, N.J.: Littlefield and Adams, 1977), and *Philosophy and Women*, ed. Sharon Bishop and Marjorie Weinzweig (Belmont, Calif.: Wadsworth, 1979).

36. Showalter, "Women in the Literary Curriculum," *College English* 32 (1971), 855–62. This paper was initially presented at the Annual Meeting of the Modern Language Association, New York, Dec. 1970.

inform it that feminists have tended to devote almost all of their critical energies to unearthing women's literary activity—seeking to reevaluate the works of recognized women authors and to reclaim "lost" writing by women.

Literary scholarship has not simply neglected the works of women, however. In addition, feminists argued, both literary works themselves and the commentaries of critics tend to interpret female experience according to sexist preconceptions that rely upon the myths of female nature prevalent in our society. Since the literary tradition is a fertile source of such myths, scholarly interpretation also serves to reinforce and perpetuate them. Mary Ellmann's *Thinking about Women* investigated the habits of mind and of language that are commonplace in our society and that find expression in both literature and criticism.[37] Ellmann began with a discussion of the phenomenon of "sexual analogy," her term for a process by which women are reduced, conceptually and metaphorically, to their specifically reproductive functions; at the same time, she claimed, metaphors of reproduction are indiscriminately applied to a range of creative and intellectual functions from which women's sexual nature supposedly bars them. Extending this analogy, Ellmann pointed out in a chapter entitled "Phallic Criticism" that male critics treat a book by a woman as if it were itself a woman. She went on to explore a subtle range of often contradictory literary and critical stereotypes that equally describe what male authors say about the females they create and what male critics say about the creations of female authors. Ellmann's investigation of "shrillness" as a dismissive label, for instance, included a brilliant catalogue of instances where critics have been at pains to emphasize its complete absence, marveling that some rare woman's writing is, in fact, *not* shrill.

Structurally, *Thinking about Women* served much the same function in literary studies as the other early critiques did in their respective disciplines. The differences between this study and most of the others we have been discussing are factors that have helped shape the subsequent history of feminist work in the field. Ellmann's book was published in the fall of 1968, which meant that its conception and execution date from a period just before the mass feminist revival in academe or in society at large. "Feminism," to Ellmann was the name of an historical phenomenon, an epithet one can sometimes catch male writers using as a contemptuous slur, but not the name of a living movement. She wrote in isolation from the

37. Ellmann, *Thinking about Women* (New York: Harcourt Brace Jovanovich, 1968).

passions and promises of such a movement. Whereas the critiques in other fields were angry and dramatically comprehensive denunciations, often collectively compiled, demanding a drastic shift in a discipline's priorities, Ellmann's tone was witty and ironic, her stance entirely individual, and her examples, though striking and apt, clearly idiosyncratic.

The rage at the heart of women's renewed attack upon their condition did find other, less academic outlets among cultural critics. Much of the best-known feminist theory of the early 1970s is actually criticism that relies on literary—or at least textual—phenomena as the basis for discussion of social experience. In these cases the sexist content of the texts was examined primarily with reference to sexist values and practices in society, which the literature both reflects and influences. Thus, in *Sexual Politics*, even though Kate Millett anchored her opening argument in a discussion of Henry Miller, Norman Mailer, and D. H. Lawrence as sexist writers, her chief target was the society that generated their oppressive displays, rather than the novelists themselves.[38]

Millett's special contribution to literary criticism consisted in identifying male dominance as the force motivating the portrayal of heterosexual relations in many contemporary male writers and in denominating that force "political." The sexual candor of a Miller or a Mailer, she maintained, serves the same ideological purpose as the explicit phallic worship of a Lawrence: the objectification, degradation, and subjection of the female. Millett's further reading of literary and historical texts—indeed, her reading of Western social history in general—proceeded from and built upon this understanding of sexuality in contemporary literature. In the course of her indictment of masculine cultural bias, Millett also implicitly called into question the critical tradition that has elevated to prominence in our culture the very writers she attacked for their profound sexism.

Theorists like Shulamith Firestone, Eva Figes, Carolyn Heilbrun, and Germaine Greer worked, like Millett, with a range of texts—psychological, religious, and philosophical, as well as literary—tending to read these diverse sources as if they were empirical rather than textual evidence for the nature and ramifications of sexism.[39] The feminist movement traces its

38. Millett, *Sexual Politics* (Garden City, N.Y.: Doubleday, 1970).

39. Firestone, *The Dialectic of Sex: The Case for Feminist Revolution* (New York: Morrow, 1970); Figes, *Patriarchal Attitudes* (New York: Stein and Day, 1970); Heilbrun, *Toward a Recognition of Androgyny* (New York: Harper and Row, 1974); and Greer, *The Female Eunuch* (New York: McGraw-Hill, 1971).

theoretical origins, therefore, to a series of books that placed sexist ideology on precisely the same plane as sexist experience, without being called upon to explain or justify an equivalency self-evident only in a conceptual universe where the text is an object. If this disciplinary habit is a limitation, it is also a strength, for it has provided contemporary feminism with a comprehensive and thorough-going appreciation of the workings of ideology in the oppression of women.

This type of criticism continues both in and outside the academic setting. The more strictly literary type of work, questioning critical standards and the ways in which women have been portrayed in literature, has led feminists away from male writers to new interest in the works of women writers and the discovery of a female literary perspective that was ignored or unsuspected by the male critical tradition. However, because textual criticism of the culture itself drew a certain amount of feminist attention away from the study of expressive culture, this work has gone forward without an initial grounding, analogous to developments in other disciplines, in the comprehensive analysis and critique of what one commentator was to call "patriarchal poetics."[40]

The cumulative effect of the feminist critiques of the disciplines was to establish incontrovertibly the existence and varieties of male bias in traditional academic inquiry. This bias, however inadvertent, accepts and perpetuates the ideology of female inferiority. Whether the particular discipline has almost completely neglected women—as in history or philosophy—or treated them as incidental to central issues of research—as in literature or anthropology—or considered gender as an important factor for research—as in education—feminist scholars have shown that the assumption that male behavior and experience are the norm for the entire human race is common to all. So, too, do all the disciplines, whatever their other differences, provide a truncated and distorted picture of women, which reflects and justifies our society's oppressive stereotypes of what it is to be female.

The importance of these critiques reaches beyond the identification of male bias to suggest directions for subsequent research. Salutary critical examination of the fundamental assumptions of traditional scholarship has prepared the

40. Sandra M. Gilbert, "Life Studies, or Speech after Long Silence: Feminist Critics Today," *College English* 40 (1979), 849–63.

way for studies that yield a fresh, even revelatory understanding of women's being. The new scholarship on women that grew out of these initial critiques of male-biased distortion is the subject of the next chapter.

2

New Visions in the Disciplines

The rich scholarship on women and women's issues that feminism has produced is far from monolithic in character. It is marked by intellectual debate and methodological difference, with varying perspectives on the interpretation of evidence and the goals of scholarship. The diverse approaches that are so striking in this work often reflect varying, even conflicting, theoretical orientations and political perspectives, but just as often they are a manifestation of the differing frameworks for research employed by particular disciplines. Although many feminists, perceiving traditional academic structures as contributing to sexism, seek to transcend disciplinary boundaries in their work, it remains true that large portions of feminist scholarship resist unified treatment and stand firmly rooted in the separate disciplines. There is thus an inescapable duality to the character of feminist scholarship: while there is an overall commonality notable in this research, it just as often bears the stamp of some particular field.

Rather than attempting to ignore disciplinary distinctions in order to present a composite picture of the discoveries of feminist scholarship, in this chapter we follow the accepted academic divisions between areas of knowledge. It is important not to lose sight of the characteristic kinds of questions each discipline pursues, both in order that we be able to be precise about the impact of feminism and also that we be in a position to identify directions for future research that emerge within each field. The limits imposed by our consideration of specifically disciplinary work in this and the previous chapter are lifted in Chapter 3, where we take a more interdisciplinary approach to the work of scholars, addressing issues that call upon the insights and methods of many fields.

Two closely related theoretical approaches may be distinguished in the fields under study here. In a broad view of the research about women that has appeared over the last decade, a debate stands out concerning the proper emphasis to place on the various determinants influencing women's situation: Should scholarship concentrate on the oppression of women in society, describing and documenting their subjugation in private and public life, analyzing the institutions and belief systems that perpetuate that subjugation? Or does this focus falsely imply that women are mere passive victims, when in fact they should properly be seen as active agents in the world, shaping their own destinies within restricted possibilities, resisting and overthrowing those restrictions, sometimes even acting in complicity with the forces that keep them in a state of social inferiority? Surveying research on women with a careful eye to the distinction between these approaches helps to clarify several aspects of feminist scholarship. It reveals shared intellectual concerns that are otherwise obscured by disciplinary boundaries; at the same time it helps to explain certain differences that fall along disciplinary lines; and it illuminates a division of opinion, often unformulated but far-reaching, concerning which perspective to take on the study of women.

At first glance, the debate over whether to approach women's role in society as one of active agent or victim of oppression would appear to be a politically grounded conflict over the value of women's activities and relationships and the amount of control women exercise over their lives. To some extent, this is the case; much of the scholarship has a frankly normative dimension. But whether one stresses the discovery of agency or the analysis of oppression is also strongly influenced by the purview of the particular discipline from which one is working. Anthropology provides an excellent example of a field where feminists of all stripes emphasize women's activity, for reasons that have much to do with developments within the field itself. Although the descriptive language they use is different and the conclusions more controversial, similar observations may be made about scholarship in history and literature. By contrast, within fields such as education, sociology, economics, and political science, where the focus is on the operation of social institutions, feminists tend to be more struck by the presence of oppressive structures affecting women and to turn their attention to analysis and critique of those institutions. Similarly, the tools of philosophy, sharpened for the fine analysis of concepts, are more readily put to use in the examination of the many aspects of oppression.

It cannot be too strongly emphasized that none of these is a strictly either/ or distinction, for while this theoretical division does mark a difference of approach, it does not inevitably result in incompatible sets of conclusions. After all, activity is activity within recognized oppressive circumstances, and oppression is oppression of conscious human beings capable of action. Precisely because each emphasis illuminates truths about female reality, together they present complex problems that must be confronted in the development of sophisticated methodological perspectives for the study of women. The theoretical question of whether to focus on women's active agency or their oppression forms the frame within which we present a picture of how feminist scholarship, building on the initial critiques discussed in Chapter 1, has developed within the disciplines.

A Rediscovered Reality

From the perspective of this debate, of the five disciplines discussed in this study, the most readily complementary work has been that produced by feminist scholars in history, literature, and anthropology. All three have come to emphasize the active agency of women. Yet each began with a tradition of inquiry that assumed that women are solely the objects of the dynamic influences shaping their world and that their roles are wholly defined through accommodation to those their male counterparts actively carve out for themselves. From the initial recognition of how male bias operates in these fields, feminists have moved to reassess and replace these premises with a different approach to the reality of women's existence.

Divesting themselves of the presumption that only men's activities had social value, feminist researchers have given us fresh pictures of female experience in diverse cultures. A distinguishing feature of anthropological research—traditional and feminist—is its emphasis on community studies that convey and explain the culture and social organization of particular groups. No longer do women lurk as shadows in the background of these studies. They emerge as conscious actors living full, deliberate, complex lives.

Betty Chiñas's early ethnographic study, *The Isthmus Zapotecs: Women's Roles in Cultural Context*, presents a useful framework for revealing women's full role in culture and society. "Perhaps we have overlooked the 'action' of women's roles in many cultures," she speculates, "because that action is qualitatively different from that associated with male roles." To redirect attention to women she challenges the traditional anthropological assumption that in any society "the sexes perceive their culture and their own sex's place in it in essentially the same way . . . and that men and women share a common culture in similar terms."[1] Instead, she claims that men and women stand in profoundly different relations to their common culture. She argues that all societies have formalized and unformalized roles and that men usually monopolize the former, women the latter. Seen in their own terms, women's social roles become significant. In her ethnography Chiñas documents women's formal roles in the family and the market, and their nonformal roles as messengers, mediators, and maintainers of order. Women emerge as strong, self-conscious actors with a sense of identity as women and a feeling of sisterhood and solidarity. Chiñas posits that their social contribution is so essential that, despite an ideology that assumes male dominance, Zapotec society should be viewed as one in which men and women approach equality.

In "Women and Politics" Jane Collier outlines another perspective for revealing women's activity by challenging the assumption that only men engage in political activities. While acknowledging that the norms of most societies assert that men are important in public life and that women are insignificant, she suggests that we need to go beyond this and look at how women do act to influence society and assert their interests. Hence she declares: "The model woman of my argument . . . is not the affectionate daughter, hard-working wife, or loving mother who gets into trouble while trying to make the best of a difficult situation, but the cold, calculating female who uses all available resources to control the world around her."[2] Recognizing that anthropologists no longer analyze male political behavior simply in terms of normative rules, but rather consider the wider constraints governing individual choices, she urges that we do the same for women. Collier suggests that this has never been done because, although anthropologists have the analytical tools to do so, they have not seen social patterns in female behavior and have assumed it to be idiosyncratic or unpredictable. She sees such a pattern in the roles women take in instigating domestic quarrels, in societies in which power rests on the size and cohesiveness of patrilocal extended families. Women's interests, in these

1. Chiñas, *The Isthmus Zapotecs: Women's Role in Cultural Context* (New York: Holt, Rinehart and Winston, 1973), 2.
2. Collier, "Women in Politics," in *Woman, Culture and Society*, ed. Michelle Zimbalist Rosaldo and Louise Lamphere (Stanford: Stanford University Press, 1974), 90.

societies, are quite different from men's because they have more control when their lineage divides, while men's power rests on the consolidation of lineages. The society itself—and sometimes the anthropologist as well—describes women's initiation of quarrels in terms of male and female character: men are cooperative, women are "immature and unstable." Collier's framework shows that women's quarrelsomeness has nothing to do with innate character, but rather with their necessarily covert efforts to defend their interests in a system in which they have no overt political power.

This sort of approach is developed at greater length in Margery Wolf's work on rural Taiwan, an ethnographic study that reveals how Chinese women have attained power despite a strongly male-dominated patriarchal social structure.[3] Previous research on Chinese society interprets women as passive pawns for male activity, but Wolf shows how women develop an influential position with their husbands and the husbands' lineage by forging strong ties with their children, and that their power increases as their children mature. In addition, she shows how adult women's gossip, though informal, is an integral part of social life and has a strong influence on men, who do not want to lose face. From Wolf's work emerges a new picture of Chinese women as politically astute and effective at bettering their situation, given the confines of their society. This understanding of Chinese women in traditional society illuminates puzzling questions in later periods, notably how the Chinese Communist Revolution could so readily and effectively involve the active participation of women. Thus, the indubitably oppressive circumstances of traditional patriarchy are seen in a new light, whereby women do not merely submit to their assigned lot, but manipulate their situations to their own best advantage.

The framework of women's active social agency has become virtually axiomatic in feminist anthropological research.[4] Not only does it make women visible and important where previously they were not, it opens up whole new areas for anthropological inquiry. For instance, studies of women marketers in Africa and Latin America are already extensive enough to constitute a subspecialty of their own, as are studies on birthing practices and gynecological care.[5]

---

3. Wolf, *Women and the Family in Rural Taiwan* (Stanford: Stanford University Press, 1972).

4. For an interesting comment on the possible Western bias in the concept of active agency, see Jane Monnig Atkinson, "Review Essay, Anthropology," *Signs* 8 (1982) 250–51.

5. See, for instance, Ann McElroy and Fran Assael, "Selected Bibliography on Reproductive Anthropology and Birthing Studies" (mimeographed, SUNY, Buffalo, Department of Anthropology, 1983).

Furthermore, this work does more than enlarge our understanding of women: It also elicits reinterpretation of old conclusions about societies in general. This sort of revision can be seen in a work such as Annette Weiner's monograph on the Trobriand Islanders, *Women of Value, Men of Renown*.⁶ The original study of the Trobrianders by Bronislaw Malinowski is a classic in anthropology and so remarkable for its fullness that before Weiner's work it seemed beyond revision, especially by feminists, since Malinowski had already acknowledged that Trobriand women had high status.⁷ But Weiner argues that Malinowski did not seriously consider women's lives nor question male dominance. Rather he made a superficial case for their high status without documenting its basis. Her research suggests that women's power in Trobriand society is not located simply in the world of politics and economics but derives from reproduction, women's role in the continuity of life. Through an analysis of women's life cycle, she shows the value that both sexes give to women, which derives from the entire society's respect for the regeneration of human life, and the complete control women have in this area. She also documents the importance of women's wealth, a phenomenon Malinowski completely missed. Women work daily to amass wealth for payments to be made at mortuary rites. This wealth both influences the entire system of Trobriand exchange and, at the same time, is important for the continuity of the matrilineage by allowing the deceased to be reclaimed for the lineage of his or her birth. Weiner argues that men's power in Trobriand society is in the world of politics and economics — what she calls historical time. Women share this domain with men, but their real power derives from the reproduction and the continuity of life, what Weiner calls cosmic time, an area where they have full control. Weiner suggests that it is our own ethnocentrism and sexism that prevents us from seeing this base of women's power and from accepting the complex balance of Trobriand gender relations.

6. Weiner, *Women of Value, Men of Renown: New Perspectives on Trobriand Exchange* (Austin: University of Texas Press, 1976). See also Weiner, "Trobriand Kinship from Another View: The Reproductive Power of Women and Men," *Man* 2 (1979), 328–48, and Weiner, "Reproduction: A Replacement for Reciprocity," *American Ethnologist* 7 (1980), 71–85.

7. See Malinowski, *Argonauts of the Western Pacific* (New York: E. P. Dutton, 1922), *Coral Gardens and Their Magic*, 1 & 2 (London: Allen & Unwin, 1935), and *The Sexual Life of Savages* (London: George Routledge and Sons, 1932).

Urban community studies have also benefited from the challenge of feminist reinterpretation. Carol Stack's research on the black urban family in the United States, for example, criticizes those scholars, notably Daniel P. Moynihan, who blame the current problems of blacks on the disintegration of the black family, hence ultimately on the black woman.[8] Stack inverts Moynihan's emphasis and centers her work on the activity of women and the relations among them that form the basic kin linkages that shape the family system of poor black people and insure community survival. Her study suggests that so long as women's activities and interactions are paid little heed urban families will never be understood on their own terms, but will only be judged by essentially abstract and external ideological norms of family life.

In addition to such studies of self-contained communities, feminist anthropologists have also examined women's activities in the context of changing economic and political conditions of Third World nations. In taking this direction feminists are supported by the recent trend in the entire field of anthropology toward research that situates communities within massive worldwide social changes. The task of feminist scholarship, however, is nonetheless distinct: to take topics such as production, development, migration, and so forth, traditionally associated with the public sphere and therefore with men, and reconceptualize them so that they include women. Such work is similar to that of feminists in other disciplines, who focus on economic development and political transformation—economics, sociology, and political science—and therefore will be considered as part of our interdisciplinary treatment of feminist scholarship on modernization theory and socialism in Chapter 4.

Here, however, we want to show how development research also contributes to new conceptual frameworks used in the anthropology of women. For instance, Kate Young's study of the impact of capitalist development on the sexual division of labor in Oaxaca, Mexico, shows how women's work was dramatically transformed as coffee production replaced the domestic manufacture of cloth.[9] Women no longer organized their own

---

8. Stack, *All Our Kin: Strategies for Survival in a Black Community* (New York: Harper and Row, 1974).

9. Young, "Modes of Appropriation and the Sexual Division of Labor: A Case Study from Oaxaca, Mexico," in *Feminism and Materialism: Women and Modes of Production*, ed. Annette Kuhn and AnnMarie Wolpe (London: Routledge and Kegan Paul, 1978), 124–54.

work in the home as weavers but had to respond to the households' need for labor in the coffee harvest. In addition, they lost their independent source of income, for their labor in harvesting was an unremunerated contribution to the household economy. These general changes, however, had varying effects on women of different classes. Poor women of landless families had to work outside the home for survival, and therefore maintained some degree of independence from their husbands, though they were scorned for their menial jobs and offered less support than their husbands in this work. The richer women also worked outside the home, but in managerial tasks, and were valued and respected. Women of the middle stratum, the families with small coffee-producing farms, became firmly locked into their domestic roles, dependent on their husbands while providing hidden labor for the coffee harvest. This kind of study reorients feminist anthropology from a vague presumption of the underlying unity in the condition of women toward specific analyses that stress historical conditions and class forces.

The explosion of feminist scholarship in anthropology is not simply due to its potential for revealing women's activity in particular societies. Because of its emphasis on comparative methods, its concern with human origins, and its focus on the specifics of culture, anthropology has the potential to answer questions about women's status and subordination prominent in the minds of contemporary feminists. Is the subordination of women universal? Are there different forms of subordination, and what determines the differences? Does economic development improve or lower women's status? Feminist scholarship on women's agency refines and multiplies these questions. Does the fact that women are conscious actors influencing society mean that they are not oppressed or not subordinate to men? Does the existence of pride and solidarity among women and the important contributions women make to the economy mean that they are equal to men? How is female power in reproduction to be evaluated in relation to male power in politics and the economy? Feminist anthropologists have generated a substantial body of analytical writing on these topics using preexisting data, new ethnohistorical research, and original field studies.

For a similar kind of analysis showing the impact of capitalist development on women of different classes in rural Indonesia, see Ann Stoler, "Class Structure and Female Autonomy in Rural Java," *Signs* 3 (1977), 74–89.

From the beginning feminist anthropologists have been interested in exploring the determinants of women's status. By comparing societies they have begun to isolate what factors in social life lead to women having a relatively high or low status. Looking at the economy, researchers have identified clearly that it is not women's participation in production that leads to high status, but rather their control over the process of production and over the distribution of goods.[10] Others have examined the degree to which systems of production institutionalize a separation between the private and the public spheres, documenting the correlation between women's low status and the degree to which women's work is limited to the domestic sphere.[11]

In addition to economic factors, scholars look at the way social organization, particularly family forms and residence patterns, shape women's status by creating the potential for solidarity among women.[12] Others have considered the influence of ideological systems. In an article which has had influence beyond anthropology, Sherry Ortner analyzes the opposition between nature and culture as an ideological universal and locates women's oppression in the symbolic association of women with the former and men with the latter.[13] At the same time there is a growing tendency to question the assumption that a society has a unitary belief system with regard to gender and to consider the possibility that men and women might hold differing views of maleness and femaleness.[14] Daisy Dwyer, drawing on her

10. See, for instance, Judith Brown, "Economic Organization and the Position of Women among the Iroquois," *Ethno-history* 17 (1970), 151–67; Ernestine Friedl, *Women and Men: An Anthropologist's View* (New York: Holt, Rinehart and Winston, 1975); and Deniz Kandiyoti, "Sex Roles and Social Change: A Comparative Appraisal of Turkey's Women," *Signs* 3 (1977), 57–73.

11. See, for example, Karen Sacks, "Engels Revisited: Women, the Organization of Production and Private Property," in *Woman, Culture and Society*, ed. Rosaldo and Lamphere, 207–22.

12. See, for example, Nancy Leis, "Women in Groups: Ijaw Women's Associations," in *Woman, Culture and Society*, ed. Rosaldo and Lamphere, 223–43. For a general discussion of the forces creating women's solidarity, see *Women United, Women Divided: Comparative Studies of Ten Contemporary Cultures*, ed. Patricia Caplan and Janet M. Bujra (Bloomington: Indiana University Press, 1979).

13. Ortner, "Is Female to Male as Nature Is to Culture," in *Woman, Culture and Society*, ed. Rosaldo and Lamphere, 67–88.

14. See, for instance, *Perceiving Women*, ed. Shirley Ardener, (London: Malaby, 1975); Susan Rogers, "Woman's Place: A Critical Review of Anthropological Theory," *Comparative*

own field data, argues that in the Moroccan town she studied men and women both agree about women's inferiority, but only men consider men more capable than women. She posits that there are four possible kinds of sexual ideologies: men and women could hold the same ideas about maleness and femaleness; they could agree about maleness but disagree about femaleness; they could agree about femaleness and disagree about maleness; or they could disagree about both. She suggests that the type of belief system is important for understanding women's role in society, for it has a significant impact on women's consciousness and the form of political action they choose.[15]

This kind of research has established the complexity of assessing women's social position and the need for a multidimensional analysis of status, which includes economic forces, social organization, and ideology.[16] Debate continues over which elements in social life are primary for determining women's status. In pursuit of clarity on these issues some scholars have shifted their framework from one which only considers women to one which analyzes patterns of gender relations and considers gender as an organizing force in society; for sexual hierarchy is a system of social relations between men and women which creates women's subordination, and it cannot be understood by looking at women alone. This direction of research is already present in the work of Young and Dwyer. Young, like a growing number of scholars, uses the analytical framework of the sexual division of labor to reveal women's changing role in production and the family in the context of changes in the entire system of gender relations.[17]

Studies in Society and History 20 (1978), 123–73; Constance Sutton et al., "Women, Knowledge and Power," in *Women Cross-Culturally: Change and Challenge*, ed. Ruby Rohrlich-Leavitt (The Hague: Mouton, 1975), 581–600; Daisy Dwyer, *Images and Self-Images: Male and Female in Morocco* (New York: Columbia University Press, 1978).

15. Dwyer, "Ideologies of Sexual Inequality and Strategies for Change in Male-Female Relations," *American Ethnologist* 5 (1978), 227–40.

16. This kind of model is proposed in Alice Schlegel, "Toward a Theory of Sexual Stratification," in *Sexual Stratification: A Cross-Cultural View*, ed. Alice Schlegel (New York: Columbia University Press, 1977), 1–40. The literature on determinants of the status of women is reviewed in Naomi Quinn, "Anthropological Studies on Women's Status," *Annual Review of Anthropology* 6 (1977), 181–225; see also Rogers, "Woman's Place." The following review essays in *Signs* on anthropology are useful: Louise Lamphere's *Signs* 2 (1977), 612–27, Rayna Rapp's, ibid., 4 (1979), 497–512; and Atkinson's, ibid., 8(1982), 236–58.

17. For examples of this approach, see Kate Young, Carol Wolkowitz, and Roslyn McCullagh, *Of Marriage and the Market: Women's Subordination in International Perspective*

In the area of cultural analyses a new development conceptualizes male and female as a culturally created system of meanings and analyzes the way that such a system is constructed and reproduced in a particular society.[18] Judith Shapiro argues for the necessity of this shift from studying women to the consideration of gender as a social fact. She states: "The task before us, as I see it, is one of making it as impossible for social scientists to avoid dealing with gender in their studies of social differentiation as it is for them to avoid dealing with such things as race, class, and kinship. The goal is to integrate the study of gender differences into the central pursuit of the social sciences and, in turn, to see what way these pursuits are modified and refined by understanding the particular features of gender as a principle of social organization."[19]

Analyses which explore the determinants of women's status and the construction of gender systems through the use of comparative methods are anthropology's most recognized contribution to feminist scholarship. They raise central, controversial questions about the origins of women's oppression and the possibilities for ending it that we shall consider in the next chapter; and they also raise methodological issues about ways to assess the status of women and the measurement of change in that status that will be considered in Chapter 4. Anthropology reveals a dialectical relationship between studies of women's activity and studies of women's oppression. Research perspectives that examine women's agency in shaping culture and society and thereby explode the myths about women's natural passivity bring into focus the need to search for the social causes of asymmetrical gender relations.

The question of whether oppression or agency should be the central focus of feminist scholarship has been a lively one among contemporary women's historians as well. While aware of the changing structures of women's oppression, they have been more intrigued by the largely unexamined questions of women's historical activity and they have insisted on the importance of

---

(London: CSE Books, 1981); and special issue on "Development and the Sexual Division of Labor," *Signs* 7 (1981).

18. See, in particular, *Sexual Meanings: The Cultural Construction of Gender*, ed. Sherry Ortner and Harriet Whitehead, (Cambridge: Cambridge University Press, 1981).

19. Shapiro, "Anthropology and the Study of Gender," in *A Feminist Perspective in the Academy: The Difference It Makes*, ed. Elizabeth Langland and Walter Gove (Chicago: University of Chicago Press, 1983), 112.

studying women's role in creating the past. This emphasis was anticipated by Mary Beard, whose writings in the 1930s and 1940s stressed the importance of investigating women as "force" in history.[20] Beard argued that too great an emphasis on oppression makes women seem the victims of history and leads to serious distortions in our study of the past. It can inadvertently reinforce the stereotype of female passivity that feminist scholars are determined to eradicate. Beard's ideas about how women's history should be studied, which received little attention when she published them, have been very influential among contemporary feminists. Sheila Johansson, for instance, has argued forcibly that Beard's focus on women as actor is preferable to Simone de Beauvoir's emphasis on women as victim. "The most interesting and significant aspect of the history of women as a field is its potential for showing us that females, handicapped or not, did things . . . that affected the structure, function and historical unfolding of their societies."[21] Many other feminist historians have also embraced Beard's ideas, although with more appreciation for the still unanswered questions about the history of women's oppression. "Implicit in Beard's work," wrote Gerda Lerner, balancing the two poles of oppression and historical agency, "was the recognition of the duality of women's position in society; women are subordinate, yet central, victimized yet active."[22] Although feminist research has proceeded in classical, medieval, European, Latin American, and Asian history, we shall focus here primarily on American history, the largest and most complex subset of women's history in the discipline.

Beard's approach to women as historical "force" has been reinforced by the general interest of contemporary historians in the historical agency of the masses of people not in positions of formal power, workers and immigrants as well as women.[23] The emphasis on women's historical activity,

20. Beard, *Woman as Force in History: A Study in Traditions and Realities* (New York: Macmillan, 1946). See also Berenice Carroll, "Mary Beard's *Woman as Force in History*: A Critique," *Massachusetts Review* 13 (1972), 125–43; and *Mary Ritter Beard: A Sourcebook*, ed. Ann J. Lane (New York: Schocken, 1977).

21. Johansson, "'Herstory as History': A New Field or Another Field," in *Liberating Women's History: Theoretical and Critical Essays*, ed. Berenice Carroll (Urbana: University of Illinois Press, 1976), 400–430.

22. Lerner, *The Majority Finds Its Past: Placing Women in History* (New York: Oxford University Press, 1979), xxi.

23. The two historians most generally associated with this perspective are E. P. Thompson (British history) and Herbert Gutman (U.S. history). Mari Jo Buhle makes some

especially in the field of American history, has also been affected by a shift away from the optimistic, "progressive" account of historical development employed by scholars of Beard's generation to the much more critical approach that contemporary historians use to probe the underside of the American dream.[24] Both shifts can be seen in research into the historical activity of women in the racial conflicts of slavery, the industrial struggles of the labor movement, and the middle-class reform efforts of the nineteenth and early twentieth centuries. They can also be seen in feminists' reexamination of the role of women on the American frontier and their consequent challenge to the entire character of this most cherished of American historical myths. Here, as elsewhere, feminist historians are not only replacing a single sex picture of historical development with an understanding that women were present and active at every moment and in every aspect of the past. They are also demonstrating that the inclusion of women's lives has the power to alter the larger historical picture in significant ways.

An early example of the focus on women's historical agency and an influential indication of its ability to recast the larger historical issues was the 1972 essay "Reflections on the Black Woman's Role in the Community of Slaves" by Angela Davis, who is an activist and a professional philosopher.[25] While tracing the particular exploitation of black women in slavery, Davis's most powerful observations had to do with the special contributions black women had made to the defense of their people, shaping daily life in the slave community and participating in outright rebellion against the master class. By treating black women as active agents rather than passive victims in this most oppressive of American institutions, Davis helped to forge a new approach to the history of both slavery and women. Instead of focusing on the big house and the slave fields, where whites were in control, she

---

observations on the impact of these historians on women's history in "Recent Contributions to Women's History," *Radical History Review* 11 (1975), 4–11.

24. Ann D. Gordon, Mari Jo Buhle, and Nancy Schrom Dye, *Women in American Society: An Historical Contribution* (Somerville, Mass.: New England Free Press, n.d.), 2.

25. Davis, "Reflections on the Black Woman's Role in the Community of Slaves," reprinted from *The Black Scholar* in the *Massachusetts Review* 13 (1972), 81–100. See also *Black Women in White America: A Documentary History*, ed. Gerda Lerner (New York: Random House, 1972); *Black Women in Nineteenth Century American Life*, ed. Bert Lowenberg and Ruth Bogin (University Park: Pennsylvania State University Press, 1976); and *The Afro-American Woman: Struggles and Images*, ed. Sharon Harley and Rosalyn Terborg Penn (Port Washington, N.Y.: Kennikat Press, 1978).

gave her attention to the slave quarters, where women helped to develop and maintain an independent Afro-American culture and politics. Her work on the historical activity of black women, arguably slavery's greatest victims, suggested the system's internal weaknesses and essential instability, the wellsprings of rebellion that constantly undermined the authority of the planter class.

While very influential for its general emphasis on women as historical actors and its powerful new approach to slave life and culture, Davis's particular suggestions about the role of black women in slavery have not been followed up by detailed scholarship.[26] For the most part the work of women's historians in reevaluating slavery in terms of women's agency has focused on the plantation mistress rather than the slave woman.[27] While the slaveholding man of the plantation class frequently hired others to oversee field labor, thereby avoiding firsthand contact with the labor force under his authority, his wife had no such option and was directly responsible for disciplining the household slaves. The portrait that Anne Firor Scott and others have given us of the women of this class emphasizes their widespread, if secret, rebellion against the society in which they lived, a hatred in part of slavery and in part of slaves. Meanwhile, the role of black women in the history of slavery has also been obscured by black historians who, as Darlene Hines has observed, "viewed black women almost exclusively in terms of their roles in the black [slave] family."[28] Here, as elsewhere, the history of black women has fallen through the cracks between women's history and black history and lags behind either field in terms of development.

26. A rare exception is Darlene Clark Hines and Kate Wittenstein's "Female Slave Resistance: The Economics of Sex," in *The Black Woman Cross-culturally*, ed. Filomina Chioma Steady (Cambridge, Mass.: Schenkman, 1981).

27. Anne Firor Scott, *The Southern Lady: From Pedestal to Politics: 1830–1930* (Chicago: University of Chicago Press, 1970); and Scott, "Women's Perspective on the Patriarchy in the 1850s," *Journal of American History* 61 (1974), 52–64, reprinted in Scott's *Making the Invisible Woman Visible* (Urbana: University of Illinois Press, 1984); Catherine Clinton, *The Plantation Mistress: Woman's World in the Old South, 1780–1835* (New York: Pantheon, 1983); Steven M. Stowe, "'The *Thing*, Not Its Vision': A Woman's Courtship and Her Sphere in the Southern Planter Class," *Feminist Studies* 9 (1983), 113–30.

28. Darlene Hines, "Black Women's History, Black Family History: Where Are the Boundaries?" paper presented at the Organization of American Historians Meeting, Philadelphia, Pa., 1983, 3. For example, see Herbert Gutman, *The Black Family in Slavery and Freedom, 1750–1925* (New York: Pantheon–Random House, 1976), and John Blassingame, *The Slave Community: Plantation Life in the Ante-Bellum South* (New York: Oxford University Press, 1972).

Like female slaves, female industrial workers have been regarded mainly in terms of their economic and social victimization. Feminist scholars have been reexamining this history as one of activity, not just oppression. Their research has established that there have been significant numbers of women workers since the earliest phases of American industrialization. Indeed, the first industrial labor force in the United States, the factory operatives of the New England textile mills of the 1820s and 1830s, was female. Away from their families and living together in what one historian calls "communities of women," the New England millgirls were aware of their pathbreaking role as both independent women and industrial workers.[29] They consistently protested their low wages, long hours, and the patriarchal rules of the textile companies. Their strikes and labor organizations, some of which grew into region-wide movements in which men participated as well, challenge the standard interpretation that the nineteenth-century American labor movement was made up entirely of skilled male workers, defending their crafts against industrial technology. The efforts of the early New England millgirls begin a long and full history of women's militant labor activities. Feminist historians have also studied women workers' participation in men's nineteenth-century unions and labor federations, cross-class organizations of women formed to advance the labor organization of women workers, and the mass women's strikes in the garment and textile industries in the early twentieth century.[30] Research is only now beginning to appear on the role of women in the industrial upheavals of the 1930s and 1940s.[31] Eventually, the discoveries being made in women's labor history will lead to a new conceptualization of the stages of the American labor movement as a whole.

29. Thomas Dublin, *Women at Work: The Transformation of Work and Community in Lowell, Massachusetts, 1826–1860* (New York: Columbia University Press, 1979).

30. *Sex, Class and the Woman Worker*, ed. Milton Cantor and Bruce Laurie (Westport, Conn.: Greenwood Press, 1977); Meredith Tax, *The Rising of the Women* (New York: Monthly Review Press, 1980); and Nancy Schrom Dye, *As Equals and as Sisters: Feminism, Unionism and the Women's Trade Union League of New York* (Columbia: University of Missouri Press, 1980). A new overview is Alice Kessler Harris's *Out to Work: A History of Wage-Earning Women in the United States* (New York: Oxford University Press, 1982).

31. Ruth Milkman, "Organizing the Sexual Division of Labor: Historical Perspectives on 'Women's Work' and the American Labor Movement," *Socialist Review* 10 (1980), 1–19. Sharon Hartman Strom, "Challenging 'Woman's Place': Feminism, the Left and Industrial Unionism in the 1930s," *Feminist Studies* 9 (1983), 359–86.

The role of women in the middle-class reform movements of the nine-teenth- and early twentieth-century United States is also being reexamined from different angles. Feminist scholars are investigating how women's rights organizations embodied the social relations and cultural values of the women who were their constituency.[32] Another approach is to explore the many reform movements to which women's rights was related, ranging from the moral reform and antislavery movements of the 1830s and 1840s to the labor reform and social welfare movements of the 1910s.[33] This research has important consequences for the larger history of American reform. For instance, research into women's activities in the late nineteenth-century temperance and social purity movements is adding a great deal to our knowledge of reform movements in general in that period.[34] In time this body of scholarship will result in a serious rethinking of the reform movements of the early twentieth-century Progressive era, which recognizes their nineteenth-century roots as well as their twentieth-century results.

Finally, women's historians are researching the active role of white women on the frontier. This has been a particularly popular area for feminist

32. Ellen Carol DuBois, *Feminism and Suffrage: The Emergence of an Independent Women's Movement in America, 1848–1869* (Ithaca: Cornell University Press, 1978); *Elizabeth Cady Stanton, Susan B. Anthony: Correspondence, Writings, Speeches,* ed. Ellen Carol DuBois (New York: Schocken, 1981); Sharon Hartman Strom, "Leadership and Tactics in the American Woman Suffrage Movement: A New Perspective from Massachusetts," *Journal of American History* 62 (1975), 296–315; *From Parlor to Prison: Five American Suffragists Talk about Their Lives,* ed. Sherna Gluck (New York: Vintage, 1976).

33. Mary P. Ryan, *Cradle of the Middle Class: The Family in Oneida County, New York, 1790–1865* (Cambridge: Cambridge University Press, 1981), ch. 5; Nancy Hewitt, *Women's Voluntary Activities in Rochester, New York, 1820–1870* (Ithaca: Cornell University Press, 1983). Mari Jo Buhle, *Women and American Socialism, 1870–1920* (Urbana: University of Illinois Press, 1981); Karen J. Blair, *Clubwoman as Feminist: True Womanhood Redefined, 1868–1914* (New York: Holmes and Meier, 1980); Estelle B. Freedman, *Their Sisters' Keepers: Women's Prison Reform in America, 1830–1920* (Ann Arbor: University of Michigan Press, 1981); Linda Gordon, *Woman's Body, Woman's Right: A Social History of Birth Control in America* (New York: Grossman, 1976); Rosalind Rosenberg, *Beyond Separate Spheres: Intellectual Roots of Modern Feminism* (New Haven: Yale University Press, 1982).

34. Barbara Leslie Epstein, *The Politics of Domesticity: Women, Evangelism and Temperance in Nineteenth Century America* (Middletown: Wesleyan University Press, 1981); Ruth Bordin, *Women and Temperance: The Quest for Power and Liberty, 1873–1900* (Philadelphia: Temple University Press, 1981); William R. Leach, *True Love and Perfect Union: The Feminist Reform of Sex and Society* (New York: Basic Books, 1980).

scholarship, perhaps because the traditional picture of westward expansion is so flagrantly all male.[35] "Nowhere has this necessity to reexamine old explanations [from the perspective of women] been more evident than in regard to the frontier . . . ," observes historian Carl Degler. "All of the characteristics . . . ascribed to Americans because they had to conquer a wilderness [individualism, competitiveness, egalitarianism] actually applied to men only."[36] Like the millgirls, women on the frontier recognized the historically significant character of their own experience and left many diaries and much correspondence, which had not been examined by historians until modern feminist scholars took them up.[37] One theme that emerges from this body of evidence is the tremendous reluctance with which women faced the prospect of leaving established communities and personal ties for the "adventure" of settling new land. Like slave women, women on the overland trail engaged in protest activity, ranging from their insistence that the wagon trains stop entirely for the Sabbath, to occasional, outright attacks on their husbands and other men they considered responsible for their suffering. In one particularly memorable example, one distraught woman burned down her wagon so that her husband could not make her go any farther.[38] Overall, the history of white women on the frontier, like that of the native peoples who fought the white settlers for control of the land, does a great deal to undermine the "heroic" story of the American frontier, an unreflective, largely mythic account, that helps to justify both national and male chauvinism.

Although research into each of these areas of women's historical activity alters our sense of general historical phenomena, some feminist scholars have pointed out the limitations implicit in seeing their task solely as one of

---

35. John Mack Faragher, *Women and Men on the Overland Trail* (New Haven: Yale University Press, 1979); Julie Roy Jeffrey, *Frontier Woman: The Transmississippi West, 1840–1880* (New York: Hill and Wang, 1979); Glenda Riley, *Frontierswomen: The Iowa Experience* (Ames: Iowa State University Press, 1981).

36. Carl Degler, "What the Women's Movement Has Done to American History," in *Feminist Perspective in the Academy*, ed. Langland and Gove, 68.

37. *Women's Diaries on the Westward Journey*, ed. Lillian Schlissel (New York: Schocken, 1982); *Let Them Speak for Themselves: Women in the American West, 1848–1900*, ed. Christine Fischer (New York: E. P. Dutton, 1978).

38. John Faragher and Christine Stansell, "Women and Their Families on the Overland Trail, 1842–1867," *Feminist Studies* 2 (1975), 160.

fitting women into an already existing picture of society and history. Gerda Lerner has written extensively about the problems of such an orientation, which produces what she characterizes as "contribution history." "The movement in question stands in the foreground of inquiry," she explains, "and women made a 'contribution' to it." This approach is limited, she believes, because it "deals with women in male-defined society and tries to fit them into categories and value systems which consider man the measure of significance."[39] Lerner suggests, for example, that Jane Addams's greatest historical significance may lie not in her work with immigrants and the beginnings of social work (the "contribution history" perspective), but in her role in developing the settlement house as a structure of living and working for the new generation of independent, educated women of the late nineteenth century who chose not to marry. Even more forcefully, Lerner argues that the lives of women far less notable than Addams cannot be fully comprehended using analytical categories derived from the male experience; feminist scholars must "find a new framework for conceptualizing the history of women." As feminist scholars have begun to give attention to the "common" woman, the domestic woman, the private woman, the "feminine" woman, they are finding that even she—perhaps especially she—cannot be seen simply as a recipient of others' actions, that she creates her own life, influences others, and must be understood as a force in her own right.

One of the central concerns in the search for a new framework for women's history is the effort to recapture the distinct consciousness of women in the past, to discover how they—as contrasted with men—felt and saw themselves in the world. This concern with historical women's consciousness is consistent with the emphasis on activity rather than oppression; it is a reaction against the assumption that male stereotypes and norms for womanly behavior determine women's sense of themselves, and thus it is similar to the change of perspective, the emergence from the shadows advocated in anthropology by Betty Chiñas. Feminist historians have gone far beyond Barbara Welter's early essay, 'The Cult of True Womanhood," which documents nineteenth-century oppressive prescriptions concerning femininity. They have criticized this approach for assuming

39. Lerner, "Placing Women in History: Definitions and Challenges," *Feminist Studies* 3 (1975), 5–14.

that dominant ideas about the feminine ideal were passively and uncritically absorbed by women into their own self-images.[40]

Thus, in *The Bonds of Womanhood: 'Woman's Sphere' in New England, 1780–1835*, Nancy Cott initially intended to study the way that dominant stereotypes of femininity were absorbed by early nineteenth-century American women, but she came to reject this approach because it implicitly denied women's active role in history.[41] She chose, instead, an approach that assumes that ideas become widespread and accepted to the degree that they help people come to terms with their experiences. In an attempt to comprehend women's experience from within, Cott shows how popular, seemingly restrictive ideas about womanhood were used or interpreted by women to justify some independence, enlarge their sphere, improve their self-image, and build sisterhood among them. She says that women were neither totally victims of history nor mistresses of their fate, but a little of both. Still, the thrust of her work is to emphasize the active role women played in formulating nineteenth-century ideas about their sex. The effort to reconstruct women's consciousness has also led feminists to reassess institutions that have long been ignored by historians. Scholars are reexamining women's clubs and organizations (the Woman's Christian Temperance Union is a prime example), women's magazines, and the literature aimed at a predominantly female audience, the better to understand how women viewed their society and how they struggled to change it.[42]

Thus ideas and perspectives that were initially attributed to an oppressive "cult of true womanhood" have largely been reinterpreted by feminist historians in terms of a rich and empowering culture of women. By the term "women's culture" (sometimes "women's subculture") historians mean to indicate a set of habits, values, practices, institutions, and a way of seeing the world common to large numbers of middle-class nineteenth-century women and distinct from the characteristic male perspective of the

40. Welter, "The Cult of True Womanhood, 1820–1860," *American Quarterly* 18 (1966), 151–74.

41. Cott, *The Bonds of Womanhood: "Woman's Sphere" in New England, 1780–1835* (New Haven: Yale University Press, 1977).

42. Keith Melder, *Beginnings of Sisterhood: The American Woman's Rights Movement, 1800–1850* (New York: Schocken, 1977); Carroll Smith-Rosenberg, "Beauty, the Beast and the Militant Woman: A Case Study in Sex Roles and Social Stress in Jacksonian America," *American Quarterly* 23 (1971), 562–84; Blair, *Clubwoman as Feminist*; Bordin, *Women and Temperance*; Epstein, *Politics of Domesticity*.

time.[43] The concept, one of the most creative and important developments in contemporary women's history, has enabled feminists to discover and make sense of an enormous amount of information about women's lives, especially private and emotional realities that were previously invisible or made no sense to historians. Clearly this historical scholarship is related to work that feminist anthropologists have done on women's distinct activities and bases of power, but it is interesting to note that anthropologists, whose discipline is defined in terms of the examination of cultures, have been much more tentative about hypothesizing an independent women's culture than the historians. In any event, for anthropologists consideration of this issue is overshadowed by (and, to a great extent, subsumed in) the controversy over the determinants and significance of women's status that we discussed earlier.

A key element in the reconstruction of nineteenth-century American women's culture is the discovery of a rich and meaningful network of relations among women, which contradicts the notion that women were totally identified with the concerns of their nuclear families. The chief interpreter here is Carroll Smith-Rosenberg, who has recreated nineteenth-century women's intimate relations with each other, established the frequency of their occurrence, linked them to relations among women in their families, and given a term — "homosociality" — to this form of same-sex intimacy.[44] Much as the discovery of these sustaining ties reflects an intersection in the perspectives of anthropology and history, their exploration reveals a confluence in the interests of history and literature, where questions about women's consciousness and culture have also emerged. Thus, Smith-Rosenberg's ideas have been taken up enthusiastically not only by women's historians but also by feminist literary critics, who find such themes in nineteenth-century English and American literature. In *Communities of Women* Nina Auerbach applies the theme of women's culture directly to

43. Faragher and Stansell, "Women on the Overland Trail"; Cott, *Bonds of Womanhood*; Kathryn Kish Sklar, *Catharine Beecher: A Study in American Domesticity* (New Haven: Yale University Press, 1973). See also Ellen DuBois et al., "Politics and Culture in Women's History: A Symposium," *Feminist Studies* 6 (1980), 26–64.

44. Smith-Rosenberg, "The Female World of Love and Ritual: Relations between Women in Nineteenth-Century America," *Signs* 1 (1975), 1–30. It should be noted that historians like Cott and Smith-Rosenberg caution against extending their ideas about women's consciousness and culture from white middle-class women, whose diaries and letters they have studied, to black women, immigrant women, or poor women.

literature and explores the relations formed by female characters who are the fictional counterparts of Smith-Rosenberg's historical women.[45] Lillian Faderman interweaves the evidence for homosocial relations in both fiction and reality in an even earlier period into an extended study on the history and literature of lesbianism.[46]

As we pointed out in Chapter 1, a number of the early documents of the women's liberation movement, such as Kate Millett's *Sexual Politics* and Germaine Greer's *The Female Eunuch*, were the work of scholars of literature who used textual criticism as a point of departure for criticizing sexism in society at large. The examination of literature as a source of oppressive ideas about women remains an important task. Yet, paralleling the cases of history and anthropology, feminist literary scholars have turned most of their attention to the study of female agency which, in this field, means literature produced by women, chiefly about the nature and lives of women themselves.

Feminist literary scholars add a distinctive dimension to the growing body of knowledge about women's lives and activity: women's artistic expression and the conditions that shape it. The methods of the feminist literary scholars include reinterpretation of the work of recognized female authors, discovery or rediscovery of female authors who have been dismissed from the literary canon, and exploration of a specifically female literary tradition.

Women have been active in the literary profession in the English-speaking world for the past 300 years. While prefeminist scholarship had admitted a handful of these authors to the first rank of writers, most have been accorded secondary status. With the advent of feminist literary studies, both the great and the less great have been reconsidered, the major figures because they have been consistently misunderstood, the minor ones because they have not only been misinterpreted but also frequently undervalued.

The outpouring of feminist commentaries on such major authors as Virginia Woolf, George Eliot, the Brontës, Emily Dickinson, and Jane Austen focuses on the relations between their writing and the lives that women—including the authors themselves—lived. For instance, Jane

45. Auerbach, *Communities of Women: An Idea in Fiction* (Cambridge, Mass.: Harvard University Press, 1979). See also Janet Todd, *Female Friendship in Literature* (New York: Columbia University Press, 1980), and Louise Bernikow, *Among Women* (New York: Harmony, 1980).

46. Faderman, *Surpassing the Love of Men: Romantic Friendship and Love between Women from the Renaissance to the Present* (New York: Morrow, 1981).

Marcus emphasizes Woolf's relationships, literary, personal, and political, with other women. Drawing on Woolf's own argument that the emergence of a woman genius requires a long prior history of women's creative efforts, Marcus links Woolf to women writers before her. Similarly, Woolf's political and social views, especially her feminism, have become of central importance in the reinterpretation of her career, with Marcus insisting that we see Woolf not "in her own room but in a meeting room with other women, in her element as a public woman (within) the sisterhood of her peers."[47] This kind of analysis has been particularly important in bringing forward the less appreciated works of recognized writers, Charlotte Brontë's *Shirley* and *Villette*, for example, or Elizabeth Barrett Browning's *Aurora Leigh*. Feminists have pointed out that it was the consciousness these books reflect of women's common problems that has made them often seem obscure to traditional critics and that condemned them to relative obscurity in the history of literature.

But in literature, as in other disciplines, reinterpretation of existing scholarship on women cannot take us very far. Because so little of women's reality and so few women writers have found their way into the body of standard disciplinary knowledge, feminist scholarship has of necessity been overwhelmingly a work of discovery and rediscovery. Feminists have rescued from oblivion a whole series of women writers whose work had gone out of print and whose reputations had diminished or utterly disintegrated. One of the first of these rediscoveries was that of the nineteenth-century American fiction writer, Rebecca Harding Davis. Contemporary feminist Tillie Olsen recognizes in Davis a precursor of her own efforts to link the perspectives of women and of working people in literature. In her Afterword to the reissued *Life in the Iron Mills*, Olsen considers why Davis never wrote anything else as powerful or significant. In a moving account of Davis's marriage, motherhood, and the constant demand on her to maintain and support her family, Olsen examines the mundane pressures that overrode artistic concerns for Davis and for other women writers.[48] The list of American women authors similarly reclaimed from critical oblivion includes Elizabeth Stuart Phelps, Kate Chopin, Agnes Smedley, Mary

---

47. Marcus, "Art and Anger," *Feminist Studies* 4 (1978), 69–98, and her "Tintinnabulations," *Marxist Perspectives* 5 (1979), 144–67.

48. Olsen, "Afterword" to Rebecca Harding Davis's *Life in the Iron Mills* (Old Westbury: Feminist Press, 1972). See also the other essays collected in Olsen's *Silences* (New York: Seymour Lawrence–Delacorte, 1978).

Wilkins Freeman, Sarah Orne Jewett, Susan Glaspell, Edith Summers Kelley, Meridel LeSueur, and Anzia Yezierska.

Black women writers have been under a double injunction, having to face a critical jury that is both white and male. A pioneer effort in rescuing and defending a lost predecessor is that of author Alice Walker to rehabilitate the reputation and writings of the early twentieth-century writer Zora Neale Hurston. Along with Hurston's biographer, Robert Hemenway, Walker has helped to revive interest in Hurston, who was driven by critical attack and rejection from an initially brilliant career into defeat, poverty, and, ultimately, total obscurity.[49]

Complementing the effort of rediscovering forgotten individual writers is that of reconsidering entire genres of writing long dismissed as inherently minor, popular, transient, and (of course) feminine. These supposedly women's genres include domestic, sensational, Gothic, and sentimental fiction. Sentimentality, for instance, is at once a stance, a style, and a literary mode associated with women, and it has long been taken for granted that the work of nineteenth-century female authors who wrote for an audience of other women was so tainted with it as to be unworthy of serious critical examination. Feminist scholars have studied the sentimental novel from a standpoint sympathetic to the conflicts experienced by the women who wrote and read it, thus considering it as a social as well as a literary document, part of the struggle for nineteenth-century women's minds. The question of whether sentimental fiction served to strengthen and justify conventional roles for women or was one aspect of an essentially subversive tradition developed by women has therefore become a central question for literary scholars, paralleling similar debates about the "cult of true womanhood" among historians.[50]

49. Walker, "In Search of Zora Neale Hurston," *Ms.* 3 (Mar. 1975), 74–79, and Robert Hemenway, *Zora Neale Hurston* (Urbana: University of Illinois Press, 1977).

50. See Ann Douglas, *The Feminization of American Culture* (New York: Knopf, 1977), for a critical assessment of sentimental fiction as literature that takes the traditional stance about its literary merits. Opposing aspects of the controversy are explored in two articles that appeared in *Feminist Studies* 2 (1975): Elaine Showalter, "Dinah Mulock Craik and the Tactics of Sentiment: A Case Study in Victorian Female Authorship," 5–23, and Katherine Ellis, "Paradise Lost: The Limits of Domesticity in the Nineteenth-Century Novel," 55–63. Showalter also uses what might be termed the "argument from subversion" to reclaim the sensational novel as practiced by popular women novelists in the Victorian period. See Showalter, *A Literature Of Their Own: British Women Novelists from Brontë to Lessing* (Princeton: Princeton University Press, 1977). In the same vein see also Ellis, "Charlotte Smith's Subversive Gothic," *Feminist Studies* 3 (1976), 51–55. For a range of feminist

Precisely because, as Olsen and others have demonstrated, the female tradition in literature includes and is, in a sense, defined by the silence of the great mass of women, feminist literary scholars have tried to determine whether, running alongside the silence, it is possible to detect the elements of a mass female voice, strains of artistic expression by women who had no professional identity as writers or artists.[51] Thus, feminist literary critics have expanded their field (and the definition of literature itself) to include women's diaries, journals, private poetry, and letters. The search for the widest forms of female creative expression has also taken them beyond the written word, to look at tales, oral narratives, bawdy stories, and even quilts as forms of female artistic expression.[52] Walker has written movingly about those black women who make art out of everyday life—their homes and their gardens.[53]

For literature as more traditionally defined, reinterpretations of previously recognized writers, rediscovery of those whose reputations have declined, and research into forms of expression ignored by most scholars have occurred in such a way that each sort of scholarship creates the intellectual context for the pursuit of the other. It is a climate that makes the hypothesis of a female literary tradition a logical, almost inevitable development. The idea of a female tradition of literary expression complements the historian's notion of a women's culture. In fact, as the discussion of unpublished writings and other forms of female creative expression indicates, the sources pursued by feminist historians and literary critics have begun to merge.

The notion of a female literary tradition is not the product of a single scholar, but has evolved out of a series of critical interpretations. Louise Bernikow's collection, *The World Split Open*, published in 1974, is the first critical expression of the idea that a tradition—in this case, a poetic

---

readings of twentieth-century popular novels, see Ann Barr Snitow, "Mass Market Romance: Pornography for Women is Different," *Radical History Review* 20 (1979), 141–63; Lillian S. Robinson, "On Reading Trash," in her *Sex, Class, and Culture* (Bloomington: Indiana University Press, 1978), 200–222; Janice A. Radway, "Women Read the Romance: The Integration of Text and Context," *Feminist Studies* 9 (1983), 53–78; and Radway's *Reading the Romance: Women, Patriarchy, and Popular Culture* (Chapel Hill: University of North Carolina Press, 1984).

51. Olsen, *Silences*.

52. Rayna Green, "Magnolias Grow in Dirt," *Southern Exposure* 4 (1977), 29–33; Elaine Hedges, "Quilts and Women's Culture," in *In Her Own Image: Women Working in the Arts*, ed. Elaine Hedges and Ingrid Wendt (Old Westbury: Feminist Press, 1980).

53. Walker, "In Search of Our Mothers' Gardens," *Ms.* 2 (May 1974), 64–70.

tradition—links women writing through the centuries. Bernikow argues that there is a continuity in women's poetry that extends across the boundaries of class and race, as well as across the more artificial frontiers separating what is designated as high culture from popular art, and even literature from music. "Where women have distilled experience into the verbal art form that in so short a space can create for the reader so total a sensation, where women have found language to shape what is in our imaginations, we have made poetry," Bernikow maintains. "We have, from the first, been singers, always."[54]

In *The Female Imagination* Patricia Meyer Spacks contributes a rather loose series of observations about how various women writers have treated key issues, such as phases in the female life cycle, suggesting, though not demonstrating, that the tradition that links them inheres in common psychological or thematic concerns shared by all women in all times.[55] By contrast, in *Literary Women* Ellen Moers argues that it is the quality she calls "heroinism" that links women writers to one another and to the women they wrote about.[56] Moers thus emphasizes the awareness that women writers had of each other as they read and learned from the works of predecessors and contemporaries and the way this informed their treatment of female characters. In *A Literature of Their Own* Elaine Showalter suggests the conscious involvement of the audience in a definition of the female literary tradition. She argues that, despite some lacunae and the occasional absence of intentionality, a literary tradition existed among women from the eighteenth through much of the twentieth century that was based on a common sexual, social, and economic history and the shared culture to which these gave rise.[57] This culture and therefore women's literary tradition are shared by writer and reader, and Showalter's argument for the subversive potential of domestic or sensational fiction depends on the establishment of a kind of conspiracy between the two. Showalter's interpretive scheme and her extensive documentation of unknown writers of the nineteenth and early twentieth centuries also make an implicit case for perceiving popular and more serious fiction as complementary parts of the same tradition. This involves replacing the usual standards

---

54. Bernikow, "Introduction" to her *The World Split Open: Four Centuries of Women Poets in England and America, 1552–1950* (New York: Vintage–Random House, 1974), 47.

55. Spacks, *The Female Imagination* (New York: Knopf, 1975).

56. Moers, *Literary Women* (Garden City, N.Y.: Doubleday, 1976). See also Rachel M. Brownstein, *Becoming a Heroine: Reading about Women in Novels* (New York: Viking, 1982).

57. Showalter, *A Literature of Their Own.*

of "excellence" with values that examine the extent to which a work reflects or serves the interests of women. Sandra Gilbert and Susan Gubar, in *The Madwoman in the Attic*, return, by way of the "attributed oddness" of nineteenth-century female authors, to the links among women writers and the connection between this and what they had to say about the female experience through the women in their books.[58]

The development of feminist literary criticism in general is recapitulated in the special efforts of both black and lesbian feminist criticism. Both begin by attacking a critical tradition—this time including mainstream feminist criticism—that omits and distorts the work with which they are concerned and both, through a process of rediscovery and reevaluation, proceed to reconstitute a lost literary tradition, which is an unacknowledged part of female literary history, yet which reflects, as well its own discrete and autonomous tradition.

White feminist critics such as Spacks and Gilbert have been severely criticized for their apparent ignorance of black women writers and of the scholarship devoted to them in recent years.[59] The major task of black feminist criticism, however, has been the more positive one of bringing to light the wealth of writing by and about black women and demonstrating its coherence and power as a literary tradition. Scholarship on individual writers has been reinforced by syntheses such as Barbara Christian's work on black women novelists and Erlene Stetson's work on poets.[60] In addition to documenting a black women's literary tradition, such research also

58. Gilbert and Gubar, *The Madwoman in the Attic: The Woman Writer and the Nineteenth-Century Literary Imagination* (New Haven: Yale University Press, 1979).

59. See Barbara Smith, "Toward a Black Feminist Criticism," *Conditions* 2 (1977), 25–44; Alice Walker, "One Child of One's Own . . ." *Ms.* 7 (Aug. 1979); Mary Helen Washington, "New Lives and New Letters: Black Women Writers at the End of the Seventies," *College English* 42 (1981). Smith also points out the shortcomings of black male criticism in regard to women writers.

60. Christian, *Black Women Novelists: The Development of a Tradition, 1892–1976* (Westport, Conn.: Greenwood Press, 1980); *Black Sister: Poetry by Black American Women, 1746–1980*, ed. Erlene Stetson (Bloomington: Indiana University Press, 1981), and *Black Sister II*, ed. Erlene Stetson (Bloomington: Indiana University Press, forthcoming). On Hurston, see the material cited above, as well as Alice Walker, "Dedication: On Refusing to be Humbled by Second Place in a Contest You Did Not Design," and Mary Helen Washington, "Zora Neale Hurston: A Woman Half in Shadow," both in *I Love Myself When I Am Laughing and then Again When I Am Looking Mean and Impressive*, ed. Alice Walker (Old Westbury: Feminist Press, 1979). For other work by black feminist critics on

significantly changes critical generalizations about the female tradition and the female voice in our literature as a whole.[61]

Most of the books that speak in terms of a single female tradition are marked by heterosexual presumptions, where they are not openly antilesbian. One strain in lesbian feminist criticism catalogues these failings and their consequences for feminist criticism generally, noting where the sexuality of lesbian writers is ignored or even deprecated and where the word lesbian is used pejoratively.[62] Like the research of black feminist critics, however, this negative effort has claimed less attention than the positive work of reclaiming a lesbian feminist literary tradition.[63] But here the parallel ends. Just what is the lesbian tradition? In the case of black literature the problem does not arise in this form. Criticism has not acknowledged that there have been important black women writers or that what they have to say about the lives of their sisters is a worthwhile or significant literary contribution. The task of black feminist criticism is to identify the writers, make their work known, and argue for its literary merit and its continuity as a tradition. No one quarrels with the essential elements: If one grants there is a black female literary tradition, it necessarily consists of the literature created by black women.

---

black women writers, see also Mary Helen Washington, "Introduction: In Pursuit of Our Own History," in *Midnight Birds: Stories of Contemporary Black Women Writers* (Garden City, N.Y.: Doubleday, 1980); Bettye J. Parker, "Introduction: Black Women in and out of Fiction: Toward a Correct Analysis," and Gloria Hull, "Black Women Poets from Wheatley to Walker," both in *Sturdy Black Bridges: Visions of Black Women in Literature*, ed. Roseann P. Bell, Bettye J. Parker, and Beverly Guy-Sheftall (New York: Anchor, 1979).

61. See Lillian S. Robinson, *Women and Fictions* (London: Methuen, forthcoming).

62. See, for instance, Smith, "Toward a Black Feminist Criticism"; Becky Birtha, "Is Feminist Criticism Really Feminist?" in *Lesbian Studies*, ed. Margaret Cruikshank (Old Westbury: Feminist Press, 1982); Maureen Brady and Judith McDaniel, "Lesbians in the Mainstream: Images of Lesbians in Recent Commercial Fiction," *Conditions* 6 (1980).

63. Adrienne Rich, "Jane Eyre: Trials of a Motherless Girl," in her *Lies, Secrets, and Silence: Selected Prose, 1966–1978* (New York: Norton, 1979). But see also Bonnie Zimmerman, "What Has Never Been: An Overview of Lesbian Feminist Literary Criticism," *Feminist Studies* 7 (1981), and her "Is 'Chloe Liked Olivia' a Lesbian Plot?" *Women's Studies International Forum* 6 (1983), 169–75. On questions related to teaching this material, see Zimmerman, "One out of Thirty: Lesbians in Women's Studies Textbooks"; Kathy Hickock, "Lesbian Images in Women's Literature Anthologies"; Evelyn Torton Beck, "Teaching about Jewish Lesbians in Literature: From *Zeitl and Rickel* to *The Tree of Begats*"; Toni A. H. McNaron, "A Journey into Otherness: Teaching the Well of Loneliness," all in *Lesbian Studies*, ed. Cruikshank.

By contrast many literary critics acknowledge that certain well-recognized women writers were lesbians for all or a part of their lives. But until recently no one suggested that the fiction of Gertrude Stein and Virginia Woolf might be part of a lesbian tradition—much less that *The Well of Loneliness*, which is not usually considered great literature, but is one of the most influential novels of the century, might partake of the same tradition. Or that certain popular paperback novels of the 1950s, addressed to an audience seeking affirmation in the experience of coming out and assuming a lesbian identity, might also be studied as part of the same lesbian literary voice. Does lesbian feminist criticism mean identifying how the writing of women like Stein and Woolf was shaped by their sexuality? Would the tradition include all kinds of writing by lesbians, whether or not the subject is the relations between women? And what sorts of relationships—other than specifically sexual ones—should be understood as lesbian?

The most inclusive responses to this last question bring us back to the shared women's culture perspective of literature and history. Demonstrating the existence of powerful primary relations among women lends strong support to the hypothesis of a culture in the more general affective and practical sense in which historians use the term. At the same time that women's world is the milieu and often the subject of literature in the female tradition, and the women who participated in the "women's culture" were that literature's natural audience. Thus, in discerning female community or its absence in women's literature Nina Auerbach employs the concept normatively, valuing works of fiction in which it is a defining force—*Little Women*, for one—over those books by female authors—*Pride and Prejudice*, for example—in which the women live in a male-defined universe, unsustained by such relations.[64] The debate is joined in terms echoing those in other fields: Does women's participation in a network of female relationships mean that they live, essentially, in a world of their own, which they actively make; or should these strong relations with other women be seen as an adaptation to oppression and situated in the larger world, in which men have more power?[65]

Because literary feminists often discuss the world of literature as an almost self-contained universe, literary critics have come rather late to the questions anthropologists have been raising about the connection between

---

64. Auerbach, *Communities of Women*.
65. See DuBois et al., "Politics and Culture" in Women's History."

what we have learned from the reevaluation of women's cultural activity and their social status relative to men. In *Women, Power and Subversion* Judith Newton places her study clearly in the cross-disciplinary tendency of feminists "adjusting our sights from women's oppression to women's agency." Although she concentrates on "power as ability," Newton never loses sight of the historical or literary constraints under which women authors and their female characters operated in a man's world. As she describes the process, "Both a preoccupation with power and subtle power strategies . . . presented themselves . . . like unlooked-for patterns in a carpet, the startling figure of a fist, say, repeated at intervals among the peonies."[66] Exploring novels by Fanny Burney, Jane Austen, Charlotte Brontë, and George Eliot, Newton makes a real contribution to the active agency position, examining female characters' activity as well as that of their creators, without confusing cultural resistance with historical autonomy.

In their different ways historians, literary scholars, and anthropologists have given real substance to the feminist assertion that women are not just passively molded by external factors but active agents in human society. Not only had such passivity been almost axiomatic in the disciplines before the development of feminism within them, but it was even carried over into early feminist analyses of women's condition. By positing the fullness of women's lives, their independent bases of power, their distinct cultures and separate traditions of artistic expression, feminist scholars are able to offer both a description of women's activities and an explanation for how they could have been overlooked so long. Such research allows us to see the reality of female existence in a more positive and more complex light than is possible with a simple focus on the effects of oppression. It also allows a reassessment of the values we place on domestic activities and private lives, on women's associations and friendships, and on all the beliefs and activities associated with them, both in the past and in cultures other than our own.

But the emphasis on women's activities raises questions of its own, and the responses to them are beginning to describe a major and vital debate among feminists, some of which is presaged in the anthropological discussion on women's status. The idea of a culture or tradition exclusive to women, most of whom live dispersed among men, experiencing their social,

66. Newton, *Women, Power and Subversion: Social Strategies in British Fiction, 1778–1860* (Athens: University of Georgia Press, 1981), xv, xvii.

historical, and creative lives in situations where male structural domination continues, raises problems of clarity and precision. There is also the difficulty in attributing only to women values and practices that also flourish within same-sex relations among men. Finally, the emphasis on women's activities inevitably raises normative questions. What value do we place on the cultures and traditions that women have created? Do we discover so much strength and richness that our previous perceptions of subordination and inequality are all but eclipsed? Or do we see women's separate world as making a poor virtue of necessity? These are the poles of debate; possible resolutions fall along a wide spectrum between them.

These problems notwithstanding, the recognition of women's independent historical and social agency and the need for an appropriate framework for analyzing it has marked a tremendous step forward in feminist scholarship. It raises provocative questions about the relations between women's activity and the conditions of women's oppression and lays the foundation for much greater sophistication about the interconnections among complicity, resistance, and oppression in the lives of women.

The Boundaries of Choice

Though notably different from one another, neither philosophy nor education lends itself particularly to discoveries about how women live and work. Consequently, neither discipline has contributed much to the proliferation of work describing women's agency that is so remarkable in history, anthropology, and literature. The work of feminist scholars in both philosophy and education tends to emphasize the sexist institutions and ideologies within which women's activity is contained. This occurs for different though complementary reasons: education examines what the schools teach; philosophy, the abstract systems of ideas that refine and reflect the fundamental beliefs of a culture and are passed on through institutions of learning. Of the fields we consider here, these two, the oldest and the newest, are the ones that turn the most direct attention to the political issues facing the women's movement today: education, because of its emphasis on policy; philosophy, because of its disposition to bring tools of analysis to matters of moral and social significance.

Since the field of education tends to rest on the assumption that learning directly mirrors what is taught, most feminist research in the discipline concentrates more on an analysis and critique of the institutions of learning and less on the independent activities of students in those institutions. The picture is rather more mixed in philosophy, where a considerable amount of early scholarship was directed to specific issues of relevance to women, such as abortion and sex equality, subjects where an emphasis on either activity or oppression does not clearly develop. Yet the pervasiveness of masculine bias in virtually all influential philosophical works has been so striking that scholars who examine the history of philosophy, political theory, or a host of concepts relevant to ideas about women find themselves engaged of necessity in charting and dismantling the foundations of that bias.

Although we wish to illuminate the ways in which the purview of a given discipline shapes the feminist research that arises within it, there is no inherent reason why these tendencies need be a permanent state of affairs. Just as feminism poses challenges to the discipline, so it must meet the challenges presented by the complexity of its own discoveries. When we conclude our discussion of specific fields, we shall consider how the two strains of feminist scholarship we have identified—research about the realities of women's lives and examination of sexist institutions and ideas—interweave into broader theoretical analyses of basic feminist questions in such a way that disciplinary boundaries begin to disappear.

Documentation of the complexity of women's lives and concern for what it means to incorporate women fully into our understanding of society make it imperative to analyze basic institutions that shape the options women have. Many of the historical, literary, and anthropological studies of women's lives and activities we have examined are also at the same time examinations of such social structures as motherhood, industrialization, and the family. But this type of institutional analysis is not the traditional concern of these disciplines. By contrast, other fields, such as economics, political science, and education, are organized around the study of particular institutions and permit the study of the restraints imposed on women. In these fields feminist scholarship focuses on such issues as the sex-segregated nature of the labor force, the marginalization of women in political processes, and the effect of schools on women's achievement; in so doing, these studies often ignore the questions about women's own activity that are so central to historians, literary critics, and anthropologists. We shall consider education as an example of a field in which the primary direction of feminist scholarship has been to look at how an institution—in this case, the schools—shapes women's lives.

While some of the early feminist critiques of educational research on sex differences in achievement suggested that those differences might not be as great as they appeared and a few even argued that the entire literature rested on dubious assumptions, most feminist scholars in education have accepted the existence of differentials. They have, however, focused attention on how these differences have been created. Miriam David, for example, shows how public policy has shaped family life and the definition of appropriate sex behavior, both of which socialize girls to feminine roles prior to their entry into school and continue to exert influence throughout the life cycle.[67] Janet Lever has emphasized the function of play in developing the sex cultures that schools reinforce. Lever shows that girls play indoors while boys play outdoors, and that girls play in smaller groups than do boys and in a less competitive fashion. In their play girls learn individualism rather than teamwork and as a result develop fewer organizational skills.[68]

The different socialization of girls and boys in the family and in the schools has resulted in differences in the ways they think and reason. Carol Gilligan's research on the way females, as opposed to males, think has shown that they pay more attention to context in making judgments than men and place a greater value on relationships and interdependence. Gilligan contrasts the degree to which women's moral reasoning is based on responsibility with men's tendency to reason on the basis of rights.[69]

While feminists acknowledge that sex differences in educational achievement exist, they argue that they reflect nurture rather than nature and so fault the schools for reinforcing dominant sex role distinctions and the division of labor. Most feminist scholarship has concentrated on investigating how and why the schools create girls' inferior pattern of achievement and attainment and contribute to both differences in the ways women and men think and their respective positions in the work force and society.[70] Although

67. David, *The State, the Family and Education* (London: Routledge and Kegan Paul, 1980).

68. Lever, "Sex Differences in the Games Children Play," *Social Problems*, 23 (1978), 478–87; Lever, "Sex Differences in the Complexity of Children's Play and Games," *American Sociological Review* 43 (1978), 471–83.

69. Gilligan, *In a Different Voice: Psychological Theory and Women's Development* (Cambridge, Mass.: Harvard University Press, 1982).

70. See, for example, Eleanor Maccoby and Carol N. Jacklin, *The Psychology of Sex Differences* (Stanford: Stanford University Press, 1974); Jeremy D. Finn, Loretta Dulberg, and Janet Reis, "Sex Differences in Educational Attainment," *Harvard Educational Review* 49

following from feminist indictments of the educational system, such research has been greatly encouraged by federal legislation, such as Title IX of the Education Amendments of 1972 and federal funding from the Department of Health, Education and Welfare. Thus, there is a strong policy impulse in much feminist research in education, an attempt to change school practices so as to remedy educational inequality.

Feminist scholars are agreed that schools as currently constituted contribute to women's oppression by providing differential education to the sexes and by attempting to socialize girls to accept narrowly defined roles as adults in both the family and the work force. The internal workings of the schools as well as the structural relations between school practices and women's postschool lives have become the major focus for the feminist educational research.

A pioneering work in the study of how schools create sex differences in achievement is Nancy Frazier and Myra Sadker's *Sexism in School and Society*, which surveys not only overt discrimination in access to technical, vocational, scientific, and higher education but also more subtle problems in the social organization of the school, formal curriculum, textbooks, and counseling and guidance practices.[71] Subsequent research has detailed precisely how these practices produce gender inequality. Reading, mathematics, social studies, and other kinds of texts have been analyzed to show male bias in the use of language, the general absence of women portrayed as active contributors to society, and their relegation to the stereotyped roles of housewife, mother, nurse, ballerina, secretary, teacher, and librarian. Studies have also documented the systematic portrayal of passivity, nurturing, and dependency as positive female traits.[72] Feminist scholars

(1979), 477–503; Jeremy D. Finn, Janet Reis, and Loretta Dulberg, "Sex Differences in Educational Attainment: The Process," *Comparative Education Review* 24 (1980), S33–S52; Jeremy Finn, "Sex Differences in Educational Outcomes: A Cross-National Study," *Sex Roles* 6 (1980), 9–26.

71. Frazier and Sadker, *Sexism in School and Society* (New York: Harper and Row, 1973).

72. See, for example, Janice Law Trecker, "Women in U.S. History High School Textbooks," in *And Jill Came Tumbling After*, ed. Judith Stacey et al. (New York: Dell, 1974), 249–68; L. D. Weitzman, E. Mokada Eifler, and C. Ross, "Sex Role Socialization in Picture Books for Pre-School Children," *American Journal of Sociology* 77 (1972), 1125–50; Myra Pollack Sadker and David Miller Sadker, "Sexism in Teacher Education Texts," *Harvard Education Review* 50 (1980), 36–46; J. Pottker, "Psychological and Occupational Sex Stereotypes in Elementary School Readers," in *Sex Bias in the Schools*, ed. J. Pottker and

have related the bias in textbooks to women's lesser educational attainment and achievement in certain subjects and, once in the work force, their concentration in low-status, relatively poorly paid occupations.

Analyses of sex bias have been extended to vocational guidance in the schools. Carol Tittle has shown how guidance testing, upon which counselors base their advice to students for future educational and occupational plans, gives women little opportunity to show either an aptitude for math and science or an interest in careers in these areas.[73] The Strang Vocational Inventory, for example, had pink forms for girls and blue forms for boys. Girls filling out the pink form could show interest in becoming a stewardess, a secretary, or a housewife. Unlike the blue form designed for boys, the pink one made no provision for expression of interest in becoming a pilot, an engineer, or a business manager.

Not only have texts and vocational guidance procedures been unmasked for sex bias, so has what can be called hidden, or informal, curriculum of the schools. Scholars have found that teachers fail to encourage female students, especially in mathematics and the sciences, interact less with them in the classroom, and reward them for social rather than academic performance.[74] This subtle lack of encouragement for women's academic achievement may be as powerful in producing gender inequality as texts, guidance practices, and other parts of the formal curriculum.

A. Fishel (Teaneck, N.J.: Fairleigh Dickinson University Press, 1977), 111–25; W. T. Jay and C. W. Schminke, "Sex Stereotyping in Elementary School Mathematics Texts," *Arithmetic Teacher* 22 (1975), 242–46; P. Z. Boring, "Sex Stereotyping in Educational Guidance," in his *Sex Role Stereotyping in the Schools* (Washington, D.C.: National Education Association, 1973), 14–22; Laurel W. Oliver, "Counseling Implications of Recent Research on Women," *School Counselor* 19 (1972), 354–59; J. J. Pietrofeska and N. K. Schlossberg, "Counselor Bias and the Female Occupational Role," in *Sex Bias in the Schools*, ed. Pottker and Fishel, 221–29.

73. Tittle, "The Use and Abuse of Vocational Tests," in *And Jill Came Tumbling After*, ed. Stacey et al., 241–46.

74. Richard L. Simpson, "Sex Stereotypes of Secondary School Teaching Subjects: Male and Female Status Gains and Losses," *Sociology of Education* 47 (1974), 388–98; Andrea M. Seewald, Gaea Leinhardt, and Mary Engel, *Learning What's Taught: Sex Differences in Instruction* (Pittsburgh: University of Pittsburgh Learning Research and Development Center, 1977); Theresa A. Levitin and J. D. Chananie, "Response of Female Primary School Teachers to Sex-typed Behaviors in Male and Female Children," *Child Development* 43 (1972), 1309–15; A. J. Gaite, "Teachers' Perception of Ideal Male and Female Students: Male Chauvinism in the Schools," in *Sex Bias in the Schools*, ed. Pottker and Fishel, 105–7.

Feminist scholars have also turned their attention to how the social organization of the schools reproduces gender relations in the society at large, arguing that the authority structures of the schools help teach girls their secondary place in society. As Suzanne Estler points out, there are few women leaders in education. Even with the same credentials as men and despite their preponderance in the profession, women do not become superintendents or even secondary school principals. They are more often than not relegated to the primary and, to a lesser extent, the secondary classroom as instructional rather than administrative staff, visibly under the authority of men. The organization of the school, in short, mirrors male dominance in the society and normalizes it in the eyes of both male and female students.[75]

Feminist research on sex bias in every facet of schooling has become the basis for much educational reform. It has resulted in guidelines for producing nonsexist learning materials, workshops for sensitizing teachers and school administrators to sexist practices in the classroom, and affirmative action programs designed to provide women in authority as role models. The reforms that have emanated from sex-bias research have, for the most part, assumed, as does much educational research, that the schools effectively and independently socialize youth for adult roles. Any failures in this educational process traditionally have been attributed to some deficiency on the part of the individual student that educators are unable to modify. In contrast to this view feminist scholars have refused to blame the victim for women's educational achievement and attainment patterns, since their basic premise is that such outcomes are the effect of nurture rather than nature. And they have shown that in the case of gender-related failures, the schools actively contribute to such outcomes, even openly create them. Still much feminist research continues to assume the learner as a passive receptacle—a *tabula rasa*—upon which schools and society imprint attitudes and capabilities.

Much educational research focusing on the way that girls internalize negative educational messages is based on the fear-of-success model mentioned in Chapter 1. This model posits that, even given opportunities to achieve and the removal of structural barriers that deny women access to the same quality and quantity of education as men, women will still underachieve. This is because, from an early age, girls are exposed to notions of

75. Estler, "Women as Leaders in Public Education," *Signs* 1 (1975), 363–86.

feminine versus masculine that are reinforced through mass media, family sex roles, and the division of labor and they come to equate achievement with a lack of femininity. So deeply embedded are these attitudes that, out of fear of losing their femininity, women choose not to achieve or at least not to enter fields of study and work, especially technical areas, that are defined as male domains.[76]

This presumption of internalization has led to several types of research and to the development of intervention strategies to correct underachievement. There are scores of studies demonstrating that women are not motivated to achieve in school and work generally. In math and sciences, in particular, research holds that women create phobias that prevent them from even attempting to master these subjects. Such research has led to reform strategies that are aimed not so much at removing structural barriers (which this type of research assumes not to be the major impediment to female attainment and achievement), but rather at changing girls' self-perceptions of their abilities and at undermining stereotypical images of what it means to be a woman. The focus is on helping the learner to overcome her victimization; the structural and social attributes of the school as an institution that reproduces dominant ideologies and allocates categories of learners into ascriptive roles becomes secondary. Reform strategies derived from this type of research have attempted to provide girls with self-assurance that they can succeed in education and careers and still be feminine. In the case of math, workshops designed to overcome psychological barriers to mastery of the subject have become a major reform effort.

Although most feminist educational research has been concerned with documenting the ways in which schools create gender inequalities and lead

76. Sheila Tobias and Carol Weissbrod, "Anxiety and Mathematics: An Up-Date," *Harvard Educational Review* 50 (1980), 63–70; Georgia Sassen, "Success Anxiety in Women: A Constructivist Interpretation of Its Source and Significance," ibid., 13–24; M. S. Horner, "Toward an Understanding of Achievement-Related Conflicts in Women," *Journal of Social Issues* 28 (1972), 157–76; R. P. Esposito, "The Relationship between the Motive to Avoid Success and Vocational Choice," *Journal of Vocational Behavior* 10 (1977), 347–57; R. R. Grifford, "Fear of Success and Task Difficulty Effects on Graduate Students' Final Exam Performance," *Journal of Educational Psychology* 69 (1977), 556–63; D. Tressmer, "The Cumulative Record of Research on Fear of Success," *Sex Roles* 2 (1976), 217–36. See also critiques of this literature: T. G. Alper, "Achievement Motivation in College Women: A Now-You-See-It-Now-You-Don't Phenomenon," *American Psychologist* 29 (1974), 194–203; T. Olsen and V. Willemsen, "Fear of Success: Fact or Artifact?" *Journal of Psychology* 98 (1978), 65–70; D. Tressmer, *Fear of Success* (New York: Plenum Publishers, 1977).

girls to internalize the schools' teachings, a recent and more radical trend has been to contest the notion that girls simply learn what schools teach. This work tends to question whether reforms designed to undermine girls' negative attitudes about educational achievement and attainment are effective. Working in the tradition of social reproduction theorists like Michael Apple, Paul Willis, and Madeline MacDonald Arnot, feminists like Mary Fuller, Katherine Clarricoates, Vandra Masemann, and Karen Biraimah have sought to determine why and how girls slip through the webs of school socialization.[77] Their starting point is not the schools and their negative messages to girls, but rather the girls themselves, especially those who are successful in schooling. They have found that girls actively and often consciously sift through the messages of the schools to become, in Fuller's words "pro-education and anti-school."[78] The girls Masemann studied were well aware of the school's attempt to undermine their educational and occupational aspirations. But they simply ignored these messages, withdrew from active participation in the classroom, and learned what they chose. Biraimah researched girls who derided both school authorities and the curriculum, yet at the same time achieved as well as their male peers and held the same occupational and educational aspirations. The girls Fuller studied did not manifest the same open hostility to the entire school system. The black girls, in particular, understood "women's place" in society, both their own and their teachers'. They perceived the teacher who attempted to allocate them into inferior social roles not as an oppressor, but as a "working girl" who functioned autonomously and had a "place of her own" because she had done well in school. Thus they learned, though not exactly what they were being taught. Fuller also found that the girls functioned as a support group, encouraging one another to succeed, countering the pressure of their male peers as well as that of the school's formal and informal curriculum.

77. Fuller, "Black Girls in a London Comprehensive School," in *Schooling for Women's Work*, ed. R. Deem (London: Routledge and Kegan Paul, 1980), 52–66; Biraimah, "The Impact of Western Schools on Girls' Expectations: A Togolese Case," *Comparative Education Review* 24 (1980), S196–S208; Masemann, "The Hidden Curriculum of a West African Girls' Boarding School," *Canadian Journal of African Studies*, 8 (1974), 470–94; Katherine Clarricoates, "The Importance of Being Ernest . . . Emma . . . Tom . . . Jane. The Perception and Categorization of Gender Conformity and Gender Deviation in Primary Schools," in *Schooling for Women's Work*, ed. Deem, 26–41.
78. Fuller, "Black Girls in a London Comprehensive School," p. 64.

Jean Anyon's study of 100 white fifth graders in U.S. schools demonstrated that girls creatively accommodated to as well as resisted the school and society's attempts to enforce femininity.[79] The girls exhibited behaviors that ranged from incorporation of school values (excelling academically and dressing in a feminine manner) to resistance (the girls distanced themselves from school, tended toward high rates of absenteeism and used feminine wiles to disrupt instruction). Anyon showed that the girls' strategies varied by social class, which shapes sex role ideologies and expectations.[80] Among working-class families girls are expected to adhere strictly to feminine behavior, defined as submissiveness and subordination to men. The expectation that girls be dependent and domestic contrasts sharply with realities of working-class life, in which women take on strong economic roles outside the home. The definition of femininity in middle-class families was less rigid but no less contradictory. Parents expected their daughters to become educated and pursue a career while fulfilling domestic roles of mother and housewife. Anyon points out that the differences in the ways girls resist and accommodate in school represent how they actively seek to accept or transcend the conflicts in class-based definitions of being female.

These woman-centered studies obviously parallel and in many cases directly draw on feminist research in other disciplines where the focus is on women's active agency. This sort of research, while relatively new and rare in education, promises to lead to the identification of innovative and more effective strategies for reforming the schools; because it recognizes that women actively negotiate their lives, it may allow feminists better to assist girls in overcoming male domination in school and in postschool life.

As we noted in Chapter 1, in the field of philosophy feminist thinking developed according to two different but complementary efforts: the extension

79. Anyon, "Intersections of Gender and Class: Accommodation and Resistance by Working-Class and Affluent Females to Contradictory Sex Role Ideologies," in *Gender, Class and Education*, ed. Stephen Walker and Len Barton (Sussex: Falmer Press, 1983), 1–19.

80. For scholarship on working-class girls and sex-role ideologies, see Madeleine MacDonald, "Schooling and the Reproduction of Class and Gender Relations," in *Education and the State*, ed. Roger Dale et al. Volume II. *Politics, Patriarchy and Practice* (Sussex: Falmer Press, 1981), 159–78; Angela McRobbie, "Working Class Girls and the Culture of Femininity," *Women Take Issue*, ed. Women's Studies Group, Centre for Contemporary Culture Studies (London: Hutchinson, 1978); D. Hartley, "Sex and Social Class: A Case Study of an Infant School," *British Educational Research Journal* 4 (1978), 75–81. For a discussion of families, see David, *The State, the Family and Education*.

of philosophical analysis to issues arising from the women's movement and the feminist consciousness it fosters, and the continuing investigation of male bias in philosophical theories and methods. The full scope of feminist scholarship emerged somewhat more slowly in philosophy than in our other fields and took slightly longer to become established as a distinctive body of research within the discipline. The discovery of male bias in this field was a more difficult, far-reaching task than in many other areas, partly because it is not a discipline conducting empirical studies and could not be faulted simply for neglecting the evidence of women's lives. From behind the veil of sex neutrality philosophy appeared to exclude women as a subject more like mathematics does and less like history and anthropology.

We have already considered some early feminist challenges to the presumption of sex neutrality in philosophy. The continuation of such challenges as a central focus of much feminist philosophy places the initial critiques of this field in a somewhat different relationship to subsequent scholarship than is the case with other fields. Especially with disciplines such as anthropology and history, those first critical revelations and the discovery of bias in methodology mainly served to clear the way so that research on women could be conducted more readily. In philosophy, however, the feminist critiques of male bias in the discipline have continued as a substantial task in themselves, revealing only gradually the profundity of the extent to which concepts of women as inferior pervade our intellectual tradition and might influence thinking on a host of seemingly remote subjects. The magnitude of this undertaking has contributed to the tendency among philosophers to investigate ideas that relate to the nature of oppression.

In contrast to the gradual and continual discovery of male bias in philosophy, the extension of philosophical analysis to contemporary issues of importance to women has been an immediate and visible response of feminist philosophers. This scholarship indicates the general renewal of interest in normative, applied questions in social and political theory that has taken place over the last ten to fifteen years. In fact, in purely quantitative terms, the greatest amount of work on women and issues of special concern to women has been produced in the areas of ethics and social philosophy. There is considerable dialogue now about topics new to philosophy such as sexual relations, the family, rape, power, women and medicine, feminist perspectives, and the environment. Feminist concerns have also revived interest in subjects such as human nature that had fallen out of fashion in the field but now are seen to have special importance in light of debates over male and female characteristics. Here we discuss the subject of abortion as an example of the philosophical debate that has developed over an issue of concern to the women's movement.

If ever there were a clear example of a relationship between a social concern and philosophical literature, it is the topic of abortion, one of the first women's issues to find its way into academic philosophy. Although the abortion controversy per se was recognized as a topic for contemporary philosophy only in the late 1960s, the subject has inherited a theoretical legacy in which certain metaphysical and ethical questions are seen as fundamental to deciding the moral permissibility of abortion.[81] The metaphysical questions concern the fetus and the type of being it has: whether it is a person or has humanity, and, if so, from what point in time. The ethical questions concern the rights of the fetus and the pregnant woman, the philosophical problems that arise when they come into conflict, and whether certain rights are subordinate to others. Most writers on the subject view the metaphysical and the ethical issues as mutually connected, so that in order to decide on the morality of abortion, one must first decide the status of the fetus.[82] A minority argues that conclusions about the permissibility of abortion may be drawn while bypassing metaphysical questions.[83]

81. See Christine Pierce's review essay of philosophical work on women in *Signs* 1 (1975), 487–503. A varied selection of philosophical treatments of abortion can be found in *The Problem of Abortion*, ed. Joel Feinberg (Belmont, Calif.: Wadsworth, 1973), and in *The Rights and Wrongs of Abortion*, ed. M. Cohen, T. Nagel, and T. Scanlon (Princeton: Princeton University Press, 1974).

82. For examples of this approach that argue for and against abortion, see Baruch Brody, "Abortion and the Sanctity of Human Life"; John J. Noonan, Jr., "An Almost Absolute Value in History"; Marvin Kohn, "Abortion and the Argument from Innocence"; Michael Tooley, "A Defense of Abortion and Infanticide"; Roger Wertheimer, "Understanding the Abortion Argument," all in *The Problem of Abortion*, ed. Feinberg; H. Tristram Englehardt, Jr., "The Ontology of Abortion," *Ethics* 84 (1974), 217–34; Lisa Newton, "Humans and Persons: A Reply to H. Tristram Englehardt," ibid., 85 (1975), 332–36; Mary Anne Warren, "On the Moral and Legal Status of Abortion," *The Monist* 57 (1973), 43–61.

83. Without doubt the most influential argument that takes this approach is Judith Jarvis Thomson's "A Defense of Abortion," *Philosophy and Public Affairs* 1 (1971), 47–66, reprinted in *The Problem of Abortion*, ed. Feinberg, 121–39. See also Daniel Callahan, "Abortion Decisions: Personal Morality," in ibid., 17–27; Norman C. Gillespie, "Abortion and Human Rights," *Ethics* 87 (1977), 237–43; Joseph Margolis, "Abortion," ibid., 84 (1973), 51–61.

Both of these approaches to the question of the permissibility of abortion focus on the conflicting rights of individuals, and the scope of debate is limited to the time when these rights are in immediate conflict, the nine months between conception and birth. A different approach to the issue can be seen among a relatively small number of articles, which introduce broader social concerns as relevant to the debate, such as economic, social, or psychological factors, or the quality of life of the mother after birth.[84] The advocacy of abortion as part of a program for women's liberation can be found within all of these approaches to the subject, although the grounds for argument in most cases are significantly channeled by the framework within which rights are customarily discussed in philosophy.

It is noteworthy that within the feminist movement at large the right to "control our bodies" is asserted on behalf of women with little attention to the issues that are posed by the philosophical literature. This may be the result of philosophers' greater awareness of the notorious difficulty involved in the assertion of a "right."[85] But at least one philosopher finds that the discrepancy suggests that accepted philosophical methods of moral reasoning contain a deeply hidden bias that makes it exceedingly difficult to turn them to the service of the best interests of women. In "Moral Revolution" Kathryn Pyne Parsons undertakes a detailed analysis of the process of reasoning that surrounds the abortion question within philosophy. She contends that the concept of rights covertly sustains a hierarchy of patriarchy and power. She contrasts reasoning based on rights as used by philosophers with reasoning based on needs as expressed by participants in an abortion clinic. Her provocative and controversial conclusion suggests that the philosophical heritage, even when it is employed in the defense of rights for women, is not to be put fully in the service

---

84. For example, Howard Cohen, "Abortion and the Quality of Human Life," in *Feminism and Philosophy*, ed. Mary Vetterling-Braggin, Frederick Elliston, and Jane English (Totowa, N.J.: Littlefield, Adams, 1977), 429–40; Alison Jaggar, "Abortion and a Woman's Right to Decide," *Philosophical Forum* 5 (1973–74), 356.

85. For example, Elizabeth Rappaport and Paul Segal argue that, lacking a fully developed social theory with relevant concepts of rights, one simply cannot decide on the abortion question. See "One Step Forward and Two Steps Backward: Abortion and Ethical Theory," in *Feminism and Philosophy*, ed. Vetterling-Braggin, Elliston, and English, 408–16. English also comments on this issue in an essay in the same collection, "Abortion and the Concept of a Person," 417–28.

of the pursuit of a meaningful, autonomous life for women, precisely because this is not its primary concern.[86] Part of Parsons's argument involves the contention that the accepted methods of moral reasoning contain many sorts of hidden biases—not just sex bias, but also bias regarding social class, race, and age. Therefore, this article also contributes to that other task of feminist philosophers: the examination of the philosophical tradition for its sexist implications concerning women. While the growth of work in normative philosophy can be seen as an extension of philosophical analysis in the service of women's issues, this other direction of research can be seen as probing the core of philosophical reasoning. We have already observed that Western cultural and intellectual history is virtually continuous in the idea that women are inferior to men. Recognizing that philosophers often epitomize the prevailing ideas of their times and weave them into the web of argument and system, feminists have begun to examine the influential classics of Western philosophy to unravel our heritage of oppressive ideology.[87] This effort unites many of the writings of feminist philosophers that otherwise might

86. Parsons, "Moral Revolution," in *The Prism of Sex*, ed. Julia A. Sherman and Evelyn Torton Beck (Madison: University of Wisconsin Press, 1977), 189–227. This argument compares interestingly with Carol Gilligan's research on the development of moral reasoning in *In a Different Voice*. In her studies Gilligan came to distinguish between moral reasoning based on "rights" (typically but not inevitably adopted by boys and men) and moral reasoning based on "responsibility" (typically but not inevitably adopted by girls and women). The link between rights and responsibilities ordinarily assumed in political and ethical theories is broken in Gilligan's analysis, or at least called into question with regard to the attitudes individuals take to moral decision-making.

87. Several anthologies in recent years have gathered together the writings of major philosophers on the subject of women. For example, *History of Ideas on Women*, ed. Rosemary Agonito (New York: Putnam, 1977), *Philosophy of Woman: Classical to Current Concepts*, ed. Mary B. Mahowald (Indianapolis: Hackett, 1978); and *Women in Western Thought*, ed. Martha L. Osborne (New York: Random House, 1979).

Plato's view of women has received particular attention. Selections from this literature include: Christine Garside Allen, "Plato on Women," *Feminist Studies* 2 (1975), 131–38; Julia Annas, "Plato's Republic and Feminism," *Philosophy* 51 (1976), 307–21; Anne Dickason, "Anatomy and Destiny: The Role of Biology in Plato's View of Women," *Philosophical Forum* 5 (1973–74), 45–53; Susan Moller Okin, "Philosopher Queens and Private Wives: Plato on Women and the Family," *Philosophy and Public Affairs* 6 (1977), 345–69; Martha Lee Osborne, "Plato's Unchanging View of Women: A Denial That Anatomy Spells Destiny," *Philosophical Forum* 6 (1975), 447–52; Christine Pierce, "Equality:

seem isolated by subfield. Much of the work on language analysis, for example, is the discussion of the imprint of an ideology on the way we speak, perhaps even the way we are predisposed to think. (This topic is discussed in more detail in Chapter 3.) Feminist political theorists have reexamined views of the individual, the state, and citizenship to reveal analytical frameworks that hamper the achievement of women's equality in theory and in practice. Recent work in epistemology and philosophy of science involves the discovery of bias in models of knowledge and scientific method.

From ancient times to the present the various views philosophers have expressed regarding women employ two related principles: that women's reproductive capacities root them more inescapably in their biology, their animal nature, than is the case for men and, consequently, that women are incapable of full development of their rationality, the element that raises human beings above the merely animal, that allows for moral choice and responsibility, and that even (according to some) partakes of the divine. The inferiority of women thus extends to all dimensions of being: the biological, where women are physically weaker and encumbered by the necessities of reproduction; the mental, where their reason is limited; and the moral and spiritual, where whatever instinct for good they may have does not compensate for their lessened freedom and responsibility.[88]

Certain feminist philosphers see in this tradition a general system of dualistic thinking that reflects and perpetuates the subordination of women. Such dualism is notably present in political philosophies, which commonly posit categories of analysis that parallel the distinction between male and female: the state as distinct from the family, production as contrasted to reproduction, public life versus private life, the world governed by reason versus that of the passions and appetites—in short, a natural

---

Republic V," *The Monist* 57 (1973), 1–11; Sarah Pomeroy, "Feminism in Book V of Plato's *Republic*," *Apeiron* 8 (1974), 33–35; and Gregory Vlastors, "The Status of Persons in Platonic Justice: Women," *Carus Lectures* (LaSalle, Ill.: Open Court, 1976).

88. The conceptions of woman's capacities are complex and conflicting, for she may be seen at once as angelic and demonic. The same duality of good and evil in woman that can be found in myth and religion, and that is frequently reflected in literature, may also be found in the works of philosophers. See, for example, Christine Garside Allen, "Nietzsche's Ambivalence about Women," in *The Sexism of Social and Political Theory*, ed. L. Lange and L. M. G. Clark (Toronto: University of Toronto Press, 1979), 117–33. For a thorough analysis of such ideas, with particular emphasis on their role in theology, see Mary Daly, *Beyond God the Father: Toward a Philosophy of Women's Liberation* (Boston: Beacon Press, 1973).

hierarchy between the governing authority, which is associated with the male, and that which is ruled, which is associated with the female.[89]

Political theorist Susan Moller Okin analyzes the significance for women of the private-public dichotomy by concentrating on the methods used to frame a concept of woman within a general philosophy of human nature. With only a few exceptions, she argues, the influential thinkers of the past have defined man by describing ideal human nature but have defined woman by her function in relation to man as wife and mother within a patriarchal family. "Philosophers," she observes, "who, in laying the foundation for their political theories, have asked 'What are men like?' 'What is man's potential?' have frequently, in turning to the female sex, asked 'What are women for?' There is, then, an undeniable connection between assigned female nature and social structure, and a functionalist attitude to women pervades the history of political thought."[90] Okin argues that most political thinkers do not take individuals but families as the units that make up societies. Since a functional concept of woman merges her with the family unit, the male head of the family is the only one provided for as citizen in political theory. On the basis of this analysis, she foresees difficulty in formulating feminist political philosophy on the foundation of even the most liberal tradition, because even here the functional view of woman is woven into the vision of society and citizenship.

A similar conclusion is reached by Lorenne Clark and Lynda Lange, who argue that since it is women who have historically been responsible for reproduction, continuing to regard this aspect of human life as private, rather than a part of public, social life entails that women will remain limited to a secondary domestic domain in the ideas of virtually all political theories. No matter how otherwise egalitarian, a theory that fails to recognize reproduction as a social and not a private concern will not yield a theoretical system in which women are the social equals of men. In other words the formulation of fully developed theories that merge the public

89. Some would add to these dualities the philosophical distinction between mind and body. See Rosemary Radford Reuther, "Misogyny and Virginal Feminism in the Fathers of the Church," in *Women in Western Thought*, ed. Osbone, 62–65, reprinted from *Religion and Sexism* (New York: Simon and Schuster, 1974). For a critique of the dualistic habit of thought itself, see Joyce Trebilcot, "Conceiving Women: Notes on the Logic of Feminism," *Sinister Wisdom* 11, (Fall 1979).

90. Okin, *Women in Western Political Thought* (Princeton: Princeton University Press, 1979), 10.

and private worlds is necessary to the progress of feminist political philosophy.[91] As we shall see in Chapter 3, this line of reasoning joins that of feminists from many disciplines who speculate about the origins and nature of women's oppression.

While the implications of masculinist philosophical perspectives are apparent in the areas of political, ethical, and social philosophy, their relevance for other fields of inquiry is also being investigated. Perhaps the newest and most recalcitrant frontier is presented by theories of knowledge and philosophy of science, where the stance of abstract objectivity and sex neutrality is most easily maintained. Feminist explorations of these areas indicate the extent to which the discovery of deeply buried male bias continues to be a prominent task for feminist philosophers. However, there is a new flavor to these writings, and one can see in the more recent work a development away from the emphasis on oppression that characterizes earlier analyses of the philosophical tradition. The first endeavors of feminists, as we saw in Chapter 1, primarily revealed concepts of female inferiority imbedded in influential theories that regularly excluded women from the realm of the fully human. More recently feminists have begun to question the idea that the concept of the "human"—the nonsexed person—is functional or even coherent and to speculate that all activities, including science and scientific investigation, thought, and knowledge, are filtered through a perspective that includes, among other factors, the sex of the perceiver or knower. Thus rather than pointing out female exclusion and negotiating inclusion into a single human voice, feminists are vigorously acknowledging the presence of a "standpoint" or "perspective" in all knowledge claims and exploring those that are particular to women.[92] Thus this work can be seen as a new dimension of earlier challenges to the ideal of objectivity—that is, an absolutely neutral, unbiased view—as a characterization of scientific method.[93] Feminists have begun to extend this critique

91. Clark and Lange, eds., *Sexism of Social and Political Theory*, introduction and several of the essays.

92. See Nancy C. M. Hartsock, "The Feminist Standpoint: Developing the Ground for a Specifically Feminist Historical Materialism," in *Discovering Reality: Feminist Perspectives on Epistemology, Metaphysics, Methodology, and Philosophy of Science*, ed. Sandra Harding and Merrill B. Hintikka (Boston: D. Reidel, 1983), 283–310; Lorraine B. Code, "Is the Sex of the Knower Epistemologically Significant?" *Metaphilosophy* 12 (1982), 267–76.

93. A number of feminist philosophers make use of the influential ideas of Thomas Kuhn, *The Structure of Scientific Revolutions*, 2d ed. (Chicago: University of Chicago Press,

of objectivity by investigating the proposition that "what counts as knowledge must be grounded on experience. . . . Women's experience systematically differs from the male experience upon which knowledge claims have been grounded. Thus the experience on which the prevailing claims to social and natural knowledge are founded is, first of all, only partial human experience only partially understood by men. However, when this experience is presumed to be gender-free—when the male experience is taken to be the human experience—the resulting theories, concepts, methodologies, inquiry goals and knowledge-claims distort human social life and human thought."[94]

The exploration of this hypothesis has begun among feminists in philosophy and in the natural sciences as well.[95] Once argument and evidence are mustered to support it, the need for alternative theories and methods becomes especially acute. The development of ideas for this approach ventures into the frontiers of speculation and the formulation of a vision of human life and understanding that is sometimes unabashedly utopian. As such this work shares the impulse of many feminist thinkers to reach beyond the comprehension of oppression to a glimpse of liberation.

This chapter has considered examples of feminist thinking that are shaped by particular disciplinary frameworks, hindered in some ways and helped in others by the available scholarly methods of each field. New questions, concepts, methods, and theories have begun to be formulated by feminist scholars to do justice to the information about women that is emerging within the various disciplines. In the next two chapters we explore the

---

1970). For two examples of such use, see Janice Moulton, "A Paradigm of Philosophy: The Adversary Method," and Kathryn Pyne Addelson, "The Man of Professional Wisdom," in *Discovering Reality*, ed. Harding and Hintikka, 149–64, 165–86, respectively.

94. *Discovering Reality*, ed. Harding and Hintikka, x. Speculation about bias in epistemology parallels some of the work on language being done by feminists in Europe. See, for example, the sample of essays in *New French Feminisms*, ed. Elaine Marks and Isabelle de Courtivron (Amherst: University of Massachusetts Press, 1980).

95. See, for example, Carolyn Merchant, *The Death of Nature: Women, Ecology, and the Scientific Revolution* (San Francisco: Harper and Row, 1980); Ruth Hubbard et al., eds., *Women Look at Biology Looking at Women* (Cambridge, Mass.: Schenkman, 1979); Evelyn Fox Keller, "Women in Science: A Social Analysis," *Harvard Magazine* (Oct. 1974), 14–19; Evelyn Fox Keller, "Gender and Science," in *Discovering Reality*, ed. Harding and Hintikka, 187–205.

growing pattern of multidisciplinary feminist scholarship as we consider the shared concerns of feminist scholars and their attempts to contribute to an integrated body of knowledge about women.

II

Oppression and Liberation: Feminist Questions as Guides for Research

3

Women's Oppression: Understanding the Dimensions

While feminist academics discovered within their disciplines methods and subjects that could contribute to our knowledge about women and their lives, their scholarship was equally affected by ideas imported from feminist politics as well, of which the search for sexist bias in research was only one manifestation. Taken as a whole, the new scholarship on women was a part of a general and widespread attempt to understand the phenomenon of sexism, to comprehend its implications for the heritage and experience of women, and ultimately to discover the conditions that would enable "liberation." We saw in the preceding chapter that the scholarship arising in our five disciplines implies explicit or implicit perspectives on the degree to which oppression ought to be emphasized in understanding women's lives. Even feminist scholars who focus on women's agency and active resistance continue to emphasize that such activity occurs within given social and cultural limits and that resistance means resistance to specific conditions of oppression. Thus, for them, as well as for those feminists whose disciplines are oriented toward the restrictions placed upon women, oppression is a central organizing concept. In this chapter we look directly at analyses of varieties of oppression, for this topic shows the importance of nonacademic political concepts and illustrates ways in which feminist scholarship from a multiplicity of disciplines is beginning to converge.

The notion of women's oppression grows out of the political consciousness of the feminist movement, not out of any academic tradition. Since it is a basic political concept, and since it involves complex cultural, social, psychological, and economic issues, scholars interested in the study of oppression have of necessity begun to cross disciplinary boundaries in their endeavors. Although chapters 1 and 2 observe the distinctions among disciplines while hinting at common concerns, in this chapter and the next we emphasize the unified nature of feminist scholarship, drawing on material from different fields and from outside as well as inside the academy. These two chapters are organized around the issues of oppression and liberation: In Chapter 3 we consider speculative analyses about the origins of women's oppression, elements of sexist ideology, and studies of the interaction between the public and the domestic spheres. In Chapter 4 we discuss research that contributes to our understanding of the meaning of liberation, including views of equality and its attainment and studies of the impact of modernization and socialism on women.

By stressing the complementary nature of work that has been done on these issues, we do not intend to imply that, taken together, this scholarship points to a single theory of women's oppression and liberation. The feminist movement in the United States today has a variety of theoretical positions, which are most often grouped in the general categories "liberal feminist," "radical feminist," and "socialist feminist." Sometimes these distinctions can be detected in research as well.[1] Varieties of political analyses are one source of diversity among feminist scholars, as are differences of methodology. One need not reduce feminist scholarship to a false unity to recognize, however, that the ideas of feminist scholars are interconnected and mutually sustaining; sometimes their research even approaches the goal of interdisciplinary scholarship. The difficulties involved in crossing disciplinary boundaries may mean that integration of research perspectives is by no means complete, but there is no question that the process has begun.

Identifying the nature and causes of women's oppression in order to put an end to it is probably the most fundamental concern of modern feminism. This project underlies all feminist scholarship, implicitly or explicitly, and provides a common framework and language for scholars in different disciplines and for intellectuals within and outside the academy. On the

---

1. For selected readings illustrating different political approaches, see Allison Jaggar and Paula Rothenberg Struhl, *Feminist Frameworks* (New York: McGraw-Hill, 1978). See also Jaggar, "Political Philosophies of Women's Liberation," in *Feminism and Philosophy*, ed. Mary Vetterling-Braggin, Frederick Elliston, and Jane English (Totowa, N.J.: Littlefield, Adams, 1977), 5–21, and Jaggar, *Feminist Politics and Human Nature* (Totowa, N.J.: Rowman and Allanheld, 1983).

one hand, such scholarship is informed by recognition of the magnitude of women's oppression: women are systematically allotted positions of lesser power, freedom, and autonomy than men not only in our society but also in most others and throughout human history. Feminists' stress on the nearly universal and extraordinarily enduring character of women's oppression underscores their conviction that it is one of the major problems facing contemporary society. On the other hand, this tendency to emphasize universality can become a barrier in analyzing women's oppression, and especially in achieving a perspective from which it might be overcome. So that in its magnitude oppression not be interpreted as a permanent and unchangeable state of affairs, feminist scholars have worked to refine our understanding of its dimensions—its origins, the historical transformation of its elements, and the particularities of its structure.

Prior to the development of modern feminist scholarship, the oppression of women was understood primarily by analogy to other forms of exploitation and domination. As far back as the mid-nineteenth century, the first women's rights activists relied on the metaphor of black slavery to describe the condition of women.[2] In the 1940s and 1950s the revival of efforts to combat racism encouraged the use of the concept of racial discrimination as a framework for understanding the oppression of women.[3] Scholarship of this sort stressed the social stereotypes of women as inferior to men and their unequal access to social wealth and political power. It used the notion of political and economic integration as a model for a society in which women would not be oppressed. Although the analogy with racism helped scholars trying to understand the situation of women, particularly by challenging the romanticization and privatization of male-female relations and showing that they conform to a predictable and unjust social pattern, it did not provide an adequate framework for understanding the particularities of women's oppression. The title of one of the most frequently cited analyses of this kind, "Women as a Minority Group," captured, perhaps unconsciously, the irony of the analogy.[4] For, as historian Gerda Lerner states,

2. Blanche Hersh, *The Slavery of Sex: Feminist-Abolitionists in the United States* (Urbana: University of Illinois Press, 1978); Ellen Carol DuBois, *Feminism and Suffrage: The Emergence of an Independent Women's Movement in America, 1848–1869* (Ithaca: Cornell University Press, 1978), ch. 1.

3. Gunnar Myrdal, *An American Dilemma*, 2 vols. (New York: Harper and Row, 1941, 1944); Myrdal has an appendix entirely devoted to the analogy between blacks and women.

4. Helen Hacker, "Women as a Minority Group," *Social Forces* 30 (1951), 60–69.

"We have not yet really solved the problems of definition, but it can be suggested that the key to understanding women's history is in accepting . . . that it is the history of the majority of mankind. Women are essentially different from racial and ethnic categories because they are the majority now and always have been at least half of mankind."[5]

In the 1960s, under the influence of anticolonial movements in the emerging nations of Asia, Africa, and Latin America, colonialism—the domination of one nation over another—became an important model for understanding women's oppression. Scholars of colonialism such as Rupert Emerson, Eric Wolf, and Cyril Black examined the economic and political exploitation of indigenous people by foreign powers as well as the cultural domination that accompanies dependence.[6] Early feminist attempts at understanding women's oppression, especially those by nonacademic intellectuals, were deeply affected by this colonial model. The most extensive investigation of colonialism as a framework for understanding the position of women was the "Fourth World Manifesto," written late in the Vietnam War by a group of Detroit radical feminists.[7] In response to the criticism that anti-imperialist efforts should take precedence over women's liberation, the authors argued that women were the first and most extensive colonial group; that the prototype of colonial oppression is to be found in the physical, economic, and cultural domination of women by men; and that underlying the control of any one nation by another was the control of all women by all men.[8]

For feminists the most important aspect of the scholarship on colonialism was the work on the psychological aspects of oppression by O. Mannoni, Albert Memmi, and, most important, Frantz Fanon.[9] This scholarship

5. Lerner, "Placing Women in History: Definitions and Challenges," *Feminist Studies* 3 (1975), 5–14.

6. Emerson, *From Empire to Nation: The Rise to Self Assertion of Asian and African Peoples* (Boston: Beacon Press, 1960); Wolf, *Peasant Wars of the Twentieth Century* (New York: Harper and Row, 1969); Black, *The Dynamics of Modernization* (New York: Harper and Row, 1967).

7. Barbara Burris et al., "The Fourth World Manifesto," *Notes from the Third Year* (New York, 1970), 102–19.

8. For a related use of these concepts, see Jill Johnston, *Lesbian Nation* (New York: Simon and Shuster, 1973).

9. See Frantz Fanon, *The Wretched of the Earth* (New York: Grove Press, 1966), and his *Black Skins, White Masks* (New York: Grove Press, 1967); O. Mannoni, *Psychologie de la Colonisation* (Paris: Le Seuil, 1950); A. Memmi, *The Dominated Man* (Boston: Beacon Press, 1968).

stressed the subjective effects of foreign domination—hatred of self, inauthenticity of daily relations, and internalization of the colonizers' perceptions and values on the part of the victims of colonial oppression. It also traced the psychological dimensions of anticolonial revolt—the expression of anger and assertion of self by which the oppressed regained what the scholars of colonialism usually termed their "manhood." As this conflation of humanity and masculinity indicates, there is considerable sexism in the anticolonial literature, and it has been criticized by feminists, but it has nonetheless proved useful and revealing as a metaphor for women's oppression.[10] Literary scholar Kate Millett devotes an entire chapter of her pioneering exploration of women's oppression, *Sexual Politics*, to the work of Jean Genet, in appreciation of his exposition of "the colonial or feminine mentality of interiorized oppression, which must conquer itself before it can be free."[11] Another early feminist writer, Robin Morgan, frequently referred to Fanon's work, especially in her article on the feminist health movement, "On Women as a Colonized People." Although acknowledging that colonialism can be only a metaphor, never an explanation for women's oppression, Morgan, a poet, was nonetheless impressed with its interpretive power, especially for women's physical victimization. "Women are a colonized people," she wrote, victims of "a gynocidal attempt manifest most arrestingly in the patriarchy's seizure of our basic and precious 'land': our own bodies."[12] Most recently poet and theorist Adrienne Rich has drawn on Fanon's work to understand women's oppression as mothers and to explore the ways that men have defined the institution of motherhood and thereby appropriated it from women.[13]

As with the analogy to racism, using the concept of colonialism to explore women's oppression has its limitations because it describes a form of subordination that is fundamentally different from that of women. Whatever the utility of "national liberation" and "self-determination" as political slogans for feminism, these concepts do not really lead us to understand the nature of relations between women and men in our culture or any other. "We are the social opposites not of a class, a caste, or a majority," writes

10. Burris et al., "Fourth World Manifesto," 113–15.
11. Millett, *Sexual Politics* (Garden City, N.Y.: Doubleday, 1970), 350.
12. Morgan, "On Women as a Colonized People," in her *Going Too Far* (New York: Vintage–Random House, 1978), 161–62.
13. Rich, *Of Woman Born* (New York: Norton, 1976), 214.

historian Joan Kelly-Gadol, "but of a sex: men."[14] She calls, therefore, for a feminist scholarship that can do more than make analogies between sexism and other forms of oppression: she asks for one that can understand the particularities of women's oppression. Having established the extent and systematic nature of that oppression, feminist scholars have begun the work to understand its reality, no longer simply by analogy, but increasingly by analysis of the particular social relations that create and perpetuate women's subordination to men.

The Origins of Women's Oppression

One of the most important ways that feminist scholars have begun to analyze women's oppression in its own terms has been through an energetic, intellectually challenging debate on its origins. Questions of the origins of social institutions, and therefore of the origins of sexual inequality, have long been out of style in academic research. Most social scientists, uninterested in questions of fundamental change, have not been concerned with the first causes of undesirable human institutions. As strict empiricists, they have considered questions of origin impossible to investigate and, as functionalists, they have treated them as unimportant. By contrast, the question of the origins of women's oppression has been important to feminist scholars from the start. Although anthropologists have played the major role in pursuing this question, the matter of origins is of such general interest to feminists that scholars in history, literature, philosophy, and other fields have also participated in its exploration.[15] Feminist scholarship on the origins of women's oppression tries to develop an account that both fits the existing information and provides a satisfactory explanation for the oppression. It is often candid in its commitment to find a way to end women's oppression. "The question of the nature and genesis of women's oppression . . . is not a trivial one," explains anthropologist Gayle Rubin, "since the answers given to it determine our visions of the

14. Kelly-Gadol, "The Social Relations of the Sexes," *Signs* 1 (1976), 814.

15. For instance, Ann Lane, "Woman in Society: A Critique of Frederick Engels," in *Liberating Women's History: Theoretical and Critical Essays*, ed. Berenice Carroll (Urbana: University of Illinois Press, 1976), 4–25; Millett, *Sexual Politics*, also discusses the origins of women's oppression, especially the ideas of Engels, at length. See, too, Ruth Hubbard, "Have Only Men Evolved?" in *Women Look at Biology Looking at Women*, ed. Ruth Hubbard et al. (Cambridge, Mass.: Schenkman, 1979), 7–36.

future and our evaluation of whether or not it is realistic to hope for a sexually egalitarian society."[16]

Feminist theoretical approaches to the origins of women's oppression fall into three general categories: those that follow the Marxist framework established in the nineteenth century by Frederick Engels, locating the origins of women's oppression in economic conditions; those that follow the suggestions of Simone de Beauvoir and Shulamith Firestone, concentrating on women's childbearing capacities; and—the newest perspective—those that hypothesize a separate structure of sexual and gender relations distinct from either economics or human reproduction. The interaction among these approaches has been extremely fruitful because each explores different aspects of the complex problem of sexual hierarchy, how it changes and how it can be changed. Although the debate has not yet provided definitive answers to the question of origins, it has already brought into focus basic intellectual issues lying at the heart of all efforts to understand women's oppression. To what degree should we look for the origins of sexual hierarchy in historical developments or in something inherent in the relations of the sexes and in "maleness" and "femaleness" themselves? Can we locate the explanation for women's oppression in the overall economic and political structures of society, or must we hypothesize a separate structure or cultural system that determines the power relations between men and women? Does the oppression of women rest primarily in the inequality of the sexes, or does it have its source in the fact of sexual distinction? And how do we balance our sense of the near-universality of women's oppression with respect for the integrity and uniqueness of societies extremely different from our own historically and culturally?

Theory that locates the origins of women's oppression in the economic system has its roots in Engels's *Origin of the Family, Private Property and the State*, written in 1884. Engels based his argument on the assertions of anthropologist Lewis Henry Morgan that in early human communities—hunting and gathering societies and horticultural societies—women were not oppressed. These societies were classless and communal, based on sharing and reciprocity rather than on private accumulation and property. In such societies men and women contributed equally to social production, and, instead of men having institutionalized power over women, the relations

16. Rubin, "The Traffic in Women," in *Toward an Anthropology of Women*, ed. Rayna Rapp Reiter (New York: Monthly Review Press, 1975), 157.

between the sexes were reciprocal and egalitarian. Theoretically, the subjugation of women developed only when an economic surplus began to develop, private property was accumulated, and classes and the state began to emerge. Once the communal structure was destroyed, women's work became privatized and the individual family replaced the clan as the primary economic unit. In the late nineteenth century, Engels saw family as the locus of women's oppression. It made women dependent on and subject to individual men, their accumulation of wealth, and their ability to pass it on to their heirs.

Among the strengths of this approach to the origins of women's oppression is its historical character. Since it presumes that sex hierarchy developed over time and through major transformations in the structure of society, it dissents from the commonly held belief that women's subordination has been universal. It is a type of analysis that presents a considerable challenge to anthropology, which also ordinarily assumes women's secondary status in all times and all places. Eleanor Leacock, a leading proponent of a modern version of Engels's theory, defends this position by observing that just as we accept the dialectical transformation of modes of economic production through history, so we should be able to envision correlative transformations of the family and women's role within it. It is ethnocentrism, she argues, that leads us to interpret all social forms as manifesting women's inferior social status.[17]

Yet Leacock's work and others in a similar vein, such as that of Karen Sacks, Ruby Rohrlich-Leavitt, and Mona Etienne, have been criticized for the assumption that men and women are social equals in classless societies when the data on the subject do not yield a clear picture.[18] Nor, say critics,

17. Leacock, "Women's Status in Egalitarian Society: Implications for Social Evolution," *Current Anthropology* 19 (1978), 247–55.

18. Ibid.; see also Leacock, introduction to Frederick Engels, *The Origin of the Family, Private Property and the State* (New York: International, 1975), 7–67; Leacock, "Women in Egalitarian Societies," in *Becoming Visible: Women in European History*, ed. Renate Bridenthal and Claudia Koonz (Boston: Houghton Mifflin, 1977), 11–35; Leacock and Etienne, introduction to *Women and Colonization: Anthropological Perspectives* (New York: Praeger, 1980), 1–24; Rohrlich-Leavitt, "Conclusions," in her *Women Cross-Culturally: Change and Challenge* (The Hague: Mouton, 1975), 619–41; Sacks, "Engels Revisited: Women, the Organization of Production and Private Property," in *Toward an Anthropology of Women*, ed. Reiter, 211–34; Sacks, *Sisters and Wives* (Westport, Conn.: Greenwood Press, 1979). For critical comments see: Michelle Zimbalist Rosaldo, "Woman, Culture and Society: A Theoretical Overview," in *Woman, Culture and Society*, ed. Michelle Rosaldo and Louise

is a satisfactory account given of why women rather than men became oppressed with the rise of private property. One response on the part of proponents of this theoretical perspective has been to reexamine the data on hunting and gathering and horticultural societies, revealing the existence of bias that has clouded the evidence on what women's lives have been like in radically different cultures. In her pioneering work on the Naskapi of Canada, Leacock has analyzed the profound impact that colonialism has had on contemporary hunting and gathering societies, destroying egalitarian relations and instituting commodity production—and male supremacy.[19] Given these changes, it is impossible to assume that contemporary hunting and gathering societies give an accurate picture of what those societies were like before the advent of colonialism. Supplementing this picture through historical research is also rendered difficult because the data on precolonial societies come from a variety of sources— missionaries, explorers, journalists, and anthropologists—and reflect the male and cultural biases of these observers. In addition, Sacks has posited another kind of bias that would affect the gathering and interpretation of data: She argues that ethnographers who are themselves natives of state societies, where difference always means inequality, apply this presumption to genuinely egalitarian societies and interpret all difference as inequality.[20]

An interesting aspect of this work is the space it allows for the exploration of the existence of matriarchies, long a topic of interest among feminists, although anathema in the academy. Rohrlich-Leavitt, for example, suggests that we should consider whether ancient Crete, where men and women had an equal role in production but where women appear to

Lamphere (Stanford: Stanford University Press, 1974), 17–24; Louise Lamphere, "Review Essay: Anthropology," *Signs* 2 (1977), 612–27; Harriet Whitehead, "A Reply," ibid. (1976), 508–11; Paula Webster, "Politics of Rape in Primitive Society," *Heresies* 6 (1978), 16–22; Elsie Begler, "Sex, Status and Authority in Egalitarian Society," *American Anthropologist* 80 (1978), 571–88; and Michelle Zimbalist Rosaldo, "The Use and Abuse of Anthropology: Reflections on Feminism and Cross-Cultural Understanding," *Signs* 5 (1980), 389–417.

19. Leacock, "The Montagnais-Naskapi Band," in *Contributions to Anthropology: Band Societies*, ed. David Damas (Ottawa: National Museums of Canada, 1969), 1–19; Leacock, "Montagnais Women and the Jesuit Program for Colonization," in Leacock and Etienne, *Women and Colonization*, 25–43.

20. Sacks, "State Bias and Women's Status," *American Anthropologist* 78 (1976), 565–69.

have been more central in politics and religion, should be reconsidered as a society where women had special prominence.[21]

Whether this direction of scholarship can eventually provide enough convincing data to establish incontrovertibly the existence of sexually egalitarian communal societies—and thereby change the entire tradition of anthropology—remains an open question. Nonetheless, feminist scholars have done enough work to raise serious questions about the correctness of assuming the universality of women's subordination and to indicate how specific economic structures can shape women's position in society. Rayna Rapp, another feminist proponent of this perspective, has suggested four areas for research that would help develop the theory and expand its potential for yielding a cogent explanation of the origins of women's oppression: the rise and development of early trade to determine its relation to the rise of private property and male control; the ways that kinship obligations generate inegalitarian social relations; the intensification of conflict from haphazard raiding to institutionalized war; and the replacement of early female-centered cosmologies with a cosmology based on God the father.[22] In these analyses of the economic and social determinants of women's oppression, we can see one of many examples of the way that feminists have adapted and transformed various theoretical perspectives in the pursuit of a further understanding of women and their social position.

A second feminist approach to the origins of women's oppression discards Engels's model in favor of a theory of universal female subordination. The universalists are especially critical of the historical hypothesis on which the economic approach is based, the existence of a time in prehistory when women were not oppressed. Michelle Zimbalist Rosaldo, one of the chief formulators of this theoretical alternative, characterizes (or perhaps caricatures) Engels's position that "at some point in human history men 'took' power away from women," as a "rather implausible assertion."[23] She

21. Rohrlich-Leavitt, "Women in Transition: Crete and Sumer," in *Becoming Visible*, ed. Bridenthal and Koonz, 36–59. For an interesting perspective on the literature on matriarchy, see Paula Webster, "Matriarchy: A Vision of Power," in *Toward an Anthropology of Women*, ed. Reiter, 141–56.

22. Rapp, "Gender and Class: An Archeology of Knowledge Concerning the Origin of the State," *Dialectical Anthropology* 2 (1977), 109–36.

23. Rosaldo, "Woman, Culture and Society," 22. It should be noted that not all modern Marxists hold the position that women and men were equal in early human society. See, for instance, the French structuralist Claude Meillassaux, *Femmes, greniers et capitaux* (Paris: Maspero, 1975).

regards it as a mistranslation of a myth about the assumption of male authority into an actual account of history. Rosaldo, Peggy Sanday, Sherry Ortner, and others reject this approach, which looks for societies and times in which women were not oppressed, in favor of one that emphasizes the "near universal character" of women's oppression and looks to structural aspects of "human social and cultural organization" to explain it.[24] "Every known society recognizes and elaborates some differences between the sexes," Rosaldo explains. Moreover, "male as opposed to female activities are always recognized as predominantly important."[25] She and others find the most likely source of this universal "sexual asymmetry" in women's responsibility for bearing and rearing children, which leads to a "differentiation of domestic and public spheres of activity."[26] It is important to observe that what is at work here is not simply a debate on the origins of women's oppression, but a redefinition of the nature of the phenomenon itself. The emphasis has moved away from inequalities of economic and political power to the fact of sexual distinction in society — "sexual asymmetry," in Rosaldo's phrase — as the essence of women's oppression.

The importance that reproduction plays in this account can be traced in particular to theoretical pioneers like de Beauvoir and Firestone, who clarified the importance of childbearing to women's oppression.[27] At the same time the universalists' account is also rooted in long-standing, nonfeminist traditions of classical sociological theory, which emphasized permanent, inherent structures common to all human societies, including the subordination of women to the demands of reproduction and the family. Rosaldo herself cites Emil Durkheim, Georg Simmel, and Talcott Parsons, sociological pioneers who are authorities for her observations about the universality of sexual asymmetry and the division between domestic and public spheres observable in all societies. The difference between these classic sociological theorists and the feminists is that the feminists do not

24. Rosaldo, "Woman, Culture and Society"; Sanday, "Female Status in the Public Domain," *Woman, Culture and Society*, ed. Rosaldo and Lamphere, 189–206; Ortner, "Is Female to Male as Nature Is to Culture?" ibid., 67–88, reprinted from *Feminist Studies* 1 (1972).
25. Rosaldo, "Woman, Culture and Society," 18–19.
26. Ibid., 23; see also Sanday, "Female Status in the Public Domain," 205.
27. de Beauvoir, *The Second Sex*, trans. and ed. H. M. Parshley (New York: Knopf, 1953); Firestone, *The Dialectic of Sex: The Case for Feminist Revolution* (New York: Morrow, 1970).

consider women's oppression as inevitable and seek ways to break the connection between reproduction and women's oppression. Rosaldo makes the
distinction between the biological fact of women's reproductive capacities
and the social and historical particularities that build on and interact with
these capacities. Another variation stresses women's exclusion from warfare
as the way their reproductive responsibilities lead to their subordination.[28]
A third emphasizes the contemporary division of labor, which is the
modern manifestation of the domestic-public split and therefore the target
of any prospects for change.[29] Nonetheless, feminists' attempts to use a
theory stressing the structural universality of women's oppression as a basis
for a strategy for change does have the character of swimming up a theoretical
stream. The proponents of this approach have been particularly criticized for
treating the split between public and private concerns as a cause rather than a
result of women's oppression, thereby contributing to its perpetuation.[30]

The power of the approach taken by Rosaldo and other feminist universalists is its ability to bring issues like domesticity, childbearing, and
motherhood to the center of explanations for sexual hierarchy and to the
forefront of social analysis in general. Whereas the economic theories of
Engels, Leacock, Sacks, and others explain the origins of women's oppression
by reference to factors that may seem external to women's daily concerns,
the approach taken by Rosaldo, Ortner, and others looks at reproduction

28. Sanday, "Female Status in the Public Domain."

29. Zillah Eisenstein, "Developing a Theory of Capitalist Patriarchy," and "Some Notes
on the Relations of Capitalist Patriarchy," in her *Capitalist Patriarchy and the Case for Socialist
Feminism* (New York: Monthly Review Press, 1979), 5–55.

30. All the references in the first part of footnote 18 are either implicit or explicit criti-
ques of this position. In addition, see Eleanor Leacock, "Class, Commodity and the Status of
Women," in *Women Cross-Culturally*, ed. Rohrlich-Leavitt, 605–16; Leacock and June
Nash, "Ideologies of Sex, Archetypes and Stereotypes," *Annals of the New York Academy of
Sciences*, 285 (1977), 618–46; Diane K. Lewis, "A Response to Inequality: Black Women,
Racism and Sexism," *Signs* 3 (1977), 339–61; and Eli Zaretsky, *Capitalism, the Family and
Personal Life* (New York: Harper and Row, 1977). Rayna Rapp, in her review essay on an-
thropology (*Signs* 4 [1979], 508–11), presents a summary of recent anthropological con-
siderations of the universality of the distinction between public and private domains.
Rosaldo makes an interesting and important revision of her original position, taking some of
these critiques into account, in "Use and Abuse of Anthropology." Finally, Carol
MacCormack and Marilyn Strathern's *Nature, Culture, and Gender* (Cambridge: Cambridge
University Press, 1980) is a collection of essays that questions the universality of the
dichotomy between nature and culture and therefore indirectly criticizes Ortner's explanation of the universal subordination of women on this basis.

and the concerns and activities that surround it—at the domestic sphere within which most women operate—to explain sexual hierarchy. To put in another way, having posed a distinction between the public and domestic spheres, these feminists shift the focus away from the former, which is associated with men's lives, to the latter, which is associated with women's, at least in industrial society. One direction in which this has led is an examination of the sources of women's power in the domestic sphere basic to women's defense of their interests.[31] Another direction, which will be considered later, is to explore the asymmetric impact on girl and boy babies of women's exclusive responsibility for early mothering. Both of these examples indicate the degree to which the focus on reproduction and the domestic/public distinction with which it is associated help to generate a dynamic analysis of women's oppression, which gives women a role in creating systems of sexual hierarchy and the potential for dismantling them.

The third and most recent approach to the origins of women's oppression attempts to conceptualize a whole system of sex and gender relations within which the development of women's subordination can be situated. This type of approach considers reproduction, but only as one aspect of a more general category of social life—sex. Historian Joan Kelly-Gadol assumes such an approach when she urges that feminist historians organize their findings about women's subordination around the concept of "the social relations of sex," much as Marxists organize their observations about working-class immiseration around the concept of the social relations of class.[32] In her history of birth control in America Linda Gordon also assumes a system of sex and gender relations that includes division of labor by sex and changing definitions of eroticism as well as the social control of reproduction.[33] The leading theoretician of this third approach is Gayle Rubin, who argues for locating the sources of female subordination in the history of what she calls the "sex gender system," which she defines as the "set of arrangements by which a society transforms biological sexuality into the products of human activity, and by which these transformed sexual

---

31. Several of the papers in *Woman, Culture and Society*, ed. Rosaldo and Lamphere, focus on this issue; see in particular the essays by Lamphere, Stack, Tanner, Wolf, Hoffer, and Leis.

32. Kelly-Gadol, "Social Relation of the Sexes," 809–24.

33. Gordon, *Woman's Body, Woman's Right: A Social History of Birth Control in America* (New York: Grossman 1976).

needs are satisfied."[34] The demands raised by biological sexuality include not only social arrangements for dealing with reproduction and childrearing, but also the creation of a cultural system for understanding and elaborating the differences between men and women, and for designating what is and is not erotic.

The hypothesis of a sex gender system, like the emphasis on reproduction, is a reaction against the tendency to explain the sources of women's oppression primarily in economic terms. Rubin insists, as do Rosaldo and Ortner, on the necessity of "a distinction between economic and sexual systems" in order to indicate that "sexual systems have a certain autonomy."[35] Similarly, sex gender and reproduction-based theories both seek to explain the origins, not simply of the economic and political subordination of women, but of the fact of the social division of the sexes itself. The difference, however, is that the sex gender approach does not focus primarily on reproduction but on sexuality, particularly heterosexuality, to explain the oppression of women. Underlying this school of feminist thought is the conviction that sexuality is profoundly mediated by culture, in Rubin's words, that "no aspect of sexuality"—most especially the primacy of heterosexuality—should be "taken for granted as natural."[36] This puts Rubin and others who seek to locate the origins of women's oppression in the systemic character of sexual relations at a somewhat greater distance from immutable biological realities and, therefore, in a more flexible position to envision a future without sexual hierarchy than those feminists who focus on childbearing.[37]

Rubin's complex elaboration of the concept of a sex gender system is one of the most fully interdisciplinary contributions to modern feminist scholarship. It incorporates the psychological insights of Sigmund Freud, the linguistic theories of Jacques Lacan, the historical methods of Karl Marx, and the kinship theories of Claude Lévi-Strauss; it is also a theory that has stimulated dialogue among scholars trained in such areas as philosophy, history, political

34. Rubin, "Traffic in Women," 159.
35. Ibid., 167.
36. Ibid., 179.
37. For a similar approach to sexuality, which acknowledges but does not focus on the problem of women's subordination, see Michel Foucault, *The History of Sexuality* (New York: Pantheon–Random House, 1978). A full analysis of the cultural construction of gender, which builds on these ideas, may be found in Sherry Ortner and Harriet Whitehead, *Sexual Meanings: The Cultural Construction of Gender* (Cambridge: Cambridge University Press, 1981).

science, and economics. Rubin considers kinship systems as "the observable and empirical forms of sex-gender systems," which are "made up of and reproduce concrete forms of organized sexuality."[38] Following Lévi-Strauss, she sees the "essence of kinship systems . . . in the exchange of women by men."[39] To Rubin, the concept of the exchange of women provides a theoretical framework adequate to describe the oppression of women, because the act so profoundly limits women's control over their own lives and establishes a deep inequality between man the giver and woman the given. Unlike Lévi-Strauss, however, Rubin is not satisfied with analyzing the social mechanisms that create women's oppression; she is intent on dismantling them. Thus, her most original contribution is to analyze and challenge the institution that she sees as underlying the exchange of women, heterosexual marriage. According to Rubin, marriage rests on the division of humanity into "two mutually exclusive [gender] categories," individual members of which are obligated to couple with each other. Rubin challenges the "naturalness" of both gender dimorphism and obligatory heterosexuality.[40] She turns to psychoanalytic theory to outline the process by which both the polarities of masculine / feminine gender identity and heterosexual eroticism are psychologically inscripted rather than biologically foreordained. For instance, she describes the way that heterosexuality among girls is imposed upon a prior homosexual inclination rooted in the infant's attachments to her mother. Since she identifies these structures as the sources of women's oppression, as well as essentially arbitrary, her analysis is a call for "rebuilding culture" without relying on coercive gender systems, compulsory heterosexuality, or the notion of property in women.[41]

Each of the three theories of the origins of women's oppression explains a different aspect of sexual hierarchy. The Marxist or political economic approach emphasizes the historical character of women's subordination; the

38. Rubin, "Traffic in Women," 169.

39. Ibid., 171; hence the title of the article, "The Traffic in Women," which Rubin, borrowing the formula from Emma Goldman, contrasts with "the traffic in goods," e.g., Engels's approach.

40. Ibid., 178.

41. Ibid., 198; see also Adrienne Rich, "Compulsory Heterosexuality and Lesbian Existence," *Signs* 5 (1980), 631–60, and the three-part symposium which responds to Rich's piece in ibid., 7 (1981): Ann Ferguson, "Patriarchy, Sexual Identity and the Sexual Revolution," 158–72; Jacquelyn N. Zitas, "Historical Amnesia and the Lesbian Continuum," 172–87; and Kathryn Pyne Addleson, "Words and Lives," 187–99.

focus on reproduction stresses its universality; and the concept of a sex gender system helps us to see how it can rest on a set of social relations that are at once deep and systematic and at the same time highly arbitrary.[42] One could regard these theories merely as hypotheses of primary causes of women's oppression and then dismiss them because of the impossibility of their proof, but such an approach misses their contribution to analyzing the dimensions of women's oppression and identifying prerequisites for change. Of necessity, these theories are concerned with early human society, but they both influence and are shaped by research on modern society. Themes and issues raised in the origins debate appear again and again, as feminist scholars approach the long-range task of creating a theory of women's oppression complex enough to apply to a wide range of modern social developments.

Ideology and Oppression

From its inception the women's liberation movement perceived sexist ideology as an important component of women's oppression and set itself to identifying the negative ideas about women that abound in all aspects of our society—the media, the schools, the law, religion, and elsewhere. For their part, scholars in the academy have demonstrated the presence and extent of sexist and misogynist ideas in our culture. The work we have discussed in earlier chapters is representative of this kind of research: philosophers who examine what the fathers of Western philosophy have to say about women as less rational, less morally autonomous than men; or literary scholars who explore how the male literary canon typically portrays women in terms of their sexuality; or historians who analyze the nineteenth-century stereotype of female domesticity and chastity.

Taken together, these and related ways of thinking about women constitute the collection of accepted beliefs that make up an "ideology." A sexist ideology may be construed as one that takes as basic truths that women are less capable than men, embody qualities tempting but dangerous to men, and are put on earth for the service of men. Sexist ideology gives rise to cultural conventions, habitual reactions, and general practices that belittle women, overlook them, or shunt them into places of secondary importance.

42. Already the debate between them has produced new analyses that seek to combine aspects of each theory; see, for instance, Ortner and Whitehead, *Sexual Meanings*; and Peggy Reeves Sanday, *Female Power and Male Dominance: On the Origins of Sexual Inequality* (Cambridge: Cambridge University Press, 1981).

This network—or, better, tangle—of ideas is so deeply rooted in ways of thinking that it often functions below the level of conscious awareness. Thus, part of the task of feminists has been to root out and identify ideological thinking at its most basic and disguised and to understand how it enters so deeply into consciousness.

Identifying the ubiquitous negative ideology that permeates our history and society is only a beginning, for, if we halted study at this point, Western culture would appear a permanent monolith of sexist belief. Fully aware of this pitfall, feminist scholars have been intent not only to reveal the dimensions of sexist ideology but also to eradicate it through argument, which shows it to be erroneous, and analysis, which explains how it is maintained and perpetuated. Although the deeper one delves into ideology, the more one is struck by its tenacity, the feminist enterprise is to work out ways to dispel sexist thinking.

The idea that women are "naturally" inferior to or dependent upon men is a common denominator of both cultural history and popular thinking. The belief that nature itself dictates the inferior social status of women has been a formidable challenge to feminists past and present. This challenge has been taken up by scholars who expose the dubious logic and rampant confusion in sexist ideas founded on the belief that nature determines the inequality of the sexes.

A fundamental difficulty with any argument from nature is that there are many inconsistent definitions of the term "natural." In an early essay on this subject philosopher Christine Pierce found a number of concepts of nature, including two especially popular and mutually incompatible meanings that are widely used in arguing for the innateness of female inferiority: "what human beings have in common with the rest of the animal world," and "what distinguishes human beings from the rest of the animal world."[43] The latter plays a large role in the history of ideas, since reason is the trait most often identified as uniquely human and, as we have seen, so many theorists have denied women fully rational capacities. The first is probably more current at present because of the popular tendency to extrapolate from

---

43. Pierce, "Natural Law Language and Woman," in *Sex Equality*, ed. Jane English (Englewood Cliffs, N.J.: Prentice-Hall, 1977), 133, reprinted from *Woman in Sexist Society*, ed. Vivian Gornick and Barbara K. Moran (New York: Basic Books, 1971). As one feminist theorist remarks, "Humans are by nature unnatural" (Dorothy Dinnerstein, *The Mermaid and the Minotaur* [New York: Harper and Row, 1976], 21).

biological evidence of nonhuman animals to conclusions about human societies: If biology did dictate gender differences—specifically that the female submit to the male—the feminist attempt to liberate women to a position of equality would be a violation of nature and a folly that would in no way contribute to a greater social good. The absence of a clear and unproblematic working concept of the "natural" is a flaw pervading arguments that the goals of feminism are unnatural.

The debate over nature versus nurture to explain gender differences engages many contemporary feminists. While probably most side with the nurture arguments, which maintain gender differences to be a product of culture and upbringing, others find the issues to be so tangled as to be virtually impossible to prove definitively one way or the other. Patrick Grim, for example, argues that to a degree we will always be ignorant about whether differences between men and women are attributable to biology or to social factors. Thus rather than first settling that question, we must decide how we ought to act, given that ignorance. He concludes that it is preferable to presume social origin of differences over what he calls "fundamental" origins, since that way we are more likely to attain a higher degree of social justice.[44] Joyce Trebilcot comes to a similar conclusion when she writes, "Whether there should be sex roles does not depend primarily on whether there are innate psychological differences between the sexes. The question is, after all, not what women and men naturally are, but what kind of society is morally justifiable."[45] Both the incoherence of the concept of the natural and its dubious relevance to considerations of justice have been grounds for the ways feminist thinkers have challenged sexist ideology. These issues go hand in hand with critiques of the concepts of femininity and masculinity, which, while purporting to be descriptions of typically female and male behavior, are often prescriptions about how women and men *ought* to behave.[46]

44. Grim, "Sex and Social Roles: How to Deal with the Data," in *"Femininity," "Masculinity," and "Androgyny,"* ed. Mary Vetterling-Braggin, (Totowa, N.J.: Littlefield, Adams, 1982), 128–47. See also, in the same volume, Alan Soble, "The Political Epistemology of 'Masculine' and 'Feminine,'" 99–127, and Jane Duran, "Nurture Theories: A Critique," 49–59.

45. Trebilcot, "Sex Roles: The Argument from Nature," in *"Femininity," "Masculinity," and "Androgyny,"* ed. Vetterling-Braggin, 48 (reprinted from *Ethics* 85 [1975], 249–55). See also Nancy Holmstrom, "Do Women Have a Distinct Nature?" *Philosophical Forum* 14 (1982), 25–42.

46. See, for example, Sarah Lucia Hoagland, "'Femininity,' Resistance, and Sabotage," in *"Femininity," "Masculinity," and "Androgyny,"* ed. Vetterling-Braggin, 85–98, and Anne Dickason, "The Feminine as Universal," ibid., 10–30.

Because of the division of human virtues into male and female camps, it has been difficult for feminists to envision and articulate a picture of a world of genuine freedom and equality for women. Given women's position of social inferiority, the first step has often appeared to be aspiring to the condition of men. Yet, ask feminists, in our efforts to escape subordination, should we not at the same time try to retain such traditionally "feminine" traits as generosity, modesty, gentleness, and sympathy? On the other hand, are not such traits precisely part of female oppression? Will retaining them hinder women in their achievements in the competitive world where men predominate?

Such questions touch on issues raised in the debates over women's culture in history and literature and indicate the moral complexities involved in challenging oppression and envisioning a new role for women that is not only "equal" to men's, but also desirable in itself. The crux of the problem is that so-called feminine virtues are easily turned into weaknesses; generosity to others may lead to exploitation or denial of one's own needs, modesty to self-effacement, deference to servility. Genuinely good ways of acting may be distorted by oppressive circumstances into traits that are undesirable. The virtues of altruism, for example, are easily freighted with the negative characteristics of self-negation.[47] Because the "feminine" virtues have been the characteristics particularly valued in women, and because women are often in dependent circumstances, these virtues can—and historically have—become tools of oppression, all the more powerful because they are virtues and women themselves are reluctant to abandon them. One writer puts the question, which she describes as "one of the central issues discussed by feminists today," as follows: "How can we explore and celebrate the life-giving, sensitive, and sensual aspects of womanhood without strengthening ancient patterns of social organization and stereotype, in which maternal capacities and 'closeness to nature' and female sexuality were the major grounds for assigning to women a distinct, confined, and subordinate space?"[48]

These investigations of traditional concepts of womanhood and femininity are elements of the extensive feminist examination of how sexist ideology is reflected in and perpetuated by social practices, institutions, and behavior.

47. Larry Blum et al., "Altruism and Women's Oppression," *Philosophical Forum* 5 (1973–74), 222–47.
48. Nannerl O. Keohane, "Feminist Scholarship and Human Nature," *Ethics* 93 (1982), 108. See also Judith Farr Tormey, "Exploitation, Oppression, and Self-Sacrifice," *Philosophical Forum* 5 (1973–74), 206–21. Tormey argues against self-sacrifice as a genuine virtue and includes a detailed analysis of the concept of exploitation.

Overt symptoms of women's exploitation, such as rape and pornography, have been a subject of debate among movement writers for years, though they have an increasing place in the work of feminists writing in academic contexts.[49] These debates, particularly vigorous on the subject of pornography and whether or not it necessarily leads to violence against women, not only bridge disciplines but also blur the edges between academic and nonacademic feminist writing. For the most part, however, feminists writing in the academy have devoted their attention to more covert forms of ideology—stereotypes and their implications, or psychological barriers to sexual equality. Although sexist ideology sometimes emerges in the form of an explicit argument, more frequently it lurks within unexamined conceptual frameworks that are not necessarily even deliberately chosen by those who employ them. Feminists have therefore examined the psychological processes by which dominant ideas become transformed into accepted intellectual convention and individual consciousness. One type of inquiry investigates ways in which sexist ideology may be embedded in how we talk, write, and think.

Philosophers and linguists, in particular, have explored issues of ordinary discourse and sexist language, investigating differences in the ways men and women use language, linguistic distinctions employed in reference to male and female, and the varying connotations of terms that make sex-specific designations.[50] Such analyses have clarified and refined the concept of sexism by applying it to language use and to behavior and have begun to reveal the extent to which sexist ways of thinking are manifest in the conventions of grammar and correct usage. Two closely connected aspects of language have received particular attention for their manifestation of the ideology of female inferiority: the employment of masculine terms for generic reference

49. A representative selection of this work includes: Susan Brownmiller, *Against Our Will: Men, Women, and Rape* (New York: Simon and Schuster, 1975); Susan Griffin, "Rape: The All-American Crime," Carolyn Shafer and Marilyn Frye, "Rape and Respect," Pamela Foa, "What's Wrong with Rape," Susan Rae Peterson, "Coercion and Rape: The State as a Male Protection Racket," all in *Feminism and Philosophy*, ed. Vetterling-Braggin, Elliston, and English, 309–75; Robin Morgan, *The Anatomy of Freedom* (New York: Anchor/Doubleday, 1983); Rosemarie Tong, "Feminism, Pornography, and Censorship," *Social Theory and Practice* 8 (1982), 1–18.

50. Perhaps the text that has stimulated the most debate on these issues is Robin Lakoff, *Language and Woman's Place* (New York: Harper and Row, 1975). A collection that gathers together a spectrum of analyses of language is *Sexist Language*, ed. Mary Vetterling-Braggin (Totowa, N.J.: Littlefield, Adams, 1981).

and the failure of certain terms to apply to men and women alike.[51] We have seen from earlier analyses of masculine bias how women are relegated to a status that is less than human. The counterpart in language is the use of such terms as "man" and "he" to refer to the human species, whereas "woman" and "she" have only specific usage. This is no mere innocent grammatical convention, some argue, for the use of the masculine for the generic continues to perpetuate sexist attitudes and practices. The use of "he" and "man," for example, can set up a context of expectation that, however unintentionally, excludes women from consideration. Analysts have considered sexist language in other forms, for instance the language that refers to sexual activities, and how and where it is used. They suggest that language that is on the face of it merely vulgar or intimate might be harmful in its contribution to attitudes, beliefs, and practices that sustain women's oppression.[52]

Scholars differ in their assessments of the capacity of linguistic conventions not only to reflect sexist beliefs but also to perpetuate oppression. One writer argues that, because sexist language sets up limitations on the activities of one sex but not the other, "elimination of sexist language is necessary for eliminating sexism in any society."[53] Others doubt anything but the most indirect causal link between social status and language use.[54] Taken as a whole, however, feminist language analysts are united in the belief that language holds one of the keys to understanding commonly held ideas about what it means to be female and the conceptual frameworks that contribute to women's oppression, for language, thought, belief, and action are close associates.

51. See, for example, Janice Moulton, "The Myth of the Neutral 'Man,'" in *Sexist Language*, ed. Vetterling-Braggin, 100–115; Marilyn Frye, "Male Chauvinism: A Conceptual Analysis," ibid., 7–22; Elizabeth Beardsley, "Referential Genderization," *Philosophical Forum* 5 (1973–74), 285–93.

52. See, for example, the following articles in *Sexist Language*, ed. Vetterling-Braggin: Robert Baker, "Pricks and Chicks: A Plea for Persons," 161–82, reprinted from *Philosophy and Sex*, ed. Robert Baker and Frederick Elliston (Buffalo: Prometheus Books, 1975), 45–64; Janice Moulton, "Sex and Reference," 183–93, reprinted from *Philosophy and Sex*, 34–44; and Stephanie Ross, "How Words Hurt: Attitudes, Metaphor, and Oppression," 194–216.

53. Sara Shute, "Sexist Language and Sexism," in *Sexist Language*, ed. Vetterling-Braggin, 31. For a more general speculation about the reflection of sex differences in language, see Merrill B. Hintikka and Jaakko Hintikka, "How Can Language Be Sexist?" in *Discovering Reality*, ed. Sandra Harding and Merrill B. Hintikka (Boston: D. Reidel, 1983), 139–48.

54. See, for example, Virginia Valian, "Linguistics and Feminism," in *Sexist Language*, ed. Vetterling-Braggin, 68–80, reprinted from *Feminism and Philosophy*, ed. Vetterling-Braggin, Elliston, and English, 154–66.

Moving from conversational discourse to the written text, we see similar issues explored in the study of sexual imagery and the portrayal of women in works of literature. Feminist critics, investigating stereotyped depictions of the female elevated into the pattern of art, also analyze literature as a reflection of the ethos of the societies that produce it. In "The American Galatea" Judith H. Montgomery considers the recurrent nineteenth-century theme of the male who creates an essentially static image of a beautiful woman, with whom he falls in love. She attributes the reiteration of the Pygmalion myth to "its successful fusion of two basic impulses in man: creation and possession—here, creation of the beautiful object and possession of that object by himself alone."[55] Similarly, Dolores Barracano Schmidt examines the emergence of the stereotype of "The Great American Bitch" between World War I and II. The emancipated American housewife as portrayed by Ernest Hemingway, Sinclair Lewis, and F. Scott Fitzgerald lives off her husband spiritually as well as materially, deriving her sustenance and strength from his emasculation. Both Montgomery and Schmidt recognize the social origins and effects of literary stereotypes. Montgomery wonders to what extent present-day relations and ideas of relations between the sexes have been influenced by literary treatment of the Pygmalion myth in the last century. Like linguistic analysts, she invites speculation as to the role fiction may play in perpetuating stereotypes as well as reflecting them. Schmidt concludes by calling into question sweeping critical judgments applied to the creators of the bitch stereotype, terms like "realistic," "acute social observer," "universal in theme and values." She argues that the view they present is specifically a male one, shaped by a postwar threat perceived to traditional masculinity. "It is in their female characters, *created not experienced*, that the nature of their fears and wishes will be found. It is from these fears and wishes that the Great American Bitch of fiction evolved."[56]

Rather than concentrating on a single stereotype, Judith Fetterley in *The Resisting Reader* constructs an overall feminist response to the sexism that defines classic American fiction. Works by Washington Irving, Sherwood Anderson, Nathaniel Hawthorne, William Faulkner, Hemingway, Fitzgerald, Henry James, and Norman Mailer provide the texts through which she examines

---

55. Montgomery, "The American Galatea," *College English* 32 (1971), 890. The theme is discussed in relation to Hawthorne, James, and Wharton.

56. Schmidt, "The Great American Bitch," ibid., 905.

the consequences of her observation that American literature is male and that, hence, not only the male world but the female one are wholly male-defined. For the woman reader, the American literary tradition is particularly destructive because it is taken as a principal source for American national identity—an identity that excludes women. To be American is to be male and to be both is to be, as Fetterley insists, *not female*. Moreover, men's power over women is the subject of much of this literature. The final indignity for the woman reader "is that she is required to dissociate herself from the experience the literature engenders. Powerlessness is the subject and powerlessness is the experience."[57]

This sort of analysis of female images in literature emphasizes their social roots, taking them out of the realm of universal myth and situating them firmly in particular historical circumstances. This is one more way that feminists are dispelling the idea that the archetypes of the female and the feminine reflect women, representing an inherent (and therefore necessary) aspect of human consciousness, and suggesting that woman's condition is an unchangeable fact of existence.

Language conventions and literary stereotypes are indicators of conceptual frameworks that are assumed, taken for granted, and barely questioned. They thus suggest the extent to which ideology is expressed not only in social expectations for women, but also in the way women think of themselves, the way they behave, and the goals they value. A number of feminists suggest that the views of women that are delineated in theory have a parallel in the concepts women have of themselves as individuals. As Sandra Bartky puts it, "The nature of psychological oppression is such that oppressor and oppressed alike come to doubt that the oppressed have the capacity to do the sorts of things that only persons can do, to be what persons, in the fullest sense of the term, can be."[58] Studies of oppressive concepts and stereotypes are thus complemented by investigation into the psychological dimensions of oppression.

Perhaps the most striking example of an intellectual source shared by feminists of different disciplinary backgrounds is provided by a group of

57. Fetterley, *The Resisting Reader* (Bloomington: Indiana University Press, 1978), xiii. For a more complex reading of the impact of masculine imagery on ways of thinking, see Annette Kolodny, *The Lay of the Land: Metaphor as Experience in American Life and Letters* (Chapel Hill: University of North Carolina Press, 1975).

58. Bartky, "On Psychological Oppression," in *Philosophy and Women*, ed. S. Bishop and M. Weinzweig (Belmont, Calif.: Wadsworth, 1979), 39.

theories that build upon psychoanalysis to construct systematic ways of understanding women's oppression. Psychoanalytic theory has been creatively used by feminists to explore further the ways that sexist ideology becomes part of common consciousness, female as well as male. Works by Juliet Mitchell, Dorothy Dinnerstein, and Nancy Chodorow all attempt in different ways to comprehend the process by which individuals incorporate the ideology of sexual hierarchy and learn to live by its dictates. All argue that the family is the primary institution within which ideas about the subordination of women and the power of men are reproduced and internalized. Mitchell is particularly concerned with women's acceptance of male power, which she identifies with the development of the feminine personality. Chodorow and Dinnerstein consider the implications of mothering for both male and female personality development and the reproduction of male-dominated social relations.

The use of psychoanalysis in these works makes them very controversial. In the United States psychoanalysis does not have much standing within the academy; it is one of the few examples of an intellectual discipline that has developed outside the university.[59] Furthermore, many feminists have dismissed psychoanalysis as itself an example of sexist ideology, rather than a tool for its analysis. In contrast, Mitchell argues that psychoanalysis is the most promising framework for developing a feminist theory of ideology because it seeks to understand the unconscious, where culture and ideology are most deeply embedded, and because gender and sexuality are its central concerns. Thus Mitchell takes classical psychoanalytic concepts, such as penis envy and the Oedipal complex, which most feminists dismiss as hopelessly rooted in assumptions about the biological inferiority of women, and reinterprets them as elements in the process by which women come to see themselves as inferior and incomplete. At the same time, while recognizing that psychoanalysis is extremely pessimistic about any possibility for escaping the nuclear family and the frustrations of desire and psychological suffering associated with it, Mitchell is optimistic. Using the intellectual tools of a different discipline, cultural anthropology, she argues that the nuclear family, in contrast to other kinship forms, makes no contribution to production, is socially and historically dispensable, and is likely to collapse from its own internal contradictions.[60]

59. Psychoanalytic literary criticism and psychohistory have found a place in their respective disciplines.

60. Mitchell, *Psychoanalysis and Feminism* (New York: Vintage–Random House, 1975). For a similar analysis, see Maria Ramas, "Freud's Dora, Dora's Hysteria," *Feminist Studies* 6 (1980), 472–510.

Dinnerstein focuses her analysis on the mothering process during the first year of life. Using the psychoanalytic method, she speculates about possible results of the fact that both male and female infants experience frustration and satisfaction of needs—good and evil—in relations to the female body and personality of the mother. Her thesis is that this early, virtually universal experience instills in all adults an extremely powerful and unconscious expectation that females will be the source of all satisfaction and also an extraordinary fear of the power of the female to frustrate. This produces a strong and constant tendency, on the part of men and women alike, to hold women as scapegoats for all misfortune. Because these associations are absorbed at a preverbal age, they do not form conscious ideas that can be unlearned by subsequent experience. Thus, Dinnerstein claims, no matter what other changes may be made in social relations, as long as the mother-child dyad remains constant and exclusive, an antifemale disposition will persist. She suggests that if women's monopoly on mothering were broken, if men and women were to share mothering, this powerful tendency would be reduced and conditions for solving the problems of gender inequality might be created.[61]

Chodorow's arguments parallel Dinnerstein's: that women's mothering is a critical aspect of personality development and, therefore, the sharing of mothering by both sexes is an essential step for changing gender hierarchy. She identifies the fostering of mothering behavior in women and the development of asymmetrical female and male personalities as the keys to the reproduction of gender hierarchy. Through their primary relationship with their mothers, girls develop the capacity to nurture and the desire to become mothers; boys' nurturant capacities are curtailed, in exchange for gaining the ability to function in the impersonal world of public life. Women's monopoly on mothering has a cyclical effect in the sense that "the sexual and familial division of labor in which women mother and are more involved in interpersonal, affective relationships than men produces in daughters and sons a division of psychological capacities which leads them to reproduce this sexual and familial division of labor."[62]

The work of Dinnerstein and Chodorow on the psychology of oppression is like that of Rosaldo's on the origins of oppression: women's ties to reproduction are the ultimate source of sex inequality. Even without this

61. Dinnerstein, *Mermaid and the Minotaur.*
62. Chodorow, *The Reproduction of Mothering* (Berkeley: University of California Press, 1978), 7.

particular analysis of origins, their psychoanalytic interpretations provide a powerful tool for understanding how oppressive ideas are reproduced, and psychological development, ideology, and basic social institutions are linked together. Because of its far-reaching implications, this approach to oppression has been extraordinarily stimulating for feminist scholars in many fields. It has, for example, been invoked by philosophers in their challenges to traditional concepts of knowledge and rationality. Sandra Harding is one of several who speculate that Chodorow's work and sex gender theories generally may provide a key to understanding the roots and flaws of "objective" value-free inquiry as a model for knowledge and scientific investigation.[63] She believes, too, that this theory can explain the basis and origin of the value placed on "masculine" domination and its connection to other relations of domination and subordination in society. "Let me stress again that it is indeed historical and material conditions to which the gender-based personality theories direct our attention. . . . The new concept of the material base of social life allows us to understand not only the historical and material conditions producing psychological interests in patriarchy and capital, but also those responsible for interests in various other kinds of dominating relationships: the interests in producing and maintaining the various dualisms where mind or intellect must dominate feelings, emotions, the body, physical nature and other social persons.[64]

Of course, psychoanalytic approaches to gender development are controversial even among feminists who acknowledge their insights. Adrienne Rich's "Compulsory Heterosexuality and Lesbian Existence" offers an important critical perspective on the work of Chodorow and Dinnerstein. Because she demands that full scholarly attention be paid to lesbianism, Rich's work is even more peripheral to the academy than is psychoanalysis. It has, however, reverberated within the women's liberation movement. Rich criticizes recent feminist scholarship in general for accepting the larger society's idea that heterosexuality is the "natural" form taken by human sexuality; she observes that this assumption leads to the invisibility of lesbianism. Commenting explicitly on Dinnerstein and Chodorow, she inquires: If women are the source of emotional caring and physical nurture for both

---

63. Harding, "Is Gender a Variable in Conceptions of Rationality? A Survey of Issues," *Dialectica* 36 (1982), 225–42.

64. Harding, "What Is the Real Material Base of Patriarchy and Capital?" *Women and Revolution*, ed. Lydia Sargent (Boston: South End Press, 1981), 154–55.

female and male children, why should female children ever redirect the search for attention toward men? Without addressing this question, any theory that posits the absence of men from mothering roles as the source of sexist ideology has a logical fault. For Rich, bonding between women is not simply sexual; it entails drawing power, strength, and identity from other women, being "woman-identified" rather than "male-identified" (not accepting the superior value and power of men). Rich elaborates the economic, political, and ideological factors that enforce heterosexuality for women and that identify the biological processes of impregnation with emotional/ erotic relationships with men. She argues that questioning the compulsory nature of heterosexuality is as important to feminism as questioning gender inequality and male dominance. In a fashion that complements Millett's initial identification of sexual relations as political, she argues for recognizing heterosexuality as a political institution.[65]

The phenomenon of what Rich terms the invisibility of lesbianism has been a subject for other theorists who consider conceptual categories that dominate thinking about women and how they obscure particular aspects of women's lives. In "To Be and Be Seen: The Politics of Reality" Marilyn Frye analyzes the language of what she calls "phallocratic reality" and demonstrates how definitions of lesbianism veil lesbians to such an extent that they disappear from the conceptual scheme that fashions prevailing views of reality. Through a series of remarkable metaphors of foreground and background perception, of actors in a play and stagehands behind the sets, Frye illustrates how what we select as real can be a matter of what we pay attention to. The phallocratic version of reality demands that we attend to male actions as the foreground activities—the play—and that we be aware of women only as the background—as stagehands whose movements underwrite what the actors do but who do not call attention to themselves. While the (female background) stagehands are presupposed by the (male foreground) actors, they are not counted among the important, the "real" elements of the play. Although the exclusion of women generally from phallocratic reality is irregular and partial, the exclusion of women who are lesbians is total. They are not needed to form the background for any part of male reality, and they are not invited to participate in it for any purpose. Therefore, the lesbian has no stake in maintaining phallocratic reality. "One

---

65. Rich, "Compulsory Heterosexuality and Lesbian Existence." See also Millett, *Sexual Politics*.

might try saying that a lesbian is one who, by virtue of her focus, her attention, her attachment, is disloyal to phallocratic reality," says Frye. "The event of becoming a lesbian is a reorientation of attention in a kind of ontological conversion. . . . Attention is a kind of passion. When one's attention is on something, one is present in a particular way with respect to that thing." Frye suggests that the potential for a reversed view of reality is so radical and dangerous that dominant ideology must exclude its possibility and that indeed "the power of those closed out" perhaps provides "the key to the liberation of women from oppression in a male-dominated culture."[66]

The Interaction between the Domestic and Public Spheres

A third aspect of feminist efforts to analyze women's oppression directs our attention to the division between the domestic, or private, sphere and the economic and political, or public, sphere. An important task of feminist scholarship has been to address this division and validate the study of the domestic sphere, which has been ignored by traditional scholarship, despite the centrality of family, reproduction, nurturance, and emotionality to women's lives. This division, at least to all appearances, is a significant aspect of modern social organization, and many feminists argue that overcoming it is a necessary step toward making women's role equal in social value to men's. Certain aspects of the origins debate as well as some of the analyses of the philosophical bases of sexist thinking take this as their working hypothesis. However, as with many conceptual advances, feminist attention to the public/private distinction has generated new theoretical problems: Is this distinction a part of social structure or rather a part of a sexist ideology that enforces women's oppression? Does this distinction have its roots in capitalist industrialization, which separated work from the family and gave rise to the corresponding definition of masculinity and femininity that we are attempting to reexamine? By using this public/private distinction are we reenforcing the oppression we are trying to remedy? A provocative direction in feminist scholarship—one that has increasing vitality—gives more emphasis to the ways that the private and public worlds are subtly and importantly connected and to attempts to understand women's situation as it is revealed in the links between the two.

66. Frye, "To See and Be Seen: The Politics of Reality," in her *The Politics of Reality: Essays in Feminist Theory* (Trumansburg, N.Y.: Crossing Press, 1983), 172.

The historical record suggests that some distinction between the domestic and the public spheres has long been present in our cultural tradition and that it has had profound implications for the ways we have been able to conceive of social organization and change. The public / private dichotomy is closely linked with a distinction drawn between that which is social or open to human intervention and that which is natural, having to do with the perpetuation and sustenance of the species. Since women are associated with the "natural" functions of reproduction and the rearing of children to a greater degree than men, their share in the sphere that is private and domestic has been viewed as an unalterable condition that any sort of social organization must accommodate. In response some feminists argue that the idea that women's reproductive role is natural is a source of sex inequality in concepts of political organization. Lorenne M. G. Clark and Lynda Lange charge that political theory from ancient through modern times has not considered women as full participants in the public life, precisely because women have been relegated to the realm of the natural, where the species is reproduced, leaving only men in the social domain. Although they agree in part with the Marxist analysis, which identifies unequal access to the means of production as the cause of women's oppression, they assert that unequal liability for reproductive labor is just as critical for understanding women's position. "We maintain that the different relation of the sexes to reproduction has had at least as profound an effect on the structure of society as the different relation of individuals to private property arising from production. The nature of this profound effect is found precisely in the fact that this different relationship is not rooted in nature at all, but in convention.[67]

Linda Nicholson has also examined the social theories of a range of thinkers throughout history and notes a persistent connection between a concept of the family and that of the sexual division of labor. She suggests that there is a link "between an endorsement of a sexual division of labor and an endorsement of the family, particularly in its nuclear form."[68] Increasing

67. Lange and Clark, eds., *The Sexism of Social and Political Theory* (Toronto: University of Toronto Press, 1979), xi.
68. Nicholson, "Women's Work: Views from the History of Philosophy," in *"Femininity," "Masculinity," and "Androgyny,"* ed. Vetterling-Braggin, 219, and "'The Personal Is Political': An Analysis in Retrospect," *Social Theory and Practice* 7 (1981), 85–98. See also Iris Young, "Beyond the Unhappy Marriage: A Critique of the Dual Systems Theory," in *Women and Revolution,* ed. Sargent, 43–69.

scrutiny has been directed at the family, its concept, ideology, and forms, as feminists have sought to understand the intricacies and varieties of women's domestic life.

Whereas there are prior traditions that feminists can use to analyze women's position in the world of work, there has been very little they can draw on for conceptualizing women's subordination in the family. Until the late 1960s the family was studied only by anthropologists and sociologists, and even then in ways that were of little use to feminists trying to understand women's oppression. Prefeminist scholars tended to describe family structures and organization as an organic whole. This meant that their methods for studying the family were not attuned to understanding profound conflicts among family members according to their different positions. Nor were they interested in change, but rather in the ways that the institution of the family maintained its viability despite social forces working to undermine it. In the 1970s historians also began to study the family incorporating many of the same assumptions and weaknesses as their anthropological and sociological predecessors.

This static and monolithic approach to the family had to be revised by feminist scholars, who tend to approach the family as an arena of sexual conflict and who are interested in family change, both in the past and in the future.[69] One of the first contributions to the feminist reconceptualization of the family was the early work of Juliet Mitchell, who challenged the assumption that the family is a monolithic unit. She disaggregated women's experience into its separate functions, which she identified as reproduction, sexuality, childrearing, and production, arguing that the last of these functions, the only one that takes place outside the family, tends to structure the other three.[70] Her emphasis, furthermore, was on change, and she was careful to point out that a history of the family that acknowledges the existence of these four components of women's subordination has to recognize that each changes in different ways and at different rates. By breaking the family down into the ways it functions in the society, her work helped to

69. Feminist critiques of nonfeminist family studies include: Rayna Rapp, Ellen Ross, and Renate Bridenthal, "Examining Family History," *Feminist Studies* 5 (1979), 174–200; Wini Breines, Margaret Cerullo, and Judith Stacey, "Social Biology, Family Studies and Anti-Feminist Backlash," ibid., 4 (1978), 43–68.

70. Mitchell, *Woman's Estate* (New York: Pantheon, 1972). Subsequent scholarship has added a fifth category, housework. See Ann Oakley, *Woman's Work: The Housewife, Past and Present* (New York: Pantheon–Random House, 1974).

lay the basis for an analysis of women's oppression that assumes women's position in the family as part of history and links it with larger social forces.

Mitchell's analysis, however, does not posit a systematic connection between women's experience in the home and the marketplace. The structures that she identified suggest discrete and incommensurate sectors of life, which have to be approached with different apparatus for analysis: In the family, sex, children, and reproduction are the relevant categories, while in the economy, work and production are appropriate. Consistent with this sharp division, the structures clustered under the rubric of family omit one of women's central domestic experiences—housework. Subsequent analyses of women's oppression have solved this problem by pointing out that women work inside as well as outside the family. In this framework housework (or domestic labor) becomes a key to understanding women's role in the family and, beyond that, an essential element in establishing the connection between the family and the economy.[71]

Margaret Benston's groundbreaking article, "The Political Economy of Women's Liberation," was the first example of modern feminist scholarship to apply to women's domestic situation the analytic categories usually employed to understand the economic universe outside the home. Using a Marxist framework, Benston maintains that because of their common responsibility for domestic work, women share a relationship to the means of production—the production of use-value in the home; this differs from men as a group, who only produce commodities (in Marxist terms, exchange value) as part of the waged labor force. Because the domestic work of women—cooking, cleaning, and childcare—remains outside the money economy, it is invisible and valueless in a society where money determines worth. Benston does not conclude from this that women constitute a distinct class. Rather, she is concerned with demystifying housework and childrearing as "labors of love," bearing no relation to the kind of "real" labor that is subject to the scrutiny of economic theorists. From this perspective, she points out that housework and childcare do possess an exchange value if performed by someone other than the wife and mother,

---

71. Mitchell's four structures were originally described in her influential and widely reprinted article, "Women: The Longest Revolution," *New Left Review* (1966), 11–37. Hence, the scholarship on domestic work that was published before the appearance of her *Woman's Estate* may rest on and extend her analysis, explicitly or implicitly commenting on its omission of housework as a distinct category. For an extensive critique of Mitchell, see Lise Vogel, "The Earthly Family," *Radical America* 7 (1973), 9–50.

whose "natural" work they are. Benston characterizes the position of the housewife as a kind of "in-law" to the fundamental relationship between labor and capital, since "at present the support of a family is a hidden tax on the wage earner—his wage buys the labor power of two people."[72]

Virtually every element of Benston's original analysis has since been the object of extensive theoretical debate. Her essential contribution has not resided in these controversial particulars, as much as in the creation of a model that adds an economic dimension to our understanding of women's experience in the family. One direction of subsequent debate centered on the applicability of Marxist categories of "value," "labor power," "productive work," and "socially necessary labor" to the housewife's job. Did the housewife produce labor power by keeping the (male) worker alive and functioning? Did she do so by replacing the current labor force with a new generation of children to become workers? Under what condition could housework be viewed as producing actual "value"?[73] By and large these attempts to reduce housework to orthodox Marxist categories did not yield fruitful conclusions for Marxist theory itself. Their lasting contribution has been to establish in feminist theory the importance of economic links among women, the family, and the larger society.

Socialist feminists, following Benston, have been less concerned with particular analytic details than with a wider historical construction and theoretical understanding of the housewife's role and its relevance to women's liberation. By arguing that women do work in the home, the way is opened to analyze women's oppression as shaped by, in service to, and changing with the wider economy. Early research emphasizes the ways housework serves capitalism. In "A Woman's Work is Never Done," Peggy Morton relates the work of childrearing to the specific needs of capitalism, a system that

---

72. Benston, "The Political Economy of Women's Liberation," *Monthly Review* 21 (1969), 13–27. In an earlier period Charlotte Perkins Gilman looked at domestic life as an example of preindustrial and inefficient economics; see her *The Home: Its Work and Influence* (1903; reprint ed. Urbana: University of Illinois Press, 1972), and her *Women and Economics: A Study of the Economic Relation between Men and Women as a Factor in Social Evolution* (1898; reprint ed. New York: Harper and Row, 1966). Selma James anticipated the more Marxist categories of modern scholarship in "A Woman's Place," in *The Power of Women and Subversion of the Community* (1953; reprint ed. Bristol: Falling Wall Press, 1972).

73. See, for instance, Ira Gerstein, "Domestic Work and Capitalism," *Radical America* 7 (1973), 101–28; Wally Seccombe, "The Housewife and Her Labour under Capitalism," *New Left Review* 83 (1973); Margaret Coulson, Branka Magas, and Hilary Wainwright, "'The Housewife and Her Labour under Capitalism'—A Critique," ibid., 89 (1975), 47–58.

requires not only labor power in general but also a work force socialized to discipline, hierarchical relations, and self-repression.[74] Subsequent scholarship explores the interconnections between housework and the economy more fully. In examining the multitude of forces that shape housework as we know it, Barbara Ehrenreich and Deirdre English consider the combined impact of advanced technology and higher education for women in the context of a system that has had to adapt both of these advances to the imperatives of profit.[75] The domestic science movement, the settlement houses and other charitable endeavors aimed at immigrant families, and advertising and the beginnings of market research all contributed to the construction not only of the ideology surrounding modern housework but also of the practical conditions under which women perform and experience it.

When feminists analyze housework as essential labor, the housewife is transformed from an isolated and irrelevant person to someone whose work gives her a central role in changing society; and her oppression in the family is revealed not only as limiting her activity, but also as generating change. Not surprisingly, then, this perspective on the family has been more productive than most aspects of feminist scholarship for political strategies for feminism. The "Wages for Housework" campaign, which is international in scope, is based entirely on the theory that women's labor in the home produces value, that such value is part of the wage and profit system. Dismissing approaches that posit women as exceptions to one aspect or another of a traditional Marxist analysis, Selma James moves women and their work to center stage on the grounds that "there is nothing in capitalism which is not capitalistic, that is not part of the class struggle." In particular, she describes the control capitalism has in shaping community and family life, and women's central role of resistance. "The community therefore is not an area of freedom and leisure auxiliary to the factory, where by chance there happen to be women who are degraded as the personal servants of men. The community is the other half of the capitalist organization, the other area of hidden capitalist exploitation, *the other, hidden source of surplus labor*. It becomes increasingly regimented, like a factory . . . where the costs and nature of transport, housing, medical care, education,

---

74. Morton, "A Woman's Work Is Never Done" (1970), reprinted in *From Feminism to Liberation*, ed. Edith Hoshino Altbach (Cambridge, Mass.: Schenkman, 1971), 211–27.

75. Ehrenreich and English, "The Manufacture of Housework," *Socialist Review* 5 (1975), 5–40.

police are all points of struggle."[76] The demand for wages for housework or its complement, the refusal of work, grows directly out of this constant resistance on women's part to the profit made from what they produce. It dignifies and recognizes women's work and seeks to give them control over their lives. Since capital relies on the housewife's labor and her continued acquiescence for its survival, proponents of this strategy see it as attacking the core of capitalist social relations.[77]

Historical changes in the economy, in modes of production, and in the family necessitate an expansion of categories of analysis traditionally used by Marxists, argues Ann Ferguson, and in her analysis she revitalizes a notion of class particular to women. To do this she identifies another kind of domestic labor that has been overlooked by social theorists because it takes place in the so-called private world of the home. She calls this "sex / affective production . . . the system of production which organizes social modes of satisfying the needs of sexuality, nurturance, and children." Because men and women systematically assume different relations to sex / affective production, they may be said to constitute classes relative to one another: "there are at least *three* different class relationships that can characterize a person at the same time: *sex class, family class,* and *individual economic class*. I argue that there is a family mode of childbearing, sexuality, and affection which I call 'patriarchal sex / affective production' and that men and women are in *sex classes* relative to their position of power and appropriation in that mode of production."[78] It is because Ferguson sees women as the major workers at sex / affective production that she views them as supporting the public world of production by rearing children to an ethos that is necessary to patriarchal and capitalist culture. Like James, Ferguson also believes that women are potentially a revolutionary force in

76. James, introduction to the English translation of Mariarosa dalla Costa, "Women and the Subversion of the Community," in *The Power of Women and the Subversion of the Community* (Bristol: Falling Wall Press, 1973), 5, 7.

77. For further writings from the wages-for-housework perspective and critical commentary, see the collection of essays, *The Politics of Housework*, ed. Ellen Malos (London: Alison & Busby, 1980). This collection has also reprinted other essays referred to in this section, those by Benston, Morton, Coulson and James. For an additional critique and response, see Carol Lopate, "Women and Pay for Housework," *Liberation* 18 (1974), and Nicole Cox and Silvia Federici, *Counter Planning from the Kitchen* (Bristol: Falling Wall Press, 1975).

78. Ferguson, "Women as a New Revolutionary Class in the United States," in *Between Labor and Capital*, ed. Pat Walker (Boston: South End Press, 1979), 281, 290–91.

society, and indeed that recent changes, such as increased participation in the paid work force, less stable marriages, and nontraditional living arrangements, have already weakened the structure of patriarchal domination over women.[79]

Another analysis of the connection between housework and the larger society emphasizes women's work as consumers. Amy Bridges and Batya Weinbaum have argued that housework is integrated into the market primarily through the process of consumption. At the same time consumption is a source of conflict between the housewife and the economic system. While others treat the modern woman consumer as manipulated by advertising and victimized by its artificially created needs, Weinbaum and Bridges see more conflict—and possibility—in the situation. "It is the housewife's responsibility for nurturance which conditions her confrontation with capital in the form of commodities."[80] There is a continuous contradiction between the housewife's responsibility for taking care of her family and the difficulty of doing so under capitalism, given women's lack of social and economic power and the kinds of goods and services available. This contradiction forms the kernel of the housewife's political perspective, allowing her to take leadership roles in community-based struggles such as tenants' and consumer organizations. (A striking example of effective housewife leadership is Lois Gibbs's work with the Love Canal Homeowners Association.[81]) These community struggles have often been viewed as less important than conflicts in the work place, but feminists are recognizing that they address major economic issues and look toward a fundamental transformation of society.

Feminist scholars have used other vantage points than domestic labor for exploring the connection between the domestic and public spheres. Weinbaum has analyzed the ways in which an individual's place within the family affects her or his place within the wage labor force, and vice versa.[82] Rather

79. Ferguson and Nancy Folbre, "The Unhappy Marriage of Patriarchy and Capitalism," *Women and Revolution*, ed. Sargent, 313–38.

80. Weinbaum and Bridges, "The Other Side of the Paycheck," *Monthly Review* 28 (1976), 193–94. An example of the authors who treat women as being manipulated by advertising is Stuart Ewen in *Captains of Consciousness* (New York: McGraw-Hill, 1976).

81. Adeline Gordon Levine, *Love Canal: Science, Politics, and People* (Lexington, Mass.: Lexington Books, 1982).

82. Weinbaum, *The Curious Courtship of Women's Liberation and Socialism* (Boston: South End Press, 1978).

than speak in terms of the abstract category "worker," she suggests we devise new categories that acknowledge the family-based realities of sex and age as they affect the structures of the labor force. In other words, she argues that not only are the experiences of male and female workers different but also those of unmarried women must be distinguished from those of married women, and those of young men without dependents from those of male heads of households. In order to capture the impact of family-based power relations, she suggests we use the categories "mothers," "sons," "fathers," and "daughters" not only with respect to the family, but with respect to the labor force as well. Weinbaum contends that such categories enable us to see how "the household has its own point of view on the economy." For instance, fathers may send their daughters out to work in order to keep their wives or sons at home. Similarly, "production has a point of view" with respect to the family, as when a new industry or area of employment opens up and is directed specifically to unmarried women, whose position in the family makes their extremely low wage rates possible.[83] Weinbaum's approach links work to the family in a concrete way and helps us see the specific avenues by which an individual woman's subordination at home translates into discrimination at work and vice versa. Such scholarship demonstrates the degree to which feminist analyses of women's oppression have advanced beyond the tendency to situate causes either in the family or in the labor force and to explore instead the nature of the links between the two areas.

A very different but equally fruitful dimension of research on the connection between the domestic and the public spheres is that which frees itself from the overly abstract concept of "the family" and looks at differences in how women live within various family relations. This approach especially illuminates women's lives in working class and Third World families, for, although women are central to family life, not all experience it in the same way, often because of the effects of race and class relations in the society at large.

The inspiration for this kind of research is both intellectual and political. In part, it reflects the feminist movement's goal of recognizing the validity of different women's experiences and understanding the tensions and difficulties that arise because of these differences, in order to develop political goals all women can share. Many researchers identify their own working-class

83. Ibid., 151.

and/or Third World family experiences as the source of their desires to reexamine the dominant assumptions about what constitutes normal family life.

Feminist explorations of the variety of family experiences also come from theoretical concerns about the family. In Juliet Mitchell's groundbreaking conceptualization, she identified three levels of analysis required for a complete study of family life: "the biological universal, the ideological atemporal, and the economic specificity." This third level recognizes that families take different forms through history, especially with respect to economic function.[84] It is only a small leap from identifying that the family changes according to economic function to understanding that class relations and racism create different kinds of families. Feminist anthropologists, whose disciplinary training stresses the differences among cultures and questions whether there is a universal family, have developed a similar conceptualization: separating the concept "household" from that of "the family." Rayna Rapp regards the household as part of the larger economic system, a set of relations within which people pool resources and perform tasks that are related to social reproduction, consumption, and in some cases economic production.[85] By contrast, she identifies the family as an ideological construction, one purpose of which is to recruit people to households. Understood in this way, the family and the household have different histories.

An early article by Mina Davis Caulfield formulates a perspective that runs through most analyses of how class exploitation and racism shape families and women's experiences within them: For working-class and Third World women the family is the center of their resistance to exploitation as well as the center of their oppression.[86] In addition, feminists are concerned to demonstrate that, contrary to common stereotypes, working-class

84. Mitchell, *Women's Estate*, 172.

85. Rayna Rapp, "Family and Class in Contemporary America: Notes toward an Understanding of Ideology," *Science and Society* 42 (1978), 278–300; see also Bridenthal, Rapp, and Ross, "Examining Family History"; Sylvia Junko Yanagisako, "Family and Household: The Analysis of Domestic Groups," *Annual Review of Anthropology* 8 (1979), 161–205; Jane Collier, Michelle Z. Rosaldo, and Sylvia Yanagisako "Is There a Family? New Anthropological Views," in *Rethinking the Family: Some Feminist Questions*, ed. Barrie Thorne and Marilyn Yalom (New York: Longman's, 1982), 25–39.

86. Caulfield, "Imperialism, the Family, and Cultures of Resistance," *Socialist Revolution* 2 (1974), 67–85.

and Third World family life is not more sexist than the middle-class version; rather, sexism takes different forms. In *Worlds of Pain* Lillian Rubin studies how white working-class people come to terms with the hard conditions and economic constraints that underlie their family disappointments and intimate conflicts.[87]

In general feminists studying the variety of family forms in the United States have concentrated more on race than on class, perhaps reflecting the impact of a powerful civil rights movement on scholarship. Here the leadership of black feminist scholars is very marked. Joyce Ladner's sociological study *Tomorrow's Tomorrow*, was an early and pioneering analysis of how racism shapes black women's roles in their families. Most sociological research has considered poor black families as broken and deviant, but Ladner regards them as effective defenses against racism and the resulting "poverty, discrimination and institutionalized subordination." She studies how young girls grow into strong, healthy, resourceful women in these families. At times Ladner seems to suggest that these black women can provide a model worthy of emulation for all women. "This freedom as well as the tremendous hardships from which black women suffered allowed for the development of a female personality that is rarely described in the scholarly journals for its obstinate strength and ability to survive. Neither is its particular humanist character and quiet courage viewed as the epitome of what the American model of femininity should be."[88]

Subsequent research follows Ladner's emphasis on institutionalized racism and imperialism as it affects black women's oppression, fostering strong bonds between black women and creating black women's strength and self-reliance. The role of institutionalized sexism in shaping black women's experience is also receiving attention.[89] In *Ain't I A Woman* Bell Hooks argues for the necessity of recognizing the tremendous toll sexism takes on black women in the twentieth century, manifesting itself in their silent resistance to pain and unnecessary suffering, and their demoralization

87. Rubin, *Worlds of Pain: Life in the Working-Class Family* (New York: Basic Books, 1976).

88. Ladner, *Tomorrow's Tommorow: The Black Woman* (Garden City, N.Y.: Doubleday, 1972), 12, 275.

89. See, for instance, Bonnie Thornton Dill, "The Dialectics of Black Womanhood," *Signs* 4 (1979), 543–55; Angela Y. Davis, *Women Race and Class* (New York: Vintage, 1981); Gloria Joseph and Jill Lewis, *Common Differences: Conflicts in Black and White Feminist Perspectives* (Garden City, N.Y.: Anchor Press, 1981); Filomina Chioma Steady, ed., *The Black Woman Cross-Culturally* (Cambridge, Mass.: Schenkman, 1981).

when it comes to building a feminist movement that will make the society more healthy and humane.[90]

This research raises fundamental issues for feminist scholarship, starting with the challenge to place black women at the center of history and society—no mean feat in its own right—and culminating with questions about whether we can speak of the universal oppression of women. These theoretical possibilities are highlighted in *Common Differences*, a dialogue between Gloria Joseph and Jill Lewis, which explores the different histories, culture, and experiences of black and white women and their implications for building feminism.[91] For instance, Joseph suggests that white feminist scholarship on the mother-daughter relationship does not encompass black women's experiences. White feminists emphasize a fundamental ambivalence in the mother-daughter relationship, in which daughters seek both to escape and reproduce their mothers' mothering. Joseph argues that in the black family there is a different basis to the mother-daughter relationship, one built on the daughter's respect for the mother's accomplishments and the mother's responsibility to cultivate in her daughter the strength required to live in a racist world.

The obvious advantages of these studies that integrate the public and the private, the family and the economy, is that they give specificity to women's oppression and provide ways of understanding cultural and historical differences in women's situation. In contrast, when the spheres are assumed to be divided, research on the family and women's oppression tends to emphasize continuity and similarities and to underplay the changes in history and differences in culture. In some sense both approaches capture different truths and, like the origins debate, remind us that the challenge in developing a theory of women's oppression is to explain the extraordinary differences in women's position and yet account for the astonishing persistence

90. Hooks, *Ain't I a Woman: Black Women and Feminism* (Boston: South End Press, 1981); see also *All the Women Are White, All the Blacks Are Men, But Some of Us Are Brave*, ed. Gloria P. Hull, Patricia Bell-Scott, and Barbara Smith (Old Westbury: Feminist Press, 1982). Sociologist Cheryl Townsend Gilkes gives a specific example of this problem in an unpublished paper (1981) based on her "Living and Working in a World of Trouble: The Black Woman Community Worker" (Ph.D. diss., Northeastern University, 1979). She argues that the Moynihan report, which she regards as representing general sexist ideas applied to black women, acted to force black women out of the leadership roles they had traditionally held in community organizations.

91. Joseph and Lewis, *Common Differences*.

and continuity of some kind of subordination. There is no doubt that feminist scholarship has begun to grapple with this problem, by providing frameworks for analyzing evidence about women's position and by transforming these frameworks as evidence requires. It is no longer a question of whether women's oppression is a serious subject of research but rather of finding—or creating—the most comprehensive system for its analysis.

4

Liberation and Equality: Old Questions Reconsidered

As feminist scholarship has collected new information on women's lives and produced a substantial body of theory on the causes and nature of women's oppression, it has also examined a complementary issue, the problem of achieving liberation. Like oppression, liberation is a concept that came into being in a universe of discourse and action well outside the normal boundaries of academe. Once again, however, it is a problem on which the resources of scholarship have been brought to bear and where feminists have contributed new formulations of both theoretical and empirical material.

Much of this work is an exploration of schools of thought that have been posited to improve the condition of societies generally. In our society the moral and legal establishment of women's rights centers on the notion of equality inherited from the liberal, democratic political tradition. We begin, therefore, by reviewing the feminist philosophical perspectives on this idea and their application to concrete strategies for attaining sex equality. The frameworks for discussing equality and social justice derived from this theoretical tradition leave a substantial mark on the feminist literature, notably in its focus on equal treatment under law and conditions for equality of opportunity—that is, on equality in the so-called public sphere of life. Some of the discussion of the previous chapter also concerns the subject of equality. Probably the material most directly relevant is that on the domestic roles of women and the ways that activity in the world of the home influences women's opportunities and positions in the world outside the home. Significantly, the literature on the relations between the private and the public domains is both highly interdisciplinary and draws heavily from material that is not in the mainstream of academic scholarship, while the work on equality of opportunity, sex discrimination, and like subjects is often framed by the academic disciplinary traditions of philosophy and political theory.

The concept of liberation is more global than equality, both literally and figuratively. In particular, claims are made that two large-scale social transformations, modernization and socialism, provide the enabling conditions for the emancipation of women. As we examine feminist approaches to these two programs for social change, parallel questions arise: In what way do these transformations bring about greater sex equality? To what degree do they fail to do so? What are the more general criticisms that this failure suggests? And how has feminist scholarship on women modified or challenged the theoretical assumptions behind modernization and socialist policies? This area of feminist scholarship raises questions about the relations between the gathering of data and the development of ways to interpret it that challenge the social sciences in their identification and measurement of social change. These empirical studies also contribute to what is one of the major debates at present within feminist theory: whether Marxism and feminism can be combined to form a unified theory or whether they are fundamentally incompatible ways of thinking.

The Concept of Equality

The idea of equality, always a difficult one in social theory, raises special problems when the individuals proposed as equals are not the same. There are biological differences between the human male and female, and the extent to which physiological difference has implications for other differences and for the appropriateness of social roles is currently a matter for intense debate among scholars, as it is in the movement.[1] Although differences between the sexes are invoked most stridently by antifeminists who aim to preserve male supremacy, feminists also have explored the possibility that sex differences, whether biologically or culturally induced, are too imbedded in our history, culture, and society to be ignored in discussions of sex equality. For instance, some of the educational intervention strategists

---

1. In the introduction to *Sex Equality* (Englewood Cliffs, N.J.: Prentice-Hall, 1977), Jane English gives a succinct summary of the complexities involved in determining equality. The essays collected in this volume represent a range of views on sex equality.

we discussed in Chapter 2 proceed on the assumptions that male and female students may well have different dispositions to learn certain subjects and that strategies need to take these discrepancies into account. Much more radical is the contention of early feminists who argued that oppression is so tied to female biology that liberation presupposes that women must no longer reproduce the species.[2] Whereas this view advocates the eradication of gender differences, other feminists see a potentially positive value in the different characteristics that their respective sex roles have fostered in women and men, viewing women's attributes as a source of diversity and richness in humankind.[3]

The task of assessing the role of biology in determining gender differences and their possible relevance for structuring a sexually egalitarian society engages the dialogue on nature versus nurture mentioned in the previous chapter. Many writers on sex equality maintain that one ought to regard reproductive functions as the only innate area of difference between the sexes and that this difference is important only in very limited contexts. All other differences currently ascribed to gender are, in fact, elements of sex oppression and ideology. An egalitarian society, therefore, should accord sex differences no importance, treating men and women the same in all aspects of public policy. In an early piece on the subject Allison Jaggar advocated that sex roles be "deinstitutionalized," remarking that they "are irrational whenever they regulate our behavior in contexts other than the reproductive, for in doing so they unwarrantably presuppose that the difference between the sexes is more than a simple physiological distinction."[4] In a later book Elizabeth Wolgast disagrees, maintaining that the social implications of reproduction are such that in families with children,

2. See Shulamith Firestone, *The Dialectic of Sex: The Case for Feminist Revolution* (New York: Morrow, 1970).

3. See, for example, Christine Garside Allen, "A Contemporary Approach to Sex Identity," in *Philosophy of Woman: Classical to Current Concepts*, ed. Mary Mahowald (Indianapolis: Hackett, 1978), 261–74, reprinted from *Values and the Quality of Life*, ed. W. Shea and J. King-Farlow (New York: Science History Publications, 1976). For other discussions of sexuality and personhood, see Anne Dickason, "The Feminine as Universal," in *Feminism and Philosophy*, ed. Mary Vetterling-Braggin, Frederick Elliston, and Jane English (Totowa, N.J.: Littlefield, Adams, 1977), 70–100, and Kathryn Morgan, "Sexuality as a Metaphysical Dimension," in *Philosophy and Women*, ed. Sharon Bishop and Marjorie Weinzweig (Belmont, Calif.: Wadsworth, 1979), 88–95.

4. Jaggar, "On Sexual Equality," *Ethics* 84 (1974), 291, reprinted in *Sex Equality*, ed. English, 93–109.

mothers and fathers develop an "asymmetrical" relationship. Thus the idea of "equal" rights for women and men continues to put women at a disadvantage, and Wolgast advocates the introduction of "special" rights that take into account the differences between the sexes and thus insure an egalitarian society.[5] While Wolgast reflects more recent consideration of the possibility of deeply rooted gender differences that have implications beyond the limits of biological reproduction, she is most uncritical about the present-day nuclear family and the primary role of mothers in childrearing (so uncritical, in fact, that her advocacy of sex equality relies upon some traditional antifeminist assumptions).

That gender differences ought to be ignored in a just society and diminished in social roles and behavior finds a particular form in the idea of androgyny. Particularly in the early years of feminist thinking, many found appealing the idea that genuine equality entails the elimination of gender differences and the encouragement of opportunities for girls and boys, women and men to develop androgynous personalities. Advocates of this position argue that culture and history have separated out sets of characteristics that are now termed masculine and feminine. Within each, there are desirable and undesirable traits: strength and decisiveness in the masculine are frequently offset by aggression and the desire to dominate; sympathy and gentleness in the feminine are often weakened by pettiness and vanity. The goal of androgyny defines sex equality as a condition in which both sexes share in the positive traits that are now sorted out by gender to the detriment of all, a redistribution that would also eliminate the reciprocal drawbacks currently associated with each set of positive characteristics.[6] While androgyny remains an ideal to some, many of its earlier advocates have since altered their views. In a recent extensive critique Kathryn Morgan argues that the concept of androgyny itself is confused and presents an ideal that turns out to be illusory.[7]

These speculations about the permanence and nature of differences between the sexes, about their desirability, and about the advisability of recognizing them in law, policy, and custom all raise questions about equality.

5. Wolgast, *Equality and the Rights of Women* (Ithaca: Cornell University Press, 1980).

6. See Ann Ferguson, "Androgyny as an Ideal for Human Development," and Joyce Trebilcot, "Two Forms of Androgynism," both in *Feminism and Philosophy*, ed. Vetterling-Braggen, Elliston, and English, 45–69, 70–78, respectively.

7. Morgan, "Androgyny: A Conceptual Critique," *Social Theory and Practice* 8 (1982), 245–83.

What does sex equality involve? What are the best means to bring it about? The principal source of complexity arises from the gap between what might be termed formal equality and equality of circumstances. Formal sex equality might exist when no overt policies are present that discriminate against women with respect to the distribution of social goods, such as job and educational opportunities, housing, and legal and social services. Formal equality is presumed to afford citizens equal opportunity, which is supposed to obtain when, discrimination having been eliminated, all persons who choose to apply for, let us say, a job are judged by their qualifications alone. But as feminists have observed in their analyses of oppression, even equal opportunity is by no means a simple achievement. Sex oppression, which persists despite the removal of explicitly discriminatory hiring policies, means that few women will find themselves in circumstances equal to men's from which they might gain relevant qualifications for those opportunities. Different constraints on choices, such as those caused by domestic responsibilities, access to skills, and self-concepts are all barriers to equal opportunity, not to mention the lingering sex-bias on the part of those who dispense opportunities.[8] Thus, in the absence of equality of circumstance formal equality may effect little change in the relative status of men and women.

Feminist scholarship in empirical fields has grappled with the difference in these two concepts, demonstrating that the elimination of overt discrimination has rarely resulted in equality of opportunity of women.[9] Blanche Fitzpatrick's study of women's higher education, for example, points out that while colleges and universities no longer have quotas that limit the number of women admitted, women hardly have the opportunity to obtain the same kind of higher education as men. Women are rarely encouraged to enter high-status, research institutions by college recruiters, high school guidance counselors, or their families. Financial aid opportunities for women are limited: women cannot qualify for football or ROTC funding or veterans' benefits. All this makes the objective costs of obtaining an education higher for girls and their parents, and these costs cannot be offset by girls working their way through school. Typing, waitressing, and babysitting — female jobs — yield lower wages than construction and road work — male jobs.

8. Onora O'Neill, "How Do We Know When Opportunities Are Equal?" in *Sex Equality*, ed. English, 143–54, first published *Philosophical Forum* 5 (1973–74), 334–46.
9. Fitzpatrick, *Women's Inferior Education: An Economic Analysis* (New York: Praeger, 1977); see also Patricia Sexton, *Women in Education* (Bloomington, Ind.: Phi Delta Kappa, 1976).

Fitzpatrick and others have shown that lifting overt discrimination has done little to provide equal access to equal kinds of education.[10] Women remain clustered in two-year junior colleges and four-year public institutions, where costs to them are cheaper. They have little access to research institutions and schools that provide sophisticated training in sciences and technology, and consequently they lack formal qualifications to enter a host of occupations. While overt discrimination is illegal, research on vertical and horizontal occupational segregation has demonstrated that women remain in low-paid, entry-level positions in the work force, clustered in a narrow range of occupations. Since the mid-1960s, when legislation barring overt discrimination in the United States was enacted, little change in female income or the pattern of female occupations has occurred. There is some evidence to suggest in recent years that under conditions of formal equality women's income and status relative to men has even eroded.[11]

Some feminist scholars have argued that formal equality does not imply equality of result, in part because growing up in a sexist society leaves women at a psychological and attitudinal disadvantage.[12] For example, Sheila Tobias suggests that women do not enter the sciences or pursue careers in business or technology because they avoid studying mathematics. Many women have math anxiety and math phobia—they cannot master the subject.[13] Others contend that women cannot compete well with men within the same career patterns because they have been taught to repress those very same personality traits of assertiveness and autonomy that allow

10. Fitzpatrick, *Women's Inferior Education*; Sexton, *Women in Education*; Bonnie Cook Freeman, "Power, Patriarchy and 'Political Primitives,'" in *Beyond Intellectual Sexism: A New Woman, A New Reality*, ed. Joan I. Roberts (New York: David McKay, 1976), 241–64; Freeman, "Female Education in Patriarchal Power Systems," in *Education and Colonialism*, ed. P. G. Altbach and G. P. Kelly (New York: Longman, 1978), 207–42.

11. Robert W. Smuts, *Women and Work in America*, 3d ed. (New York: Schocken Books, 1974); Marianne A. Ferber, "Women and Work: Issues of the 1980s," *Signs* 8 (1982), 273–95; Martha Blaxall and Barbara B. Reagan (guest eds.), "Women and the Workplace: The Implications of Occupational Segregation," *Signs* 1 (Spring 1976 Supplement).

12. M. S. Horner, "Toward an Understanding of Achievement-Related Conflicts in Women," *Journal of Social Issues* 28 (1972), 157–76; Georgia Sassen, "Success Anxiety in Women: A Constructivist Interpretation of Its Sources and Its Significance," *Harvard Educational Review* 50 (1980), 13–24; David Tressmer, "Do Women Fear Success?" *Signs* 1 (1976), 863–74.

13. For a review of this scholarship, see Tobias and Weissbrod, "Anxiety and Mathematics: An Up-Date," *Harvard Educational Review* 50 (1980), 63–70.

men to succeed.[14] Others, notably Matina Horner, argue that women fear success and that they equate successful careers with loss of femininity and are therefore ambivalent about their work.[15] While this literature on women's socialization and attitudes has generated controversies on its own terms, it has contributed to a growing recognition that equality is unobtainable if social policy is directed solely at removing discrimination. It has shown that in the absence of equality of circumstance formal equality has little or no impact on gender inequality in American society.[16]

The provision of equality of circumstances has increasingly become seen as the enabling condition for equality of outcome once formal discrimination has been eliminated. Therefore, many feminists advocate preferential treatment or affirmative action to deal with continued inequality between men and women.[17] Those who take this position most often base their argument on an appeal to justice: an avowedly democratic society with entrenched patterns of discrimination violates in practice what it advocates in principle. Giving preference to women (and minorities, for the arguments in both cases are similar) in hiring practices, promotions, and educational opportunities is one method that should be employed to achieve real egalitarianism.[18]

A substantial philosophical literature has developed in response to the claims of justice for affirmative action. Opponents of this strategy argue that an unjust situation cannot be righted simply by reversing the direction of discrimination and that preferential treatment is both itself unjust and inconsistent with the principles of equality. Furthermore, they argue, since injustice is perpetrated against individuals, not groups, it makes no sense to try to compensate the damage done to some individuals in the past by favoring other individuals in the present. Whereas some advocates of affirmative

14. See, for example, Rosabeth Kanter, *Women in the Corporation* (New York: Praeger, 1977); Kanter, "Women and the Structure of Organizations," in *Another Voice*, ed. Marcia Millman and Rosabeth Kanter (New York: Doubleday, 1975).

15. Sassen, "Success Anxiety in Women".

16. Suzanne E. Estler, "Women as Leaders in Public Education," *Signs* 1 (1975), 363–86; Marion Kilson, "The Status of Women in Higher Education," ibid., 935–42.

17. A long-running debate on this subject appears in the journal *Analysis* from 1970 onward. See also a number of articles in *Philosophy and Public Affairs* 1971 and onward.

18. The problems raised by inequality of circumstance are sometimes repeated in the articulation of what is meant by affirmative action. The principle of affirmative action is often formulated in such a way that only if a man and a woman candidate are already equally qualified should the woman be given preference.

action hold that compensation for past wrongs is indeed a sound foundation for argument, others justify preferential treatment on the grounds that it is a means to achieve greater equality of circumstances among all members of society in the future.[19]

Apart from differing views about the reasons justifying preferential treatment, advocates of such a strategy may also differ regarding ultimate goals. For many, the sex equality that is the aim of affirmative action is simply true equality of opportunity, including equality of circumstances: the sexes would be able to compete fairly for positions, and neither would be at an advantage as far as access to obtaining the necessary qualifications.

Others see the equality to be sought differently. Preferential treatment is one means of recognizing the injustice of a whole social system. It is not only discrimination against certain groups that needs to be changed, but the wholesale competitive ethos that pits individual against individual in the pursuit of unequally distributed social goods. Marlene Gerber Fried, for example, argues that most current concepts of equal opportunity actually mask oppression because opportunity is cast in the framework of market relations and individualism. Thus, the failure of women and minorities to gain in relative status despite affirmative action programs is continually interpreted as a failure of individuals, rather than a persistent pattern of social oppression.[20] Whereas the first view would see the end of sex oppression resulting in equal numbers of men and women at all strata of society, the second would aim at the eradication of the hierarchy of social stratification itself. Generally speaking, the first view can be considered a "liberal" and the second a "radical" perspective. In fact, the views of many feminists partake a little of both, since some feminist aims, such as the abolition of sex roles, entail more fundamental social change than others, such as access to equal opportunity.[21] This is another reminder of the relevance of analyses of domestic work to questions of equality, for unequal distribution of

19. Judith Jarvis Thomson, "Preferential Hiring," *Philosophy and Public Affairs* 2 (1973), 364–84. Irving Thalberg, "Reverse Discrimination and the Future," and Marlene Gerber Fried, "In Defense of Preferential Hiring," both in *Philosophical Forum* 5 (1973–74), 294–308, 309–19, respectively, take different positions on this issue.

20. Fried, "The Invisibility of Oppression," *Philosophical Forum* 11 (1979), 18–29.

21. For a general discussion of "reformist" versus "revolutionary" characteristics of feminism, see Sandra Harding, "Feminism: Reform or Revolution," ibid., 5 (1973–74), 271–84. See also Zillah Eisenstein, *The Radical Future of Liberal Feminism* (New York: Longman, Green, 1981).

responsibilities in the home contributes to the inequalities of circumstance that put women at a disadvantage in the first place.[22]

Affirmative action is a strategy requiring that women be integrated into the male-dominated institutions of society. Some feminists have opted for another method of eradicating sex inequality, one not necessarily inconsistent with preferential treatment, but that offers an alternative perspective on practical strategy as well as on the more general values of feminism. This is the advocacy of female separatism, which involves the withdrawal of women from male-dominated institutions in order to permit women to develop strengths, abilities, and confidence that might be stunted by the sex-role expectations and discrimination they experience in the male world. The problem with integrationist strategies, separatists argue, is that women enter a situation profoundly weighted against them, and they do so as individuals, alone. Frequently, they are also psychologically hampered by the idea that they must overcome their femaleness in order to "make it in a man's world." A woman among women, on the other hand, is already in a situation in which she operates with equals, protected from many of the oppressive circumstances she would otherwise face.[23] Shifting emphasis from protection to power, Marilyn Frye defends separatism as an act of liberation from male control. Part of men's traditional power over women, she argues, is the access men have to women—their services as wives, mothers, secretaries, and so on. "The slave is unconditionally accessible to the master," she observes. "Total power is unconditional access; total powerlessness is being unconditionally accessible." Separating from men is a way of denying this power, for "when those who control access have made

---

22. Some of these connections are brought out in Virginia Held, "The Equal Obligations of Mothers and Fathers," in *Having Children: Philosophical and Legal Reflections on Parenthood*, ed. Onora O'Neill and William Ruddick (New York: Oxford University Press, 1979), 228–39; a revised version was published in *"Femininity," "Masculinity," and "Androgyny": A Modern Philosophical Discussion*, ed. Mary Vetterling-Braggin (Totowa, N.J.: Rowman and Littlefield, 1982), 242–58.

23. For a discussion of different kinds of and reasons for separation, see Sara Ann Ketchum and Christine Pierce, "Separatism and Sexual Relationships," *Philosophy and Women*, ed. Bishop and Weinzweig, 163–71. Separatism is sometimes advocated as an element of the concept of "woman-identification." See the discussion of Adrienne Rich cited in ch. 3 herein; also see Mary Daly, *Gyn / Ecology: The Metaethics of Radical Feminism* (Boston: Beacon Press, 1978).

you totally accessible, your first act of taking control must be denying access, or must have denial of access as one of its aspects."[24]

Separatism is advocated by many radical feminists, and thus it is an important theoretical position represented within the women's movement. We mention it only briefly in this chapter, however, because it is essentially a new strategy and does not rest on or modify an existing scholarly school of thought. The remainder of this chapter is devoted to feminist considerations of two kinds of large-scale social transformations: modernization and socialist revolution.

Modernization: A Social Policy for the Liberation of Women?

Feminist scholarship on modernization and whether the changes it effects improve the condition of women is grounded in a tradition of social science research that has dominated the American university since the 1960s. Generally speaking, modernization is a theory that analyzes the social, political, and cultural changes accompanying industrialization and, at the same time, provides a prescription for social policy in industrializing societies. American feminist scholars particularly became enmeshed in such studies, since many of the programs intended to modernize societies were funded by U.S. government and private agencies. In general, feminists ask: What does modernization theory posit as the impact of industrialization upon women? Is it the same as the impact on men? When modernization theory guides actual social policy, what is its impact on women's lives? On male-female relations? Is it for the better? Does it alleviate the oppression of women?

Modernization is understood by its proponents as "the process by which historically evolved institutions are adapted to the rapidly changing functions that reflect the unprecedented increase in man's knowledge permitting control over his environment that accompanied the scientific revolution."[25]

24. Frye, "Some Reflections on Separation and Power," in her *The Politics of Reality: Essays in Feminist Theory* (Trumansburg, N.Y.: Crossing Press, 1983), 103, 104.

25. Cyril Black, *The Dynamics of Modernization* (New York: Harper and Row, 1967), 7. For other influential examples of modernization theory, see also S. N. Eisenstadt, *Modernization: Protest and Change* (Englewood Cliffs, N.J.: Prentice-Hall, 1966); J. A. Krahl, "Some Social Concomitants of Industrialization and Urbanization," *Human Organization* 18 (1959), 3–7; Edward Shils, "Political Development in New States," *Comparative Studies in Society and History* (Spring-Summer 1960), 265–92, 379–411.

Modernization theory takes the experience of western Europe and the United States in the eighteenth and nineteenth centuries as a model of how industrialization transforms a society. Most scholars working in the area follow the lead of the pioneering sociologist Talcott Parsons, who identified five variables to describe the movement from "traditional" to "modern" societies: from simple to complex social organization; from functionally diffuse to functionally specific institutions; from lesser to greater divisions of labor; from stratification based on ascription to stratification based on individual achievement; and from belief systems that are particularistic and fatalistic to those that are universalistic and assume that humans can control their fate.[26] Social change is viewed as unidirectional and as impelled by changes in the economy, in particular the transformation from subsistence agriculture to large-scale industrial production. In theory these economic changes bring greater numbers of people into the work force while increasing their productivity and hence both individual and national wealth. From these economic developments flow changes in political organization, in social organization, in the bases of stratification, and in family life and sex roles. As a theory of social change, modernization emphasizes structural factors and development that appears inevitable and predetermined, rather than political forces and their unpredictable resolution through conflict.

Most modernization theorists assumed that industrialization and the social transformations that accompany it necessarily raise women's position and lessen their oppression. Female oppression is understood as part of traditional society in which women live in an extended family, contribute to subsistence economies, and therefore lack opportunity to participate in the work force, political processes, and educational institutions.[27] At the same time modernization theorists differ on whether the sweeping social changes that are implied by industrialization affect both sexes in the same way.

Parsons, for one, explicitly described modernization in terms of basic changes in men's productivity, their possibilities for social mobility, and changes in their mobility patterns from ascription to individual achievement.[28] Others, like Marion J. Levy, explicitly argue that the process of modernization would mean the same thing for women as for men. Indeed,

26. Parsons, *Structure and Process in Modern Societies* (New York: Free Press, 1959).

27. Richard Brown, *Modernization: The Transformation of American Life, 1600–1865* (New York: Hill and Wang, 1976).

28. This point about Parsons in made in Alex Inkeles and David Smith, *Becoming Modern* (Cambridge, Mass.: Harvard University Press, 1974), chs. 1–3.

since Levy thought that the modernization process would do away with all forms of ascription, including those based on gender, and would increase role options for women, one measure of modernity he develops is the extent to which women do enter the work force and participate as the equals of men.[29]

Feminist scholars initially addressed modernization theory with the question of whether the process did have the same significance for women as for men. Their approach involved not only analyses of where women were in the work force but also investigation of changes in the structure of the family and relations within it and the impact of institutions and programs aimed at promoting modernization. The landmark feminist works on modernization, Ester Boserup's *Women's Role in Economic Development*, Helen Safa and June Nash's *Sex and Class in Latin America*, and Judith van Allen's "Modernization Means More Dependency," began to challenge modernization theory and argue that industrialization is more likely to exacerbate sexual subordination than to weaken it.[30]

Boserup and others found that a shift from subsistence agriculture to machine-based economies, rather than liberating women, often transforms women's oppression in such a way as to intensify it. This occurs for several reasons. First, as feminists have shown, women's oppression has cultural variants, the nature of patriarchal relations varying from society to society. There is, in other words, no one traditional society, and whether industrialization changes women's lives for the better depends very much on their position in the particular traditional society under discussion. In much of Africa and Asia, for example, women traditionally constitute the bulk of the agricultural work force, producing for both subsistence and exchange.[31] In such societies modernization of the economy does not introduce women into productive labor, since they have always been part of it. Scholars who are not working from a feminist perspective frequently do not count such

29. Levy, *Modernization and the Structure of Societies: Setting for International Affairs*, 2 vols. (Princeton: Princeton University Press, 1966).

30. Boserup, *Women's Role in Economic Development* (New York: St. Martin's Press, 1970); van Allen, "Modernization Means More Dependency," *Center Magazine* (May / June 1974), 60–67; Nash and Safa, *Sex and Class in Latin America* (New York: Praeger, 1975).

31. Boserup, *Women's Role*. See also *Women in Africa: Studies in Social and Economic Change*, ed. Nancy J. Hafkin and Edna G. Bay (Stanford: Stanford University Press, 1976); and *Women in the World: A Comparative Study*, ed. Lynne B. Iglitzin and Ruth Ross (Santa Barbara, Calif.: Clio Books, 1976).

women—for instance, petty traders or women who farm for subsistence—as workers and calculate the female labor force solely in terms of the modern sectors: cash crop agriculture, industry, and service.[32] Thus, women who appear to be entering the labor force have often been there all along.[33] As productive laborers, they have possessed economic independence, which has traditionally meant considerable autonomy in the household, marketplace, and community. Moreover, in many traditional societies, families were extended social units, often polygamous, and childrearing was not necessarily the preserve of one woman; women therefore were not defined solely in familial terms.

Second, feminist scholars have observed that the process of industrialization often tends to remove women from productive labor or worsen their position in the labor force relative to men over time, thus producing greater stratification in the work force. This trend continues even as the gross national product, a major indicator of successful modernization, increases. Such developments have been clearest in Latin America and Africa. Weeding and hoeing, frequently women's work, are often the first to be mechanized, displacing women from production. In many places women have not been able to shift into the nonagricultural work force, either because employment in manufacturing does not grow as rapidly as the displacement of agricultural workers or because childbearing and childrearing are harder to reconcile with manufacturing jobs than with agricultural labor and trade. Where women displaced from agriculture have entered nonagricultural employment, they are allocated the lowest-paid service occupations, labor-intensive manufacturing associated with women (such as garments), or work in even more marginal areas, notably prostitution, while men enter the industrial and bureaucratic work force.[34]

32. Rati Ram, "Sex Differences in the Labor Market Outcomes of Education," *Comparative Education Review* 24 (1980), S53–S57; *Industrialization and Society: Proceedings*, ed. Bert Hoselitz and Wilbert E. Moore (Paris: UNESCO, 1963).

33. Van Allen and Safa and Nash concentrate on this problem in their critiques of modernization.

34. Norma S. Chinchilla, "Industrialization, Monopoly Capitalism and Women's Work in Guatemala," *Signs* 3 (1977), 38–56; Nadia Haggag Yousseff, *Women and Work in Developing Societies* (Berkeley: University of California Institute of International Studies, 1974); Lourdes Arizpe, "Women in the Informal Labor Sector: The Case of Mexico City," and Elizabeth Jelin, "Migration and Labor Force Participation of Latin American Women: The Domestic Servants in the Cities," both in *Signs* 3 (1977), 22–37, 129–41, respectively. For a collection of essays that includes discussion of the many effects of modernization on black women in Africa, South America, and the Carribbean, see *The Black Woman Cross-Culturally*, ed. Filomina Steady (Cambridge, Mass.: Schenkman, 1981).

Third, women's entry into the modern work force is further constricted because women have less access to education than men. This inequality is due to a variety of reasons: the nature of transitional economics, the colonial heritage, and the deliberate development policies of national governments and international agencies. For instance, Marjorie Mblinyi has documented that in female-farming areas, age-specific schooling precluded girls' participation in the educational system because girls become productive at the age of six, while boys are not productive until later.[35] To send a girl to school is to forego earnings; to send a boy to school is to keep him busy. In most Third World nations attempting to modernize, boys have approximately four times as much access to education as girls at the primary level, while the discrepancy is even greater at the secondary and tertiary levels.[36] The colonial heritage in education has exacerbated the trend to deny women what Elsa Chaney and Marianne Schmink call "access to tools."[37] Thus, whether women are excluded from productive labor and stay at home or enter the modern work force in an inferior position, the process of modernization worsens their position relative to men and lessens their ability to be self-supporting. As documented by evidence of increasing malnutrition of women and children, women's status has so deteriorated in areas of the Third World that some observers suggest modernization threatens women's very existence. From their perspective the urgency of the situation requires feminists to shift their focus from whether social programs liberate women to whether they can ameliorate the declining standard of living for women and children and counteract the devasting effects of the world economy.[38]

35. Mblinyi, *The Education of Girls in Tanzania* (Dar-Es-Salaam: University College, 1969).

36. Isabelle Deble, *The School Education of Girls* (Paris: UNESCO, 1980); Audrey Chapman Smock, *Women's Education in Developing Countries: Opportunities and Outcomes* (New York: Praeger, 1981); Mary Jean Bowman and C. Arnold Anderson, "The Participation of Women in Education in the Third World," in *Women's Education in the Third World: Comparative Perspectives*, ed. G. P. Kelly and C. M. Elliott (Albany: SUNY Press, 1982), 11–30.

37. Chaney and Schmink, "Women and Modernization: Access to Tools," in *Sex and Class in Latin America*, ed. Nash and Safa, 160–82; see also Marie Eliou, "Scolarisation et promotion féminines en Afrique francophone (Cote d'Ivoire, Haute-Volta, Sénégal)," *International Review of Education* 19 (1973), 30–46; Jacqueline Chabaud, *The Education and Advancement of Women* (Paris: UNESCO, 1970).

38. See, for example, Ingrid Palmer, "Rural Women and the Basic Needs Approach to Development," *International Labor Review* 115 (1977), 97–107; Elsie Boulding, "Integration into What? Reflections on Development Planning for Women," *Convergence* 13

With respect to European and American history, the most comprehensive refutation of modernization theory and its optimistic assessment of women's experience in the industrialization process is Joan W. Scott and Louise A. Tilly's *Women, Work and the Family.*[39] Like the feminists studying the Third World today, Scott and Tilly find that women in England, France, and the United States were at a disadvantage in comparison with men as industrialization introduced them into the the wage economy. While most historians of Europe and the United States have taken the female textile operative as the representative woman worker of early industrialization, Scott and Tilly emphasize that most women were not drawn to such highly mechanized industries but rather stayed in traditional, unmechanized, and homebound manufacturing, worked in marginal service occupations such as petty trader or laundress, and, above all, labored as domestic servants. An even more important disagreement between their approach and modernization theory, however, is in the area of women's experiences within the family. They argue that, throughout the industrializing process, women continued to be subjected to the demands of their family roles. This is an explicit response to the work of historian Edward Shorter, who relies on modernization theory to contend that the spread of the market economy and wage labor led to new personal, especially sexual, freedom for women.[40] Scott and Tilly argue that, although unmarried women increasingly earned wages, they usually contributed them directly to the "family wage economy" and enjoyed little or no control over the money they earned. Even when women left their parents' home to earn money, the personal independence they gained was offset by their personal vulnerability to market forces, the fullest expression of which was prostitution. For married women, whose primary responsibilities were housework and childrearing, industrialization meant increasing conflict between their own unpaid domestic labor and the family's need for money.[41] Overall Scott and

---

(1980),50–59; Rajendra Kumar Saxena, *Education and the Social Amelioration of Women: A Study of Rajasthan* (Jaipur: Sagni Prakashan, 1978).

39. Tilly and Scott, *Women, Work and Family* (New York: Holt, Rinehart and Winston, 1978).

40. Shorter, *The Making of the Modern Family* (New York: Basic Books, 1975).

41. Scott and Tilly, *Women, Work and Family.* See also Laura Oren, "The Welfare of Women in Laboring Families," in *Clio's Consciousness Raised,* ed. Mary Hartman and Lois Banner (New York: Harper and Row, 1974), 226–44, for an analysis of how married working-class women in nineteenth-century England cut into their own food consumption to extend the purchasing power of what little money was available to their families.

Tilly contend that women's experiences with industrialization were that of continuing and at times intensifying subordination and that industrialization did not obliterate their oppression but reorganized it around inequality in the labor force, subordination of the individual to the family system, and the tension—usually harder on women than on men—between the two spheres.

Feminist scholars of the Third World have asked whether policies designed to facilitate modernization need always have such depressing results for women. Several have pointed out that the programs that led to the deterioration of women's position are themselves the handywork of men in international agencies or national governments who have little or no concern with improving the lives of women, much less in liberating them.[42] As Barbara Rogers's study of the United Nations Development Program (UNDP) points out, development planners have deliberately excluded women from access to programs that would enhance their ability to gain economic equality with men or to be self-supporting. UNDP programs that are open to women, as Rogers demonstrates, have focused almost exclusively on fertility planning, nutrition, and child health, presuming women's roles either are, or ought to be, confined solely to the domestic sphere. Rogers argues that policies designed to promote modernization need not undermine women's status or erode the conditions of life. The issue is who controls these programs: she claims male-controlled international development agencies and national governments cannot help but reproduce patriarchy.

While Rogers posits that as long as men control development planning, programs aimed at modernization will do nothing to liberate women, not all feminist scholars share this emphasis. In a pioneering work Norma Chinchilla began to argue that the deterioration in women's status is not intrinsic to modernization but to the political system in which development occurs.[43] She and other scholars, working in a Marxist tradition, rely on dependency theory—the major school of criticism of modernization theory in academic scholarship—to explain the experience of women in industrialization. In brief, dependency theorists argue that Third World nations

42. Deble, *School Education of Girls*; Rogers, *The Domestication of Women: Discrimination in Developing Societies* (New York: Tavistock, 1980).

43. Chinchilla, "Industrialization and Women's Work in Guatemala"; see also Glaura Vasques de Miranda, "Women's Labor Force Participation in a Developing Society," *Signs* 3 (1977), 261–74.

must be seen in the context of international monopoly capitalism rather than considered as autonomous nation states, which is how they are viewed in modernization theory.[44] In her study of the position of women in Guatemala, Chinchilla attributes the displacement of women from agricultural work, their growing unemployment, and their declining status within service and industrial sectors to world market forces in general and the investment policies of international corporations in the Guatemalan economy in particular. International capital investment drains wealth from Third World nations, making them poor and dependent. Dependency theorists argue that, instead of experiencing the economic development predicted by modernization theory, such nations are prevented from development. Their manufacturing sectors often remain underdeveloped and unable to absorb labor freed by the mechanization of agriculture and other sectors. This process affects men and women differently. Women, previously the mainstay of agricultural work, handicrafts, and petty trade, find their earning power undermined and themselves more dependent upon men. Men, in turn, become more dependent on international corporations for their survival. Chinchilla concludes that, as long as the Guatemalan economy is controlled from the outside, women's condition will continue to worsen.

Chinchilla's thesis is corroborated by research conducted in other parts of the world;[45] however, recent studies of development in socialist nations raise serious questions about whether dependent capitalist development alone can explain why modernization has failed as a strategy to liberate women or improve women's lives uniformly. Elisabeth Croll, with data marshaled from China, Cuba, and Tanzania, concludes that when industrialization

44. See, for example, *Imperialism and Underdevelopment*, ed. Robert I. Rhodes (New York: Monthly Review, 1970), and James D. Cockcroft, Andre Gunder Frank, and Dale L. Johnson, *Dependency and Underdevelopment* (Garden City, N.Y.: Doubleday-Anchor, 1972). This tradition gives birth to world systems theory. See, for instance, Immanuel Wallerstein, *The Modern World-System; Capitalist Agriculture and the Origins of the European World-Economy in the Sixteenth Century* (New York: Academic Press, 1974); Wallerstein, *The Capitalist World-Economy* (Cambridge: Cambridge University Press, 1979); and Samir Amin et al., *Dynamics of Global Crisis* (New York: Monthly Review, 1982).

45. See, for example, *Women and Development, The Sexual Division of Labor in Rural Societies*, ed. Lourdes Benería (New York: Praeger, 1982); María Patricia Fernández-Kelly, *For We Are Sold, I and My People: Women and Industry in Mexico's Frontier* (Albany: SUNY Press, 1983); *Women, Men and the International Division of Labor*, ed. June Nash and María Patricia Fernández-Kelly (Albany: SUNY Press, 1983).

is a priority, regardless of whether a government is capitalist or socialist, the issue for policy makers becomes the efficient exploitation of labor, not women's rights or the improvement of women's lives.[46] The political system, or the extent to which economies are tied into world capitalist systems are not the key variables for Croll.[47]

While feminist scholars may debate whether women's condition improves under socialism (a subject to which we shall turn shortly), they are generally agreed that policies designed to modernize society over the past decades in Africa, Asia, and Latin America have not improved women's lives, much less produced equality or liberation. These findings have led to a series of critiques of modernization theory itself. Taken as a whole, feminist research has shown modernization theory to be a tangle of contradictions. Although modernization theory assumes that industrialization leads to lesser ascription, feminist scholars have demonstrated that it increases gender ascription, which is built into the economy in the form of a sex-stratified labor force. Similarly, feminist analyses of the family suggest that the emergence of the modern nuclear family with its sex role division of labor has reinforced women's oppression by increasing their dependence on men and isolating them from other women. Modernization theory usually posits the development of the nuclear family as an example of the role proliferation that industrialization necessarily brings, but feminists have shown that the nuclear family actually works to limit women's roles to those of childbearer, childrearer, and homemaker.[48] In societies of scarcity, as is the case in most Third World nations, such limitations not only produce greater inequalities between males and females, but they also may even pose a threat to women's physical well-being. Feminist scholars have also shown that the nation-state is inappropriate as the major analytic category of modernization theory, for international systems affect work-force patterns and family relations in any given nation. Findings such as these stand

46. Croll, "Women in Rural Production and Reproduction in the Soviet Union, China, Cuba and Tanzania: Socialist Development Experiences," *Signs* 7 (1981), 361–74; Croll, "Women in Rural Production and Reproduction in the Soviet Union, China, Cuba and Tanzania: Case Studies," ibid., 375–400.

47. For a helpful analytic comment on these problems, see Lourdes Benería and Gita Sen, "Class and Gender Inequalities and Women's Role in Economic Development," *Feminist Studies* 8 (1982), 157–76.

48. A classic work taking this position is William J. Goode, "Industrialization and Family Change," in *Industrialization and Society*, ed. Hoselitz and Moore, 237–55.

as fundamental challenges to the Parsonian variables on which modernization theory is based and reinforce as well as broaden other critiques of the
theory on the basis of its ethnocentrism and its inability to account for
changes that are neither unilinear nor unidimensional.[49]

Not all feminist scholarship on the impact of industrialization has posed
itself as a critique of modernization theory. Feminist historians who have
focused on the impact of industrial transformation on middle-class women in
Europe and the United States have arrived at somewhat different conclusions, not refuting modernization theory, but rather modifying and reconcil-
ing it with new findings in women's history.[50] They incorporate the notion
that industrialization encouraged the development of a specialized domestic
and maternal role for women, as well as the argument that this led to an increase in women's power and autonomy. In contrast to classic nonfeminist
modernization theorists, however, they give due emphasis to the fact that
women often experienced their new family roles as confining and traumatic
and found their greatest power and freedom, not in serving their families, but
in sharing their experience and grievances in the family with other women.[51]
Feminist historians who use the modernization framework do not argue
simply that the industrialization process contradicted and weakened traditions
of sexual hierarchy, but rather that it helped to generate new resources,
cultural and psychological as well as economic, that women were able to use
to challenge their age-old subordination. This perspective seems to have little
attraction for feminist scholars of the Third World, however, perhaps because
there the size and importance of the indigenous middle class shrink to in-
significance beside the experience of the masses of women.

49. See, for example, Dean C. Tipps, "Modernization Theory and the Study of National Societies: A Critical Perspective," *Comparative Studies in Society and History* 15 (1973),
199–226; Joseph Gusfield, "Tradition and Modernity: Misplaced Polarities in the Study of
Social Change," *American Journal of Sociology* 72 (1972), 351–62.

50. Carl Degler, *At Odds: Women and the Family in America from the Revolution to the
Present* (New York: Oxford University Press, 1980); Daniel Scott Smith, "Family Limitation,
Sexual Control and Domestic Feminism in Victorian America," in *Clio's Consciousness Raised*,
ed. Hartman and Banner; Regina Markell Morantz, "Making Women Modern: Middle
Class Women and Health Reform in Nineteenth Century America," *Journal of Social History*
10 (1977), 490–507.

51. Nancy F. Cott, *The Bonds of Womanhood; "Woman's Sphere" in New England,
1785–1850* (New Haven: Yale University Press, 1977); Carroll Smith-Rosenberg, "The Female
World of Love and Ritual: Relations between Women in Nineteenth-Century America," *Signs*
1 (1975), 1–30. This material is discussed from a different perspective in ch. 3 herein.

Socialism: Revolutions and Women's Studies

Socialism, like modernization, is both a theory of how social and political structures and human relations change and a prescription for guiding policies intended to undermine inequalities born of social class, ethnicity, race, and gender. Unlike modernization theory, however, socialist theory is also an explicit politics that has been the basis for mobilization of more than one-third of the world's population in its struggle for liberation. Moreover, socialist theory has included an analysis of women's oppression and a strategy for ending it for the past hundred years; concomitantly, policies and programs directed toward this goal have been a deliberate part of government planning in those countries in which a party based on such theory has assumed state power. Feminist scholars have contributed to the critique and elaboration of socialist theory as regards women's oppression and emancipation, as well as to the examination of women's condition in socialist countries.

From our discussion of the origins debate, it should be clear that feminist approaches to that issue have always had to take Engels's classic socialist position into account. Moreover, even those theorists like Michelle Rosaldo and Gayle Rubin, whose perspective on the origins of women's oppression departs most dramatically from the views of Engels and his modern interpreters, continue to situate their theoretical work squarely within socialist-feminist tendency. Similarly, the theories about women's work and family developed by Juliet Mitchell, Nancy Chodorow, and Batya Weinbaum, however little they may rely on traditional Marxist sources, are founded, at least implicitly, on a critique of capitalist institutions and an assumption that the kind of massive transformations for women that they envisage require overall revolutionary transformation.

Essentially socialist-feminist theory represents an attempt to elaborate a more comprehensive vision of women's situation and the conditions for liberation than is available in the socialist tradition. To this end, many — though by no means all — of the scholars in this camp employ the concept of patriarchy as a structure coequal with capitalism in the characterization of the system under which we live. Others prefer to use the concept mode of reproduction, while still others have developed a new concept, the sex-gender system. In all cases these terms denote what Zillah Eisenstein characterizes as the "hierarchical sexual structuring" that exists in a "mutually reinforcing dialectical relationship [with] capitalist class

145

structure."[52] Research in this area involves either theoretical analysis of that mutual reinforcement or empirical examinations of patterns of domination along the entire spectrum of women's experience.[53]

Modernization theory has been attacked by feminists for failing to consider women and is demonstrably weakened as both a descriptive tool and a policy instrument when information about women in development is taken seriously. By contrast, Marxist theory, even when it ignores women, continues to be accepted by socialist-feminists as at least a partial explanation of reality, albeit one that needs to be radically revised by feminist insights. It is therefore in the examination and assessment of socialist practice that feminist scholars have produced a body of critical literature that resembles the work on modernization somewhat more closely. This literature has asked to what degree socialist policies have resulted in women's liberation; if not, why not; and what implications the results, if any, have for theories about socialist revolution.

Such a revolution, which brings about vast changes in the ownership of the means of production, theoretically creates the conditions for ending social inequality. In particular, classical socialist theory claims that female liberation will result from promoting women from unpaid domestic workers to equal participants in social production. Entry into productive labor is theorized as the key to women's liberation because it provides women with meaningful social labor and ends their dependency on men. In addition, women's liberation is assumed to be furthered by collectivizing domestic work, such as child care, housekeeping, meal preparation, and laundry, away from the household. The entry of women into productive labor and the socialization of domestic labor, taken together, are intended to transform the family from a compulsory economic institution to one of voluntary, emotional relations that allows both sexes to develop full personal lives.[54]

52. Zillah R. Eisenstein, "Developing a Theory of Capitalist Patriarchy and Socialist Feminism," in her *Capitalist Patriarchy and the Case for Socialist Feminism* (New York: Monthly Review Press, 1979), 1.

53. See the essays in Eisenstein's collection, *Capitalist Patriarchy*, as well as those in *Feminism and Materialism: Women and Modes of Production*, ed. Annette Kuhn and AnnMarie Wolpe (Boston: Routledge and Kegan Paul, 1978), and in *Women and Revolution*, ed. Lydia Sargent (Boston: South End Press, 1981).

54. Frederick Engels, *The Origin of the Family, Private Property and the State*, ed. Eleanor Leacock (New York: International, 1975); August Bebel, *Woman under Socialism*, trans. Daniel DeLeon (rpt. New York: Schocken, 1971).

Feminist scholars have investigated the position of women, especially in respect to the labor force, in countries that have actually experienced socialist changes in the ownership and control of the means of production and that apply socialist theory to policy. Initially, they posed a simple question: Does socialism liberate women? The debate this generated was essentially a dead end and provided no method of resolution, for each side was able to select facts to support its assertions, without substantiating what it meant by liberation or even equality, and without confronting the other side's set of facts.[55] The vitality of feminist scholarship enabled it to move quickly to a less polarized examination of the way that the transition to socialism affects women's subordinate status and what this teaches us about women's liberation in general. Extensive studies have been made of the Soviet Union and other Eastern European nations, for which considerable statistical data are available, and, to a lesser extent, Third World countries such as China and Cuba.

In studies of modernization feminist scholars often have confronted sanguine generalizations with data about women's declining status and possibilities. By contrast, studies of women under socialism almost invariably include an acknowledgment—more or less enthusiastic, depending on the particular country—that the lives of women in that country have, indeed, been substantially improved by the new order. But these changes are usually contrasted to the prior status of women in that country, not contrasted to the current status of men. Hence, feminists began by examining women's entry into the work force in socialist countries and discovered that they engaged in productive labor on an unprecedented scale in comparison with their presocialist participation.[56] The more difficult question that feminists have moved on to is the extent to which entry into productive labor signals sex equality. To determine whether there has been an end to gender inequalities, they point out, it is necessary to determine whether women workers enjoy equal status with men, earn an equal wage, and have been

55. See, for example, Janet Salaff and Judith Merkel, "Women and Revolution: The Lessons of the Soviet Union and China," in *Women in China*, ed. Marilyn B. Young (Ann Arbor: University of Michigan Center for Chinese Studies, 1973), 145–78; Nancy Milton, "A Response to Women and Revolution," ibid., 179–92.

56. William Mandel, *Women in Soviet Society* (New York: Vintage–Random House, 1975); Norton Dodge, *Women in the Soviet Economy* (Baltimore: Johns Hopkins University Press, 1966); *The Role and Status of Women in the Soviet Union*, ed. Donald Brown (New York: Teachers' College Press, 1968).

freed from the responsibilities of children and household to the same degree as men. To answer these questions, feminist scholars have developed sophisticated analytic tools, which seek to assess both inequality in the workplace and unequal divisions of labor within the family.

Feminist scholars first compared the occupational status and income levels of women and men in socialist countries. They looked at the segregation of women in specific occupations, as well as at questions of leadership and status inequality in the work force as a whole. The books of Gail Lapidus on the Soviet Union, Delia Davin on China, and Hilda Scott on Czechoslovakia are fine examples of such work.[57] These women agree that, although the labor force participation of women has substantially increased, it is still far from equal to that of men. Further, they have found that women have tended to be segregated into specific occupations, such as teaching, insurance, childcare, and housing allocation. Women have also entered the lower rungs of the agricultural labor force, replacing men who have moved into either heavy industry or aspects of agriculture that have been mechanized. Considering the labor force as a whole, women have been concentrated in the lowest echelons and underrepresented in managerial positions or work that involves independent decision-making. In other words, the pattern of occupational segregation and massive inequalities of rank — what is usually called horizontal and vertical sex segregation — found in the capitalist economies of Western Europe and North America, is characteristic of many socialist countries as well.

This vertical and horizontal occupational segregation has also resulted in wage inequality. Lapidus estimates that women in the Soviet Union earn approximately 62 percent of men's wages. Such disparities indicate that entry into the work force has not resulted in lessening women's economic dependence on men or in eliminating the economic dimensions of the institution of the family. Lapidus argues that, given the cost of living, these wage disparities mean that women, especially if they have children, cannot be economically self-sufficient, but must rely on men's incomes to survive.[58]

---

57. Scott, *Does Socialism Liberate Women?* (Boston: Beacon Press, 1974); Lapidus, *Women in Soviet Society* (Stanford: Stanford University Press, 1978); Davin, *Woman-Work: Women and the Party in Revolutionary China* (Oxford: Clarendon Press, 1976). See also Barbara Wolfe Jancar, *Women under Communism* (Baltimore: Johns Hopkins University Press, 1978).

58. Lapidus, *Women in Soviet Society*, ch. 5. Lapidus also points out that Soviet men's wages, although higher than women's, are low enough that wives usually must work to sustain a family; this too reinforces the family as an economic institution.

Feminists also inquire into the persistence of gender inequality in socialist countries by comparing the impact of the family—marriage, childrearing, and childbearing—on women and on men. Most feminists hold that inequitable divisions of labor within the family prevent women from participating equally in public life. Studies of women in socialist countries have sought to document this process. Scott and Lapidus, for example, measure the differential impact of the family on the sexes by comparing work force participation rates of single women, married women, and women with children, and then comparing these figures with those of single men, married men, and men with children.[59] They find that in socialist economies, as in capitalist, once a woman has a child, she tends to withdraw for a time from the work force; furthermore, no such trend is observable among men. This, they argue, accounts for much of the vertical segregation and wage dependence of women, since women who leave their jobs lose seniority and opportunities for advancement. The persistence of sex role divisions of labor within the family also helps to account for occupational segregation, since women cluster in occupations such as teaching and medicine, which give them greater flexibility in meeting their family responsibilities as they work for a wage.

The unequal impact of domestic responsibilities on women and men, a problem that reaches far beyond socialist societies, makes feminist researchers particularly interested in the efficacy of policies designed to socialize housework, which constitutes the other major element of the socialist program for women's liberation. Scott devotes a great deal of attention to this question in her research on Czechoslovakia and finds the situation far from encouraging.[60] Although the Czech government established commercial laundries, they were too few and took too long to return clothes, making it difficult for women to use them as the primary source of clothing care. Similarly, the child-care centers were often far away from home and work, and women had to devote extra time to delivering and calling for their children. As a result, women's special domestic responsibilities remained a problem that had far-reaching implications for their general position. The failure of the government's programs to relieve women of their extra domestic responsibilities meant women had fewer children—to relieve the pressure on their time; this necessitated government

59. See Scott, *Does Socialism Liberate Women?*; Lapidus, *Women in Soviet Society*, ch. 5.
60. Scott, *Does Socialism Liberate Women?*, chs. 3–7.

incentives for childrearing and disincentives for abortion; these policies, in turn, deterred women, suffering from the strains of two jobs, from striving for equality in the labor force.

Researchers have studied socialist efforts to free women from domestic responsibilities in other countries as well. Lapidus demonstrates the inadequacy of the Soviet system of child-care, after-school, and camp programs to meet the full demand for such facilities.[61] Similarly, Ruth Sidel finds that child care in China, while considerably more developed than most systems in the West, can still accommodate only a small percentage of the children and is concentrated in urban centers.[62] In their work on Cuba, Carollee Bengelsdorf and Alice Hageman emphasize the efforts of the government to solve the problem of housework, not just by taking some of it out of the home, but by writing into law the principle that husbands "must share equally the responsibility for tasks related to the household and the raising of children."[63] Although stressing that the distance between the law and practice is great and must be examined by others in the future, the authors are enthusiastic about this new direction: housework is removed from the privatized arena not solely by institutional means but by making the issue itself a matter of public policy, and hence of open discussion and debate in the society.

Most feminist scholars are agreed that the entry of women into the work force and the incomplete socialization of domestic labor have not obliterated inequality between the sexes, but there is considerable debate about the reasons for this failure and whether it is inherent in socialism. Some feminists argue that persistence of gender inequality in socialist nations has its roots in the continuing challenge of industrialization, which forces these nations to make efficiency in production, rather than sex equality, their priority. Both Scott and Hageman and Bengelsdorf explain the failure to socialize childcare and housework in terms of the channeling of funds into industrialization. In addition, Scott notes that in Czechoslovakia in the interests of efficient production women were barred from work in heavy industry for fear of absenteeism supposedly caused by the demands of pregnancy

61. Lapidus, *Women in Soviet Society*, ch. 7.
62. Sidel, *Women and Childcare in China* (Baltimore: Penguin Books, 1973). For a historical perspective on the development of China's policies on women, see Croll, *Feminism and Socialism in China* (London: Routledge & Kegan Paul, 1978).
63. Bengelsdorf and Hageman, "Emerging from Underdevelopment: Women and Work in Cuba," in *Capitalist Patriarchy*, ed. Eisenstein, 271–95.

and childrearing. (These commentators take for granted that there is a certain conflict between the needs of women and the imperatives of industrialization, a point of view which has interesting implications for modernization theory as well.)

Feminist scholars on the whole are not convinced that current levels of sex inequalities can be expected to disappear with the full industrialization of socialist countries. In fact, only Hageman and Benglesdorf take this position, arguing that once Cuban society is fully developed a priority on industrialization will no longer be necessary and women will be able to achieve the same wages and status as men. In contrast, Scott believes that the political priorities that favor industrialization in Czechoslovakia are so institutionalized as permanently to resist change. Similarly, Lapidus maintains that, even though the Soviet Union has already industrialized, the disparities between men and women in the work force, in political participation, and in the household are increasing rather than decreasing. She believes that women have solved the problem of two jobs—one in the family and one in the factory—by withdrawing from economic and political life. As industrialization increases the wealth in their society, women have opted to leave the labor force and become even more dependent on men, thus strengthening the patriarchal family.

The persistent sex inequality that empirical scholarship has detected in socialist nations returns us to the question of socialist theory as it relates to women's liberation. Some scholars take the position that research on women in contemporary socialist nations has little relevance to the theory, either because these societies are not really guided by socialist principles or because they have yet to carry out the entire socialist program. Others, however, use the empirical findings to challenge the theory itself as it pertains to women. Jane Flax observes that, even while Cuban law requires men to share housework with women, it outlaws homosexuality. She asks whether the socialist program as the Cubans interpret it does not lead the state to support and maintain the nuclear family and if it is possible to achieve women's liberation under such conditions.[64] Batya Weinbaum questions the deterministic basis on which she maintains the theory of socialism rests, particularly the supposition that economic factors fully account for women's oppression and that economic changes in the ownership

64. Flax, introductory commentary to "A Look at the Cuban Family Code," *Quest* 4 (1978), 87–88.

of production and in the composition of the labor force alone can effect sex equality.[65] Similarly, Norma Diamond points out that, despite enormous changes in the economic position of Chinese women since 1949, patriarchal relations in and around the family still prevent their equal advancement into political leadership. Local political leadership, for instance, develops on the basis of long association with a particular village. In a system, therefore, in which men stay in the village of their birth, while women tend to leave upon marriage to work in a new village where they do not have the same ties, experience, or respect, the male monopoly of leadership is perpetuated.[66] Thus scholarship on the conditions of women's liberation returns to the controversy over the origins of women's oppression and the range of theoretical issues it raises.

Feminist debates over the ability of socialism to liberate women are not likely to be resolved easily. In fact, controversy over the interpretation of evidence in socialist societies contributes to the theoretical debates about the ultimate compatibility of Marxist theory and feminism. Despite a general wariness of the continued presence of patriarchy in socialist societies, Marxist-feminist theory in its early stages assumed that feminism could be combined with Marxism, particularly since an element of the latter had always been concerned with women's oppression and liberation. But as analytical tools and empirical studies developed, the task of reconciliation proved much more difficult than anticipated. The uneasiness of the union of Marxism and feminism is captured by such phrases as "The Curious Courtship of Women's Liberation and Socialism" or the "Unhappy Marriage of Marxism and Feminism."[67]

65. Weinbaum, "Women in Transition to Socialism: Perspectives on the Chinese Case," *Review of Radical Political Economics* 8 (1976), 34–58.

66. Diamond, "Collectivization, Kinship and the Status of Women in Rural China," in *Toward an Anthropology of Women*, ed. Rayna Reiter (New York: Monthly Review Press, 1975), 372–95. For further contributions to the study of patriarchy in China, see Phyllis Andors, *The Unfinished Liberation of Chinese Women, 1949–1980* (Bloomington: Indiana University Press, 1983); Kay A. Johnson, *Women, the Family and the Peasant Revolution in China* (Chicago: University of Chicago Press, 1983); and Judith Stacey, *Patriarchy and Socialist Revolution* (Berkeley: University of California Press, 1983).

67. Batya Weinbaum, *The Curious Courtship of Women's Liberation and Socialism* (Boston: South End Press, 1978); Heidi Hartmann, "The Unhappy Marriage of Marxism and Feminism: Towards a More Progressive Union," in *Women and Revolution*, ed. Sargent. For further contributions to this dialogue see the other essays in *Women and Revolution*, ed. Sargent, and Catharine MacKinnon, "Feminism, Marxism, Method, and the State: An Agenda for Theory," *Signs* 7 (1982), 515–44.

If Marxism provides a comprehensive analysis of the system of production, and if feminism adds to it an analysis of either the system of reproduction or of the sex-gender system, the central issue becomes how to develop an analysis that integrates the two rather than an analysis that degenerates into two unrelated systems or subsumes one under the other. Can women simply be added to class analysis, or does the entire class analysis have to be reshaped to take into account the sexual division of labor? Can an analysis of the psychological formation of gender in the family simply be added to the analysis of the economy, or does it change the entire understanding of social structure?

Although the future of these controversies is important for feminist theory, the significance of the material presented in this chapter for the academy is as much a matter of raising important and general methodological issues as of developing new theory and settling theoretical questions. The empirical research on socialist societies has aided in the development of woman-centered measures, which take into account the multidimensional character of sex equality and social change. Such research has led to the development of new analytic tools which recognize that, particularly given both women's role as childbearer and the division of labor within families and in the larger society, change for women cannot be assessed in the same way as it is for men.

These theories of equality, the studies of how women fare under the programs of socialism and modernization, and the analyses of oppression in the Chapter 3 indicate some of the complexities involved in developing comprehensive feminist theories. Although we have been able to present only a selection of work in these areas, it should be clear that these studies touch upon numerous disciplines—challenging, borrowing, correcting, and building on research methods and scholarship across the social sciences and humanities. The new dimensions of our understanding of women's lives constitute an expanding intellectual achievement.

III

The Response of the Disciplines

5

Ten Years of Feminist Scholarship:
The Response of the Disciplines

The foregoing chapters have explored the wealth and diversity of feminist scholarship and the challenges it poses to scholarly inquiry. We have pointed out that feminist scholarship is both a product of the disciplines and a reaction against them, that it is rooted both in the women's movement and in the academy. Feminist scholarship began with critiques of the male-biased assumptions that had hitherto guided most academic research, and it has emerged as a literature that attempts to supplement and correct the beliefs about the world held within the various disciplines. The persistence, strength, and steady growth of this new scholarship has established the study of women as a focus for academic inquiry, and the critiques of disciplinary bias have rendered problematic much of what was previously assumed to be true in academic fields, the ways that research had long been interpreted, and the assumptions and methodologies guiding its conduct.

In this chapter we return to the disciplines to investigate more closely the impact that feminist scholarship may be having on disciplinary inquiry. The preceding chapters have surveyed a range of scholarship on women that expands, modifies, or even overturns the presumptions of what, by contrast, can be considered "traditional" academic inquiry. This new scholarship calls the academy to judgment with the challenges it poses, but have the disciplines responded to the challenge? We know that there has been a virtual explosion of new scholarship on women over the last decade or more, but has that scholarship been recognized by or found its way to the center of established disciplinary inquiry? Sometimes feminists declare that the new scholarship has changed the face of academic work and at other times that this new research on women is being ignored, shunted to the margins of the disciplines.[1] Although individual cases confirm each of these contradictory impressions, neither is correct as a generalization.

Our intent here is to conduct a limited but methodical analysis of the extent to which feminist scholarship has influenced the academic disciplines. We pose two questions: Has the study of women become an accepted enterprise within the academy, so that it is now a recognizable component of disciplinary research? And second, to what degree has the study of women become part of general scholarly inquiry, recognized as pertinent even to research that is not exclusively focused on women? Our method of analysis is to "count" scholarship, an enterprise somewhat reminiscent of the early days of women's liberation, when scholars incessantly counted the numbers of women who occupied various positions in proportion to men to assess the extent of discriminatory patterns of employment. The similarity is not entirely coincidental, for we are at an early stage in examining the disciplines' response to feminist scholarship, and we are attempting to provide concrete data from which we can speculate about the influence of feminist scholarship and its potential impact in the future.

Women as Topic of Inquiry

There are various data that one could use to gauge the reception of feminist scholarship in the disciplines: convention programs, dissertation topics, journal publications, university curricula, books in print. We have chosen what we believe represents the most conservative core of academic research: the publications in leading scholarly journals. Since the first and most basic challenge that feminism poses to the academy is that it direct serious attention to the study of women and women's concerns, we surmised that the most noticeable impact of feminism on the disciplines should be a rise of publications on the subject of women coinciding with the advent of the recent women's movement and the development of feminist scholarship. We surveyed a sample of ten leading journals in each of the five fields of anthropology, education, history, literature, and philosophy (Table 1.) We

---

1. *A Feminist Perspective in the Academy: The Difference It Makes*, ed. Elizabeth Langland and Walter Gove (Chicago: University of Chicago Press, 1983), and *Men's Studies Modified: The Impact of Feminsm on the Academic Disciplines*, ed. Dale Spender (Oxford: Pergamon Press, 1981), for example, present a range of assessments.

Table 1. List of Journals Surveyed in Anthropology, Education, History, Literature, and Philosophy.

Anthropology

Africa
American Anthropologist
American Ethnologist
Anthropological Quarterly
Anthropologica
Current Anthropology
Ethnology
Journal of Anthropological Research
Journal of the Polynesian Society
*Man: The Journal of the Royal
    Institute*

Education

*American Educational Research
    Journal*
Child Development
Elementary School Journal
Harvard Educational Review
Journal of Educational Measurement
Journal of Educational Psychology
Journal of Educational Research
Review of Educational Research
School Review
Teacher's College Record

Philosophy

Canadian Journal of Philosophy
Ethics
International Philosophical Quarterly
Journal of Philosophy
Mind

Philosophical Forum
Philosophical Review
Philosophy
*Philosophy and Phenomenological
    Research*
Philosophy and Public Affairs

History

American Historical Review
French Historical Studies
Historian
Journal of American History
Journal of the History of Ideas
Journal of Modern History
Journal of Negro History
Journal of Social History
Pacific Historical Quarterly
William and Mary Quarterly

Literature

American Literature
Comparative Literature
Criticism
English Literary History
*Journal of English and Germanic
    Philology*
Modern Philology
Nineteenth Century Fiction
*Publications of the Modern Language
    Association*
Studies in English Literature
Studies in Philology

159

included the publications of the umbrella academic organizations of each field, as well as several other generalist journals that claim to address the entire range of subfields within their respective disciplines. The remainder of the journals were selected to represent the subdivisions of each field, with special attention to those with particular relevance to women, such as social history and cultural anthropology, for example, or ethics and social philosophy. In general we did not include multidisciplinary journals.[2] We also excluded journals devoted primarily to publishing research on women, women-related issues, and, in the case of education, sex roles. Our central concern is the degree to which research on women has achieved a place in the mainstream of the disciplines where it had previously been absent.

While by no means exhaustive, the scholarly periodicals on which we base our analysis are representative of the leading journals in their respective disciplines, and publication there indicates that an article is considered, in the judgment of both the editors and established authorities within that discipline, to be a significant contribution to the field. Thus when an article is accepted for publication, it would seem to have satisfied the standards of the "gatekeepers" of knowledge, in which capacity scholarly journals function.[3] The presence, especially if sustained, of research on women and related subjects in such journals provides a rough indication of whether these disciplines have met the most elementary challenge feminism poses.

The following analysis is based on a study of the patterns of publication of articles on the subject of women from 1966 through 1980. We take the years 1966–70 as our baseline for assessing changes, since before 1970 feminist scholarship was sparse and had yet to achieve the growth fostered by

2. The exceptions are: *The Journal of the History of Ideas*, which is the major journal in intellectual history, and *Africa* and the *Journal of the Polynesian Society*, to which anthropologists are substantial contributors.

3. For an analysis of the concept of gatekeepers of knowledge, see Lewis Coser, "Publishers as Gatekeepers of Ideas," in *Perspectives in Publishing*, ed. P. G. Altbach and Sheila McVey (Lexington, Mass.: Lexington Books, 1976) 17–26. See also Dale Spender, "The Gatekeepers: A Feminist Critique of Academic Publishing," in *Doing Feminist Research*. ed. Helen Roberts (London: Routledge and Kegan Paul, 1981), 186–202.

the women's movement. The work before 1970 also provides some information about the attention paid to the study of women prior to the reemergence of the feminist movement. It is particularly important to establish such a baseline in disciplines like anthropology, education, and literature, each of which has some long-standing tradition of studying women or gender differences.

For this fifteen-year period we counted titles that indicated that an article concerned women or a subject especially associated with women. While this most basic measurement of publication appears rather simple, it presumes a solution to a difficult problem: Our method had to take into account the significant differences in the way feminist scholarship emerges in various disciplines. Precisely because women are a part of society and have a place in most of its structures and institutions, they do not always form a discrete subject for study, and the line to be drawn between what is "about women" and what is not varies from field to field. This is particularly true when it comes to subjects like the family or sexuality, which in some disciplines have long served to obscure women from scholarly view, while in others have brought them into sharp focus. Another kind of problem arises from the tendency, particularly strong in literature but observable elsewhere, to employ concepts like "femininity" and "womanliness" but so abstractly that they have little or no relation to women themselves. For these and other reasons, what qualifies as research "on women and women's issues" is itself a challenge to determine. However, both the difficulties and the variations are themselves interesting for understanding the process by which feminism moves through the disciplines.

The field of anthropology grew out of studies of exotic kinship systems in the late nineteenth century, and even the most sexist of researchers had to notice that women were important links in the chains of familial relationships. But as a rule the study of kinship does not illuminate our knowledge of women per se, their position in society, their work, play, responsibilities, power, or oppression. So our study of anthropology journals had to exclude titles on topics that, had they appeared in another discipline, might have been evidence for feminist influences. Articles on such subjects as kinship, marriage, family, children, conception theory, incest, and sexuality were excluded, unless their titles specifically referred to women or sex differences, since the dominant tradition in anthropology is to address these subjects from a point of view that sees women merely as a kinship category. By contrast, the subjects found in anthropology journals that were counted in our survey as being "about women" include those that focus explicitly on women's consciousness, experience, or oppression; and those studying female roles such as mother, grandmother, midwife, nurse, and exclusively female experiences such as birthing, menstruation, and menopause. The topics of matrilineality and matrilocal residence presented certain problems, because of their place in kinship studies. However, since such studies might also concern some aspect of women's lives, to allow for the most generous interpretation of the data they were included.

For the literary scholar especially there are considerable problems in defining what constitutes a study about women. One difficulty is that much of the scholarly or critical attention devoted to individual women writers ignores the fact or significance of their gender. It would, of course, be possible simply to omit articles on issues such as Jane Austen's style or George Eliot's religion, assuming that such work has as little bearing on our concerns as do studies of Samuel Johnson's style or Algernon C. Swinburne's religion. However, since the rise in feminist interests has increased the attention to gender in such studies, as well as increased their number, such omission would distort our findings. Therefore, studies of women writers were included in this survey regardless of their focus.

Another set of difficulties is created by a significant body of literary criticism on love, courtship, sexuality, and marriage. In literary studies, as opposed to history, there is nothing new about this material. The subjective world, the world of private feelings and relationships, has long been a subject of literature itself and hence of commentaries upon literature. The problem is that, although these feelings and relationships necessarily concern women, and although the literature itself is likely to involve female characters, criticism and scholarship are curiously alienated from this fact and its consequences. There is an enormous body of scholarship about love theory and love conventions, about the poetry of courtship and betrayal, about epithalamiums and marriage plots, which, although implicitly heterosexual, hardly acknowledges the existence of two sexes, much less says anything about women. Similarly, criticism devoted to finding specifically sexual allusions in literary works also manages to ignore women, even though mammaries and pudenda are identified in every reference to hillocks or pools. For the purposes of this study, therefore, and in full recognition of the irony involved, we did not categorize titles about love, sex, and marriage as scholarship on women and women's concerns unless the article made a connection between the subject and real women.

Similar considerations urge caution in the treatment of scholarship about female myths and archetypes. It is not possible to dismiss this entire area, because there are, of course, strong connections between literary myths and a society's conception of women. Therefore, more precise judgments had to be made. For instance, scholarship that concentrates on the Greco-Roman goddesses has little to do with nonmythical women and has not been included in our analysis. However, work on more primitive or universal types, the Great Goddess or Earth Mother, is more likely to have some bearing on the subject of women, and titles implying such relationships have been included.

Education is another field with a tradition of attending to gender difference in research, which complicates the discernment of influence from feminism. In our survey, not categorized as scholarship on women were studies in which gender was but one of many variables guiding research. However, all research concerning the educational achievement of women and its predictors or on the female learner was included, as was all research dealing with sex bias in instruction or sex differences in the educational and social outcomes of schools.

Of the disciplines under consideration, history and philosophy have the weakest traditions of scholarship concerning women. Accordingly, almost any article with a title referring to a women's issue or sexuality can be taken to indicate a response to the challenge of feminism. In addition to articles explicitly on the history of women as a group, individual women, or ideas about women, articles in history journals about sexuality, marriage, and divorce were included as being about women. For the most part, research on these topics has tended to recognize the existence of women, even before the growth of feminism affected the disciplines, and does not treat the people whose history it researches as if they were without gender. Only two collateral topics were excluded. The first, and by far the most important, were studies of family history that make virtually no distinction between the family experience of men and of women and tend to treat the family as a monolithic unit. This judgment also involved distinguishing between the history of fertility patterns, which is usually considered from a narrowly statistical perspective, and the history of birth control, which tends to treat people as the subject and not simply the objects of their reproductive capacities, and therefore recognizes the distinction between men and women. Articles on witchcraft, which make up a small but persistent area of historical interest, were also excluded, except for a few pieces that draw attention to the fact that the majority of witches were female.

Since there is no previous modern tradition of considering women or related issues as a philosophical subject, the task of determining which articles need be considered in this field was relatively simple. All articles whose titles included any mention of women or any sex-distinguishing term or which had to do with sex equality, sex discrimination, affirmative action, abortion, feminism, sex oppression, prostitution, rape, marriage, love, and so forth were included. While much of this selection was fairly straightforward, it did require distinguishing between very general treatments of relevant subjects, and treatments that are specific enough to have particular pertinence for women per se. For example, many discussions of the nature of social equality can be applied to women, but those that maintained the analysis only at an abstract level that does not explicitly consider gender were not categorized as research about women.

In summary, we see that an assessment of the import of feminist scholarship in terms of increased studies of women and related topics presumes an ability to distinguish among the relevant disciplinary traditions and the type of research involved. A striking example of this fact is that in history articles on love reflect a response to feminist scholarship and usually contribute to an understanding of women's history, while in literature articles on love long preceded feminist scholarship and are part of a tradition that ignores women's lives and consciousness. Thus what is a traditional, even male-biased area of study in one discipline may signal a pathbreaking consideration of women in another.

To our first question as to whether central disciplinary journals show an appreciable, sustained increase in the amount of research published on women's concerns, the answer is a subdued and modest "yes." Despite marked and unexpected differences among disciplines, discussed below, there has been a small but definite rise of attention paid to women as a subject for scholarly inquiry. Table 2 and Figures 1–4 chart the pattern of publication in all five disciplines taken as a whole and show an increase both in the number and the proportion of published research on women and women's concerns. In 1966 in all fifty journals surveyed only twenty-nine articles on women were published. By the mid-1970s the number of articles had steadily increased. In 1975 the number was eighty-one, and by 1980 over 110. Not only did the number of articles published yearly rise, but the proportion of articles increased noticeably. In 1966 only 1.9 percent of all articles were on women; as of 1975 it had risen to about 5 percent, and as of 1980 it had climbed to 7.4 percent.

Table 2. Publication Rates of Articles on Women
and Women's Issues in the Journals of History, Literature, Education,
Philosophy, and Anthropology, 1966–80.

Year	Total Number of Articles	Articles on Women and Women's Issues	
		Number	Percentage
1966	1,546	29	1.88
1967	1,591	38	2.39
1968	1,624	28	1.72
1969	1,610	36	2.24
1970	1,597	32	2.00
Average rate, 1966–70		32.6	2.05
1971	1,665	50	3.00
1972	1,693	43	2.54
1973	1,759	54	3.07
1974	1,788	88	4.92
1975	1,638	81	4.95
Average rate, 1971–75		63.2	3.70
1976	1,671	74	4.43
1977	1,678	72	4.29
1978	1,677	83	4.95
1979	1,539	84	5.46
1980	1,484	110	7.41
Average rate, 1976–80		84.6	5.31

Because the proportion and number of articles on women fluctuates from year to year, we have computed five-year averages (see Table 2). In the period 1966–70 an average of 2.05 percent of all articles focused on women, or about 32.6 articles per year. In the next five years articles on women averaged 3.7 percent of all research appearing in these journals. The numerical increase was more marked—on an average the number of articles per year just about doubled to 63.2. By the period 1976–80 the yearly average of journal articles rose to 84.6, accounting for an average of 5.31 percent of all research published.

While the general trend in all of the disciplines surveyed is toward increasing receptivity to scholarship on women, there is considerable variation among the disciplines both in their acceptance of that scholarship and the ways in which it has been diffused (see Tables 3 and 4). The discipline where the increase is most marked is history. In the first five-year span, 1966–70, articles on women accounted for an average of only 1.1 percent of all research published, while for the five years 1976–80 such articles accounted for 6.45 percent. In addition, the increase in consideration of scholarship on women appears to have affected the field broadly: Before 1970 the rare articles on women were confined to but four of the journals considered, those emphasizing either social history or American history. By the mid-1970s, however, every journal surveyed, including those in political and intellectual history, carried such scholarship.

Table 3. Publication Rate by Discipline, 1966–80.

Year	Anthropology	Education	History	Literature	Philosophy
		1966–70			
1966					
Total number	244	499	196	335	273
Number on women	1	9	1	18	0
Percentage on women	0.41	1.80	0.51	8.36	0
1967					
Total number	192	534	235	337	293
Number on women	10	6	4	17	0
Percentage on women	5.21	1.12	1.70	5.04	0

Table 3 – *Continued.*

Year	Anthro-pology	Education	History	Literature	Philos-ophy
		1966–70			
1968					
Total number	212	577	215	336	284
Number women	8	5	2	13	0
Percentage on women	3.76	0.87	0.93	3.87	0
1969					
Total number	214	516	219	340	321
Number on women	12	5	3	16	0
Percentage on women	5.61	0.97	1.37	4.71	0
1970					
Total number	197	501	221	353	325
Number on women	8	6	2	16	0
Percentage on women	4.06	1.20	0.90	4.53	0
1966–70					
Total number	1,059	2,627	1,086	1,701	1,496
Number on women	39	31	12	80	0
Percentage on women	3.68	1.18	1.10	4.70	0
Frequency rate per year on women	7.8	6.2	2.4	16	0
		1971–75			
1971					
Total number	225	508	242	326	364
Number on women	8	16	7	15	4
Percentage on women	3.56	3.15	2.89	4.60	1.10
1972					
Total number	221	540	237	327	368
Number on women	8	4	6	22	3
Percentage on women	3.62	0.74	2.53	6.73	0.81

Continued on next page

Table 3 – *Continued.*

Year	Anthro-pology	Education	History	Literature	Philos-ophy
		1971–75			
1973					
Total number	241	569	237	323	389
Number on women	6	4	7	18	19
Percentage on women	2.49	0.70	2.95	5.57	4.89
1974					
Total number	229	613	245	314	387
Number on women	14	17	13	23	21
Percentage on women	6.11	2.77	5.30	7.32	5.43
1975					
Total number	255	502	221	299	361
Number on women	16	6	13	34	12
Percentage on women	6.27	1.19	5.88	11.37	3.32
1971–75					
Total number	1,171	2,732	1,182	1,589	1,869
Number on women	52	47	46	112	59
Percentage on women	4.44	1.72	3.89	7.05	3.16
Frequency rate per year on women	10.4	9.4	9.2	22.4	11.8
		1976–80			
1976					
Table number	271	504	256	291	349
Number on women	25	9	15	18	7
Percentage on women	9.23	1.79	5.86	6.19	2.01
1977					
Total number	253	548	248	284	345
Number on women	22	4	11	21	14
Percentage on women	8.69	0.73	4.44	7.39	4.06

Table 3 – *Continued.*

Year	Anthro-pology	Education	History	Literature	Philos-ophy
		1976–80			
1978					
Total number	252	533	248	284	360
Number on women	19	24	15	18	7
Percentage on women	7.54	4.50	6.05	6.34	1.94
1979					
Total number	264	432	237	279	327
Number on women	18	27	11	23	5
Percentage on women	6.82	6.25	4.64	8.24	1.53
1980					
Total number	233	444	221	251	335
Number on women	24	27	26	24	9
Percentage on women	10.30	6.08	11.76	9.56	2.69
1976–80					
Total number	1,273	2,461	1,210	1,389	1,716
Number on women	108	91	78	104	42
Percentage on women	8.48	3.70	6.45	7.49	2.45
Frequency rate per year on women	21.6	18.2	15.6	20.8	8.4

Anthropology, like history, records a noticeable increase in publication on women, both numerically and as a percentage of total articles published, though the increase begins somewhat later. Unlike history, this field had a tradition of studying women before the emergence of contemporary feminism. As Table 3 indicates, 3.68 percent of the articles appearing between 1966 and 1970 were on women, a higher percentage than any other field except literature. Not until 1974 and 1975 does a definite increase become apparent, and thereafter the upward trend continues steadily through 1980.

Table 4. Change in Rate of Publication of Articles on Women and Women's Issues, 1966–80.

Categories of Change	Anthropology	Education	History	Literature	Philosophy
In number per year 1966–70 vs. 1976–80	+ 13.8	+ 12	+ 13.2	+ 4.6	+ 8.2
In percentage per year 1966–70 vs. 1976–80	+ 4.8	+ 2.52	+ 5.35	+ 2.72	+ 2.38

During this period 108 articles on women were published, constituting 8.48 percent of the total. This is the largest percentage of any of the disciplines studied.

In philosophy, literature, and education the increases in numbers and percentages of articles on women are less marked than in history and anthropology. In philosophy we see the small but clear influence of the feminist challenge in a discipline that has long ignored women. Before 1970 in all ten philosophical journals there was not one article in five years on women or women's issues. Beginning in 1970 the disciplinary journals began consistently publishing research on women and on issues of particular concern to women, principally abortion and affirmative action. Discounting a large special issue, which swells the rate for 1973–74, the rate of publication appears to show a more or less steady increase in consideration of women throughout the 1970s. However, in philosophy research on women is poorly distributed throughout the field; three of the journals here surveyed have never published an article on the subject in the fifteen-year period examined. Others, especially those devoted to fields like ethical and political philosophy, have consistently integrated such research into their publications.

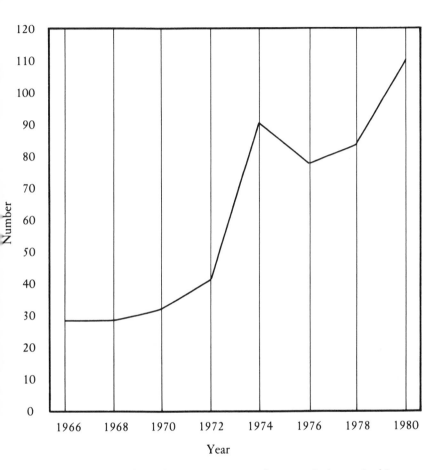

Figure 1. Number of articles on women and women's issues in history, philosophy, education, literature, and anthropology, 1966–80.

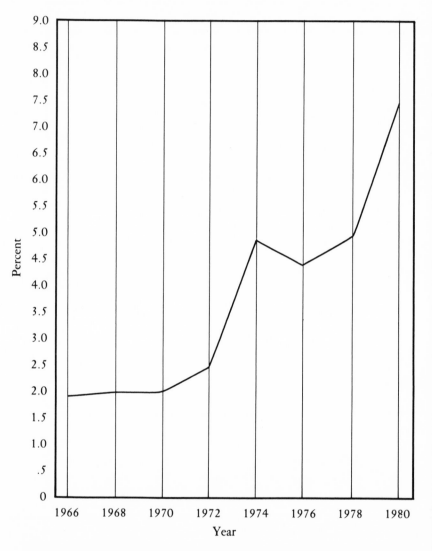

Figure 2. Percentage of articles on women and women's issues in history, philosophy, education, literature, and anthropology, 1966–80.

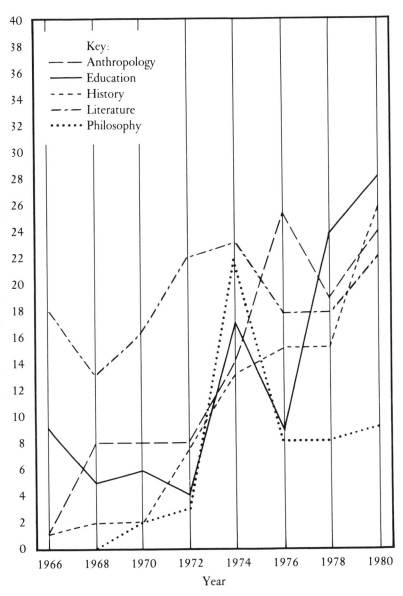

Figure 3. Number of articles on women and women's issues by discipline, 1966–80.

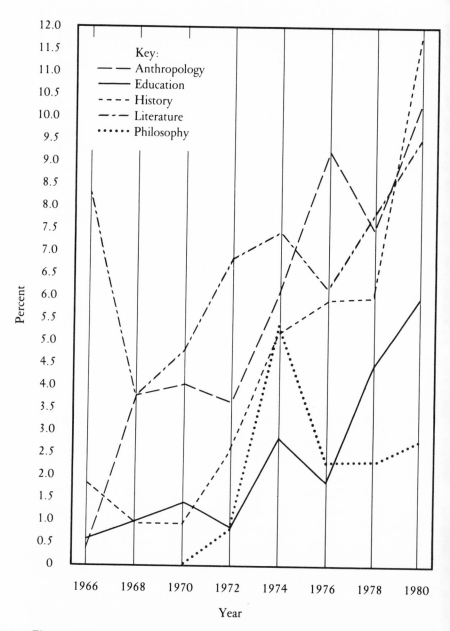

Figure 4. Percentage of articles on women and women's issues by discipline, 1966–80.

While philosophy exhibits some stability in its publication patterns on women, literature surprisingly does not. We had expected that here, where the study of women writers had long-standing legitimacy, feminism would generate greater scholarly publication on women and disciplinary journals would be more receptive to such work than in disciplines that had systematically ignored women and women's issues. In 1966 eighteen articles were published on the subject of women in the literature journals, accounting for 8.36 percent of the total. However, the advent of feminism brings little change to this situation. Not until 1972 do as many articles appear again, and, given increases in the intervening years in total number of articles published, the percentage of articles on women actually declines to 6.73 percent. Not until 1975 do both the number and percentage of articles exceed 1966 levels. In the years 1976, 1977, and 1978 the percentage of articles on female writers and women's issues once again falls to below 1966 levels. Overall, as Table 4 shows, the change in the percentage of articles on women was but 2.72 percent between 1966–70 and 1976–80, as compared with 5.35 percent and 4.8 percent for history and anthropology, respectively.

Although this pattern of publication is not what one would expect given the quantity and often the popularity of feminist scholarship in the field of literature, it is possible that the diversity of topics that can count as being "on women" in this field somewhat obscures our measurement of the development of a body of literary scholarship on women. As we noted earlier, interest in feminism has spurred interest in the study of women writers, yet at the same time a few women authors have always figured in the established literary canon. Both before and after our pivot year of 1970 one finds numerous articles on the works of women authors, including many which have nothing to do with the author as a women or with a women's issue. The presence of such studies may blur our analysis of change in publication patterns. In order to correct for such a problem, the articles on women in literature journals were noted as one of two sorts: those on women in literature (social position, imagery, creative climate, realities, and consciousness), and those on women authors that do not consider their sex a relevant topic for study. We hypothesized that the advent of feminism would affect both sorts of publication but would galvanize the former sort particularly, with its emphasis on the realities that women live as reflected in literature. This hypothesis is borne out by our study. Until 1971 the number of articles on works by women authors far outweighs that of other sorts of studies on women. Then rather abruptly the trend shifts and articles that take into account women's social issues and consciousness begin to balance and eventually to outnumber studies solely devoted to female authors. The recent studies that reclaim the works of forgotten writers invariably consider gender an important subject for comment. It remains the case that the total proportion of work on women is far less in literature than one would anticipate in these central, gatekeeper journals. Yet in the content of this work, its focus, and often in its social and political orientation, one can see the marks of a feminist consciousness working within the field of literary studies.

We are surprised at the weakness of the trends we have discerned in literature. Given the willingness of the field to consider women and women's issues and the enormous attention to literary scholarship in women's studies journals like *Signs*, we would have expected more change in the journals' response to feminism and the growth of scholarship on women. It may be that a greater number of feminist literary scholars are publishing in women's studies journals, for *Signs*, *Feminist Studies*, and others do show a large proportion of literary criticism. However, women's history is equally well represented there and yet has made a clear mark within the disciplinary publications as well.[4]

The trend in education has certain similarities to that of literature. As Tables 3 and 4 show, there is a numerical increase in articles on women and women's issues, but the proportion of articles—a better indicator, since it measures change in the general level of publication—increases at a lower rate. The educational psychology journals tend to run research on women, which is not surprising, given their long-standing tradition of research on sex differences. Otherwise, most of the journals either ignore women's concerns entirely, run a special issue on the topic without publishing such research in subsequent years, or after 1970 slow down the rate of publication of such research. This pattern suggests that the disciplinary journals in education are more ambivalent toward research on women and women's issues than those of the other disciplines we surveyed. This ambivalence translates into token special issues, not into sustained consideration. The

4. A large amount of literary and historical scholarship appears in interdisciplinary journals devoted to women's studies. A glance through four of the most widely read, *Women's Studies*, *Feminist Studies*, *Frontiers*, and *Signs*, suggests that literature and history are the fields most published there.

response is, as with literature, somewhat unexpected. In both, the prior tradition of considering women and women's issues does not necessarily imply any greater receptivity to feminism than in other disciplines. In education this is particularly surprising, given the host of federally mandated policies aimed at reducing sex bias in education. One would have expected greater consideration of these issues, if not in direct response to feminism, then in response to changes in educational policies that have gone into effect since the 1970s.

It is possible that since education is a practice-oriented field, those receiving federal funds for correcting sex bias in education are primarily practitioners and do not conduct research appropriate for publication in the journals surveyed. However, an alternate hypothesis worth considering is that this reluctance to welcome the new scholarship on women is a function of education's relative newness to the academy and that it has long been considered a "woman's field." These factors may combine to discourage the discipline from accepting new scholarship on women until the others, whose legitimacy in the academy is less tenuous, have already done so.

The presence of special issues on women within all of these fields requires cautious evaluation, for the phenomenon of special issues speaks ambiguously to the question of the impact of feminism on scholarship. On the one hand, special issues can and often do indicate recognition of a topic of particular interest and importance, one for which published dialogue is most exciting when collected together. Special issues are often preceded by a call for papers, thus stimulating publication to a certain extent. That our survey shows one special issue on women prior to 1970 and fourteen thereafter is evidence that feminism has influenced journal publication. On the other hand, special issues can also serve to isolate their subject from the rest of a field, suggesting that it is not sufficiently accepted to be dispersed among more standard research. Thus they may also indicate that the subject of women has been ghettoized within a discipline. Both of these contradictory effects are apparent in our survey. In education, for example, after journals publish a special issue they virtually drop the subject from future issues. In literature, however, the appearance of special issues seems to stimulate more publication on the subject.[5]

5. On this point mention should be made of *College English*, the journal of the College Section of the National Council of Teachers of English. This journal has frequently run

The clustering of work on women is, of course, not just the result of editorial decisions, for many feminists themselves refrain from submitting their work to disciplinary journals, preferring to publish in journals devoted to women's studies. The belief that the latter will give them a more sympathetic reading may be a factor, but also many find the special focus of a women's studies publication a salutary and productive atmosphere. What seems a ghetto from one point of view may be a crucible from another.

In all the disciplines we have noticed some sort of trend toward greater consideration of women and women's issues. However, we must exercise caution in what we make of this. There is evidence to suggest that in some disciplines research on women is confined to one or two subfields and has not been considered by the entire discipline. This is emphatically the case with philosophy, where a sizable amount of the scholarship published in major journals has been directed at a handful of issues in political and social philosophy and ethics. In fact, close to half of all research published between 1966 and 1980 focuses exclusively on two issues: affirmative action / sex discrimination and abortion. Proportionately little scholarship in these major journals has addressed the other feminist issues discussed earlier. Philosophy's willingness to consider analyses focused on women has largely been limited to issues raised by legislation and general public controversy. The broader range of feminist concerns has yet to be represented in major journals.[6]

---

special issues on women and also consistently publishes articles on women in other issues. *College English* is not included in our survey because it is not refereed and hence does not meet one of our criteria for inclusion. Similar evidence that special issues may stimulate further publication is provided by *Philosophical Forum*. A special issue in 1973–74 was subsequently published as a book, *Women and Philosophy: Towards a Philosophy of Liberation*, ed. Carol Gould and Marx Wartofsky (New York: G. P. Putnam's Sons, 1976); and this journal subsequently published numerous articles with a focus on women, as well as articles on other subjects that note the relevance of women and feminist issues to their research.

6. The degree to which the journals focus on the two issues of abortion and sex discrimination / affirmative action is highlighted when compared to the range of scholarly topics considered at the conferences of the Society for Women in Philosophy (SWIP). Looking at eight SWIP conferences in the years 1975 and 1976, we observed a markedly different distribution of concerns, for only two of the more than sixty papers presented focused on abortion or affirmative action. Instead, the papers spanned a diverse array of subjects, including socialism, capitalism, language, sexuality, rape, the family, consciousness-raising, philosophical methods, separatism, prostitution, and androgyny.

There is also evidence to suggest that anthropological research on women clusters in the social and cultural fields. The journals covered in this survey include both generalist

What all this means for the future is unclear. We do not know whether the new scholarship on women will diffuse through all subfields of each discipline, address itself to the broad spectrum of issues feminism raises, or lead the disciplines to reconsider their assumptions and what they perceive to be "true." We certainly do not know whether the growth in consideration of women and women's issues that we have cautiously noted over the last fifteen years will continue. It is important to remember that there have been previous periods in which academic scholarship on women seemed to be growing and gaining influence, for instance in the social sciences in the 1920s and 1930s, only to be halted and excluded from any further impact on the discipline.[7] Established patterns of thinking are slow to change and quick to reassert themselves, and we are convinced that the academic disciplines will continue to develop their ability to consider women only in the presence of a feminist movement that exerts continuous pressure on them to do so.

This limited quantitative study of disciplinary journals gives some clue as to why one may receive the contradictory impressions that feminism has changed the face of scholarship and that feminism is virtually ignored, for the evidence is not easy to interpret. It is clear that not every piece of scholarship that appears to be about women should be counted as such, particularly in fields such as anthropology and literature, where research traditions have in the past abstracted and removed gender categories or feminine imagery from the realities of women's lives. In addition, the burgeoning of work on women and related topics is so dramatic that one may lose sight of the fact that it is not proportionately reflected in established journals of disciplinary research. On the other hand, it is incorrect to argue

---

publications and those devoted to social and cultural anthropology; had we considered the specialties of archeology, physical anthropology, and linguistics, the picture would have looked rather different. For instance, *American Antiquity* (1965–78) shows no publications on the subject of women, other than three obituaries of women archeologists. Feminist archeologists are still probing the reasons for their subfield's resistance to including women as research focus. Adrienne Zilman, "What Happened to Woman the Gatherer?," paper presented at the 81st American Anthropological Association Meeting, Washington, D.C., Dec. 3–5, 1982.

7. For a study of the first period of feminist academic scholarship within the modern disciplines, see Rosalind Rosenberg, *Beyond Separate Spheres: Intellectual Roots of Modern Feminism* (New Haven: Yale University Press, 1982).

that the academy has been utterly unresponsive, for the rise in publication about women charted here is undeniable. Given that we have deliberately chosen to measure what we take to be the most conservative type of published material, the importance of this small response should not be gainsaid.

The Integration of the Study of Women into General Research

It is evident that at least one of the effects feminism has had on these academic fields has been to clear space for the study of women and women's issues. However, the critiques of the disciplines that gave rise to this new scholarship on women demand more than the publication of a small portion of work devoted to women. In all these fields feminist scholarship arose through critical analyses of dominant scholarly practices that omitted women from study or presented distorted views of them, not incidentally but systematically. Therefore a further challenge of feminism is the correction of basic assumptions and methods that prevent a satisfactory inclusion of women as subject for research in the first place. That is to say, feminist scholarly perspectives call for change in the framework of scholarship generally, not merely the addition of a body of research about women. In this section, therefore, we attempt to gauge the more general influence of feminist work upon the world of scholarship, that is, upon the methods, perspectives, and purviews of research that does not focus primarily on the subject of women.

Making qualitative judgments about feminist influence or its absence requires two sets of questions. The first concerns whether or not research shows evidence of any influence, and the most fundamental issue here is whether the author has overcome the dominant male-biased approaches to the collection of data or conceptualization of a problem. However, the picture is complicated because even if traditional research frameworks are still employed, one might yet discern some smaller influences, such as the recognition of the relevance of a particular point to women, the citation of feminist works, or even sensitivity to women's issues such as the avoidance of generic masculine pronouns. While these may indicate influence from the women's movement at large and not from feminist scholarship itself, they are not irrelevant changes in scholarly practice.

The second set of questions to be confronted involves a more clearly normative judgment, and that is, if an article does not show any influence from feminism, should it yet have done so? Although the critiques of male bias in traditional scholarship suggest that entire disciplines could benefit from rectifying this problem, it is possible that this is a rhetorical claim and that a good portion of research is immune from such reconceptualization. Ascertaining this requires consideration of whether the immediately relevant scholarship, which the author can have been expected to have researched, has a significant feminist component and also whether reference to women and gender could have been incorporated, at least without major change in the subject matter the author pursued. This latter point is an uncomfortable one. Even in cases where recognition of women might have been included, one shies away from insisting it should have been out of respect for scholarly independence and diversity. Nonetheless, this is an issue that must be confronted, precisely because it is so often the very conceptualization of what is an appropriate topic for research that results in the neglect of women's issues in scholarship.

To facilitate comparisons among our five disciplines we decided to think about these questions by selecting for evidence a small cross-section of recent work from the fifty journals surveyed above. For the years 1979 and 1980 we examined the content of articles that were not counted as being "about women" that were published in two journals from each field, presuming that if feminism has had any general impact, it ought to be most evident in the more recent publications. For the best possible picture of any such influence, the journals we chose included those with relatively strong records on women.[8]

Our reading of these articles indicates that despite the growing body of feminist scholarship, by and large male-biased disciplinary frameworks remain firmly entrenched. Occasional examples to the contrary, however, do provide glimpses of the ways that feminist scholarship may be beginning to infiltrate the disciplines, and they suggest specific ways that disciplinary frameworks can be receptive to change.

In history and anthropology, despite the general weakness of influence from feminist scholarship, we can detect definite possibilities for the way that male-bias in research can be eliminated. A few articles even show the

---

8. The 1979 and 1980 issues of the following journals were examined: *Ethnology, American Ethnologist; Journal of American History, Journal of Social History; Ethics, Philosophy and Public Affairs; Publications of the Modern Language Association, Nineteenth Century Fiction; Teachers' College Record, Harvard Educational Review.*

full impact of feminist perspectives for general research. Such research treats gender as consequential in history and culture and understands that it makes a difference whether the historian or anthropologist is examining women, men, or both. Thus, for example, a study of reforms in nineteenth-century Prussian universities considers both women and men throughout because the motivations, university experience, and impact of education on students' lives consistently differed by gender.[9] Or a study of family policy in revolutionary China recognizes that reform affects men and women differently and examines its effects on each to explain patterns of continuity and change in Chinese families.[10] Such articles also acknowledge that it is important to separate and distinguish historical and social experience by gender because men and women sometimes operate differently in the larger society. For instance, an examination of adolescent initiation rites challenges the dominant interpretation that they are more dramatic and common for boys than for girls.[11] This thorough awareness of gender can sometimes be detected by the use of language, as in a labor history article on unions that consistently speaks of "male workers" and "female workers" rather than "workers" and "women workers."[12] These studies are proof that scholarship that includes women as a subject for study need not be isolated under the special rubric of women's studies, for women are a part of the world and likely present in the picture, no matter what aspect of social reality is under investigation.

Perhaps the strongest indicator of the profound impact that feminist research and thought can have on the disciplines is that some research begins to recognize that men and women not only live side by side in human society but also exist in relation to each other in a way that is frequently marked by conflict. A study of the development of domestic tastes and practices in early modern England and the United States takes as its starting point the fact that "men and women have waged a silent power

9. Konrad H. Jarausch, "The Social Transformation of the University: The Case of Prussia, 1865–1914," *Journal of Social History* 12 (1979), 609–36. See also Cissie Fairchild, "Masters and Servants in Eighteenth Century Toulouse," ibid., 368–93.

10. Martin King Whyte, "Revolutionary Social Change and Patrilocal Residence in China," *Ethnology* 18 (1979), 211–27.

11. Alice Schlegel and Herbert Barry III, "Adolescent Initiation Ceremonies: A Cross-Cultural Code," ibid., 199–210.

12. Ronald Schatz, "Urban Pioneers: The Founders of Local Unions at General Electric and Westinghouse, 1933–1937," *Journal of American History* 66 (1979), 568–602.

struggle in the home"; "the family," including the specific practices of homemaking, is the outcome of this struggle.[13] The ability to acknowledge the existence and sociohistorical significance of conflict between men and women is the unique contribution of feminism and perhaps its hardest premise to absorb into general social analysis. That a small portion of general historical and anthropological research has adapted even to this concept indicates that feminism is having some impact on the larger discipline.

In philosophy we see a more subtle kind of impact on research that is not directly about women. The feminist critiques of this discipline amount to challenges to entire ways of thinking and of conceptualizing philosophical questions. A few authors have adopted a perspective or method that challenges the disciplinary tradition in ways that are similar to those of feminist scholarship at its most powerful and radical. One such article is a study of the rights of children and parents which argues that the abstract approach taken by most traditional moral and social philosophy (with its concentration on the relations between the individual and the state) tends to ignore or distort the character of intimate relationships such as those that make up a family.[14] This study challenges the disciplinary tradition from a perspective similar to that of feminists when they criticize philosophy for omitting women from its scope of study, but we can only presume that actual influence from feminist scholarship is at work here.

Consistent with our findings in the preceding section that education and literature do not show a clear and steady recognition of women as a topic for study, we could not find similar examples of how feminist scholarship might positively influence traditional scholarship in these fields. In fact, for literature no article not primarily about women in the two journals surveyed even cites a work of feminist scholarship. For education the observation in our last section that this field is especially prone to isolate work on women in special issues is supported by the fact that virtually no attention is paid to women or to gender difference in research that is not specifically devoted to women. Although our research is not comprehensive enough to

---

13. Carole Shammas, "The Domestic Environment in Early Modern England and America," *Journal of Social History* 14 (1980), 3–24.

14. Ferdinand Shoeman, "Rights of Children, Rights of Parents, and the Moral Basis of the Family," *Ethics* 91 (1980), 6–19.

be conclusive, it certainly suggests that special problems might exist in the interaction between feminist scholarship and these two fields.

In addition to these few striking examples of fruitful disciplinary response to the ideas and concerns of feminist scholarship, in all five fields there were articles that made passing reference to women, even if only in a phrase, acknowledging the particular relevance for women of an issue under study. Sometimes, particularly in anthropology and history, articles might even include specific paragraphs or particular footnotes about women in articles otherwise about men. While such references often provide useful information and demonstrate the author's awareness that generalizations about men must be proved if they are to be extended to women, they do not meet fully the challenge of feminist scholarship, for they continue to regard the male experience as standard and treat the female experience as a modification.

Whether these kinds of incidental references to the existence of women indicate an incipient trend toward greater influence of feminist scholarship or the reverse – the revision of male bias so that it incorporates references to women without losing its strength – is a provocative issue raised by our research. A closer look at the fields of history and anthropology, the fields with the most numerous references to women, demonstrates the complexity of the issue and the difficulty in making an interpretation at this point.

For history, which rarely noted the existence of women before the current feminist movement, the inclusion of women in research seems to be attributable at least to the presence of the feminist movement, if not to the rise of feminist scholarship. The area of social history publishes a high proportion of articles that recognize the importance of considering gender in the writing of history, probably because the quantitative methods of the field lend themselves to a recognition of the importance of gender distinction. To put it simply, male versus female is one of the easiest things to count when surveying a large population, whatever the topic under consideration. However, some of these quantitative articles merely count and do nothing more, while others incorporate their statistical findings into their analytic frameworks. To take an example of the former category: the first statistical table in an article on delinquency among nineteenth-century German teenagers compares the arrest rates of girls and boys, yet the text itself says nothing about the findings.[15]

15. Eric A. Johnson and Vincent E. McHale, "Socioeconomic Aspects of the Delinquency Rate in Imperial Germany, 1882–1914," *Journal of Social History* 13 (1980), 384–403.

An example of the latter type is provided by an article which counts admissions into a Boston asylum for the "feeble-minded" and uses its statistical findings about the accelerating admissions among women to arrive at one of its major conclusions, that hereditary insanity was increasingly becoming a diagnosis applied only to women.[16]

Looking at history alone, one might speculate that it is simply a matter of time until scholars move from the mere mention of women to a full incorporation of them in the analysis of research. However, anthropology suggests a more pessimistic interpretation. Since anthropology, unlike history, is a field that noted the existence of women before the feminist movement, the mere mention of the existence of women can hardly be taken as due to the influence of feminism. Rather, the traditon of anthropology that includes reference to the relevance of gender in collecting and analyzing data and the current powerful feminist critique draw attention to the continued presence of a substantial number of articles which still do not note the existence of women at all. These stand as eloquent testimony to the strength of male bias in the tradition and raise serious questions about whether the simple noting of women in some research can be taken as a harbinger for change in an entire discipline. Furthermore, the majority of articles in anthropology that note the existence of women do not take the next step of incorporating gender into their analysis.[17] The prevalence of this phenomenon in both history and anthropology suggests that we might be seeing a new kind of male bias, which gives lip service to the existence of women but refuses to incorporate women into the overall analytical framework of research.

It is clear already that these five fields show varying degrees of response to feminist scholarship. When we come to ask the prescriptive question, whether the articles surveyed should have registered more influence from feminist work and scholarship on women than they do, even more dramatic differences emerge among disciplines. In anthropology, history, and education it seems appropriate to expect such influence in the majority of articles,

16. Peter Tyor and Jamil Zainaldin, "Asylum and Society: An Approach to Institutional Change," ibid., 13 (1979), 23–48.

17. For example, Billie R. DeWalt, "Drinking Behavior, Economic Status, and Adaptive Strategies of Modernization in a Highland Mexican Community," *American Ethnologist* 6 (1979), 510–30. See also Ralph Bolten, "Guinea Pigs, Protein, and Ritual," *Ethnology* 18 (1979), 229–52.

while in literature and philosophy only in a very few. As we shall see, it is the different conceptualizations of topics for study in different disciplines that account for this disparity.

An analysis like this must take into consideration the relative ease with which women can be incorporated into general studies in a field, and once again certain differences between empirical and nonempirical research are relevant. Since women do form a part of all societies, the full realization of this long-overlooked fact is a possibility for scholars in anthropology, history, and education, even when their focus of inquiry is not an issue that pertains specifically to women. By contrast, the purviews of philosophy and literature are less suited to the incorporation of women, being fields the scope of which is not defined by lived social realities. As a result, we can expect more influence of feminist scholarship in some areas than in others.

Anthropology and history are devoted to the study of societies, lives, and daily realities, and with the exception of certain sex-segregated activities, war or hunting, perhaps, or in some societies diplomacy and government, women are always present in society. Therefore, when feminists first charged the fields with the use of male-biased research frameworks that excluded women from view, they opened up the possibility of adjusted studies which would reflect a world of two sexes, where men and women mingle in work, domestic life, religion, politics, and play. Similarly, feminist critiques in education paved the way for studies of educational institutions in which women were fully represented and accurately portrayed.

However, for all three of these fields our survey showed numerous articles where research frameworks have not been reformulated to include women or to explore gender distinctions, even though they are on topics where a significant amount of feminist scholarship exists. These point to the tenacity of the presumption that male experience and points of view are universal and exhaustive. Standard analytic concepts such as family, class, race, community, socialization, social control, and social conflict have not been modified to take into account the relations between men and women or to encompass existing research on women.

In education researchers repeatedly omit attention to sex differences while noting differences in educational access or achievement by race or class. A study of open admissions policies in New York, for example, and another on community colleges both deal with minority populations but not with the gender of those populations.[18] And even though the affirmative action controversy has involved women and minorities alike, an article on the Bakke case and admissions policies does not even mention women in passing.[19] Certain other studies, such as ones on aptitude testing, also fail to attend to sex differences in testing populations, though again the authors note class and race.[20]

In anthropology a good portion of the published articles are on such topics as class formation, state formation, or economic change. Despite the significant body of feminist scholarship on women and development, women and work, Marxism and feminism, and the rise of the state, women and the sexual division of labor are completely absent from these articles. A typical example is an article on rural Guyana which discusses class formation in supposedly sex-neutral terms but actually has a male-centered point of view, never looking at differences of men and women in waged labor or women's domestic labor.[21] Similarly, numerous articles purport to interpret rituals for an entire community, but take the male experience as the norm for all. This is particularly striking in an article that interprets a quantity of sexual symbolism, including sexual attack by men on women, but does not consider that the meaning of such rituals might need to be interpreted separately for each sex.[22] Ironically, some of the areas most resistant to feminist critiques of male bias are ones that are particularly

18. David E. Lavin, Richard D. Alba, and Richard A. Silberstein, "Open Admissions and Equal Access: A Study of Ethnic Groups in the City University of New York," *Harvard Educational Review* 49 (1979), 53–92; Fred L. Pincus, "The False Promises of Community Colleges: Class Conflict and Vocational Education," ibid., 50 (1980), 332–61. For an example of a major study of women relevant to the above, see Blanche Fitzpatrick, *Women's Inferior Education: An Economic Analysis* (New York: Praeger, 1976).

19. John Sexton, "Minority Admissions Programs after Bakke," *Harvard Educational Review* 49 (1979), 313–39.

20. For example, David B. Pillemer and Richard J. Light, "Synthesizing Outcomes: How to Use Research Evidence from Many Studies," ibid., 50 (1980), 176–95, and Warner V. Slack and Douglas Porter, "The Scholastic Aptitude Test: A Critical Reappraisal," ibid., 154–75.

21. Marilyn Silverman, "Dependency, Mediation, and Class Formation in Rural Guyana," *American Ethnologist* 6 (1979), 466–90.

22. Robert Paul, "Dumje: Paradox and Resolution in Sherpa Ritual Symbolism," ibid., 274–304. See also James B. Pruess, "Merit and Misconduct: Venerating the Bo Tree at a Buddhist Shrine," ibid., 261–73.

close to the traditionally recognized interests of women, analyses of sexuality and of the family.

It has been noted repeatedly that scholarship on the family presents a complex problem for evaluation from a feminist perspective, since it may both deal with aspects of women's lives and distort the reality of those lives by falsely conceiving of the family as a unit, harmonious and—or because—unanalyzed. A remarkable number of history articles which purport to examine the family make no reference to gender or allow men to stand for entire families.[23] A parallel problem can be seen in anthropological studies that acknowledge the presence of women but overlook their special activities and interests because of assumptions about the homogeneity of the family, a problem particularly glaring given the growing body of research on women in urban families.[24] Family experience, of course, is not only a topic of analysis in empirical fields. The persistence of the traditional concept of the harmonious family also emerges in a philosophy article in normative ethics which deals with the policies of nations to control population.[25] While this study does take into account some factors that apply particularly to women, the authors' tendency to speak of "individuals" or "individual families" obscures the fact that men and women may respond differently—or even with tremendous conflict—to issues involving contraception.

Articles on topics that do not have a relevant body of feminist scholarship to draw on cannot be faulted for not integrating feminist work, but they suffer from similar problems in their conceptualization. Given the depth of criticism of male bias and the growing body of scholarship on the possible role of women or relevance of gender-related issues, neglect of this dimension is increasingly serious and testifies to the fact that feminist scholarship has had too little impact on the way the majority of researchers conceptualize their work in the first place.

The obligation to reexamine how research frameworks are conceptualized is most obvious in history, though it exists in other fields. At first glance,

23. For example, David Brower, "Urban Russia on the Eve of World War I: A Social Profile," *Journal of Social History* 13 (1980), 424–37. See also Stephen Meyer, "Adapting the Immigrant to the Line: Americanization of the Ford Factory, 1914–1921," ibid., 14 (1980), 67–82.

24. For example, Susan Emley Keefe, "Urbanization, Acculturation and Extended Family Ties: Mexican Americans in Cities," *American Ethnologist* 6 (1979), 349–65.

25. Frank Miller and Rolf Sartorius, "Population Policy and Public Goods," *Philosophy and Public Affairs* 8 (1979), 148–74.

many of these articles in our sample that omit mention of women seem to concern topics that by their nature exclude women, since none was present at the scene of the subject under study. Thus an article on nineteenth-century German business leaders or on Harry Truman's decision to drop the atomic bomb would seem to evidence no particular blindness to the demands of feminist scholarship in their lack of reference to women. However, in many examples where women appear irrelevant, this is due more to methodological approach or conceptual apparatus rather than to the absolute irrelevance of women to the topic at hand. For instance, a common approach in intellectual and political history is to look at the writings of two or three individuals. Unless the researcher is following a private affirmative action agenda, the individuals selected will almost always be male (and white).[26] In such cases women are excluded, not because they were not engaged in the activity under consideration, but because the author chose to look at others, who "happened" to be men. Similarly, many articles continue to rest on analytic categories developed by historians before women's history was well-researched. Many of the articles that make no mention of women do so because they focus on mass activities in which only men are assumed to have participated. Yet even here the exclusion of women is interesting. Articles on sports, for instance, could (but usually do not) address the "gender meaning" of sports enthusiasm and participation, or its centrality to male culture and self-definition. More seriously, women are still habitually excluded from studies of popular political history because they have not, until recently, been voters. Other sorts of mass political activity in which women have participated in the past, for instance lobbying and political rioting, either disappear in the equation of voting and political participation, or are assumed to be as exclusively male as the pre-twentieth century suffrage. Archaic interpretive frameworks act like old rusty gates to keep out all that we now know about women's history.

Envisioning a reconceptualization of philosophy and of literature so that women's issues and feminist perspectives are integrated into general scholarship is considerably more difficult than for anthropology, history, or education. Perhaps because feminist scholarship has developed more unevenly in these areas, only occasionally could one criticize articles which appeared

---

26. For a general critique of the biases of published manuscript materials, see Jesse Lemisch, "The Papers of Great White Men," *Maryland Historian* 6 (1975), 43–50.

in the two years of our survey for ignoring an immediately relevant body of feminist work. Such a criticism could be made of a philosophy article that dealt with the distinction between the public and the private and one that analyzed character traits and morals.[27] The feminist material on both these subjects, especially the former, is significant, and, even if the arguments of these two authors are not seriously flawed by its neglect, taking it into consideration could have made the studies more thorough. However, the possible inclusion of mention of women in most other articles would have amounted to little more than a routine acknowledgment of the relevance of various social issues to women, hardly altering the overall study.

There were even fewer articles in the literature journals where the exclusion of women or related subjects involved an obvious neglect of relevant feminist scholarship. There were several pieces that would have been enriched by some consciousness of the woman question, such as one about an obnoxious female character in *Peregrine Pickle*.[28] There is, however, no specific feminist work on this novel that the author should have known; though were someone with greater sympathy for the female condition to treat this character from a feminist perspective, our understanding of women's social position evinced in literature would likely have benefited. The same may be said of an article about the shrinking from sexuality that characterizes William Morris's fiction, which would have been much enhanced by setting Morris's work in the context of relations between nineteenth-century feminism and utopian socialism, as well as by the specific approach of Victorian feminism to questions of sexuality.[29]

By far the largest category of articles in literature and philosophy, however, are those that admit no obvious place for mention of women or women's issues or for the use of feminist scholarship. That there should be some such topics is to be expected. Ethics and social philosophy do cover areas and problems which apply generally to men and women, where taking

27. Howard B. Radest, "The Public and the Private: An American Fairy Tale," *Ethics* 89 (1979), 280–91; Stephen D. Hudson, "Character Traits and Desires," ibid., 90 (1980), 539–49. The omission in the latter article may be because it is a commentary on another piece. For discussion of this factor in assessing feminist influence, see below.

28. R. G. Collins, "The Hidden Bastard: A Question of Illegitimacy in Smollet's *Peregrine Pickle*," *Proceedings of the Modern Language Association* 94 (1979), 91–105.

29. Nancy D. Mann, "Eros and Community in the Fiction of William Morris," *Nineteenth Century Fiction* 34 (1979), 302–25.

sex or gender into account is not particularly relevant. Technical problems of decision theory, normative issues involving organ transplant or plea bargaining, and metatheoretical questions in ethics are a few of the philosophical topics where the lack of reference to scholarship on women is not, as a rule, reasonably criticized. Similarly in literature, there is a range of topics— poetic conventions, relations among art forms, or certain themes of certain authors—which can be pursued without cognizance of feminist scholarship or mention of women.

However, the scant or perfunctory attention paid to women in general work in these fields leads one to speculate that it is something other than the type of areas these disciplines cover that is preventing greater dissemination of influence from feminist scholarly perspectives. In both fields it is common practice to frame a study as a commentary on a text, and this convention is highly exclusionary with regard to the feminist citations, issues, and critical perspectives that might be relevant. For example, a large number of articles from these philosophy journals are critical analyses which start from (or are even confined to) consideration of an important text, either a classic treatise or a contemporary work. If the purpose of an author is to analyze a particular theory, and if that theory itself does not include mention of women or related issues, it is difficult to insist on a shift of attention to women. Some similarity in the field of literature results from the practice of framing research as commentary on a single author. So many of these are male and so much feminist scholarship has dealt with female authors that a large body of scholarship is on subjects with no direct commentary to act as a precedent. Generally speaking, the convention of philosophers and literary critics—and perhaps others as well—of framing an analysis as a commentary on a "text" seems to be a disciplinary inhibitor to the dissemination of influence, method, or content from feminist scholars.

A summary view of the influence of feminism on general scholarship in these five fields juxtaposes the real possibility for change in disciplinary frameworks with the inertia of scholarly research traditions that conceive of research in a way that readily neglects or ignores women. The examples of research that fully include women and gender, although few, allow us to imagine how feminism could influence the disciplines and demonstrates the significance of feminist research beyond the field of women's studies. At the same time the strength of male bias in all five fields remains undeniable.

Achieving a distanced perspective from which one can evaluate and alter the entrenched presumptions of a discipline is extremely difficult, since feminist scholars themselves are members of these disciplines, at once respecting and rebelling against their traditions. It is noteworthy that among those studies that could be criticized for omitting women or not incorporating gender into their analytical framework, there are four articles written by feminist authors.[30] It is possible that these authors elected to focus their attention on aspects of their subject that did not include women, that for some reason consideration of gender was not feasible or would have required a different study. However, it is also possible that traditional frameworks for conceiving of the research process were influential in this omission. We are not so much interested in making the case that every study should include women, as in pointing out that, in those numerous instances where they could have been included but were not, their omission may indicate a persistence of exclusionary conceptualization that continues to inhibit the scope and advance of research.

Despite the shared problem of combating the inertia of disciplinary traditions, there are yet profound differences among disciplines in the ease with which one can envision adjustment of research frameworks to encompass women and their concerns. An anthropologist can, and indeed must, take note of sex and gender to achieve a satisfactory understanding of all but a few social phenomena. The claims for history are somewhat more prescriptive, for since women have been excluded from certain aspects of life, studies directed to those aspects, if unreflectively conceived, will exclude them, too. However, since women have often been present in parallel or related activities that are now achieving recognition as important, it is to be hoped that the views of historians will alter so as to see the past in a fuller,

---

30. Two anthropological studies on forces of change in different communities do not consider the possible role of women as agents in that process: Karen Sacks, "Causality and Chance on the Upper Nile," *American Ethnologist* 6 (1979), 437–48, and Jane Collier, "Stratification and Dispute Handling in Two Highland Chiapas Communities," ibid., 305–28. An education study of history texts criticizes their presentation of the past in ways that obscure labor struggles, class and racial inequalities, but does not extend the critique to the treatment of women's history: Jean Anyon, "Ideology and the United States History Textbooks," *Harvard Educational Review* 49 (1979), 361–86. Less obviously, a literary study of guilt in *Little Dorrit* seemed to have potential for consideration from a feminist perspective, but this was not developed: Elaine Showalter, "Guilt, Authority, and the Shadows of *Little Dorrit*," *Nineteenth Century Fiction*, 34 (1979), 20–40.

less exclusionary way. Since women are fully present in the educational system as well, and since a good deal of research here could be sensitive to gender difference, one can hope that the pressure of feminist work will bring about a general attention to women as subject for research in this field, even though that process has hardly begun.

It is harder to envision such wholesale changes in literature and philosophy. Partly this is because both fields include areas of study that do not focus on social issues where sex is significant, and so have a larger proportion of research subjects that will not require inclusion of women specifically. But it is also the case that the conceptualization of topics suitable for literary criticism and philosophical analysis appears to be less amenable to the changes feminism requires. For literature, such changes would mean an orientation of criticism toward attending to the social bases for literature, grounding the fictional or poetic worlds in reality so that their significance for concepts about women and sexuality, for lived subjectivities, for the position of women and men in society clearly emerges. In a discipline that has a number of ahistorical schools of thought that prefer a more abstract approach to the study of literature, these changes would involve profound disruption of standard scholarly assumptions.

Judging from the evidence at this time, the expectable influence of feminist perspectives in philosophy is likely to be rather lopsided. Certainly with the expansion of interest in normative ethics a good many issues of special relevance to women can secure a place in philosophical studies. And as feminist analyses of political theory become increasingly systematic and widespread, it is also possible—and certainly to be hoped—that feminism will gradually influence the concepts that dominate work in this area. However, while feminist critiques of other areas, such as epistemology and philosophy of science, are trenchant and relevant to a range of subjects, they are far less readily accommodated within established methods and frameworks of the discipline. As we have noted in previous sections, several feminist thinkers suggest that male bias is so deeply entrenched in the philosophical tradition that it is doubtful that an adequate perspective on women can be founded within that tradition at all. No doubt this view is too pessimistic, but at present it would at least suggest caution in anticipating the magnitude of feminist influence in all areas of this field.

However cautious or pessimistic we are inclined to be about the prospects of the integration of feminist perspectives into disciplinary research, it yet remains that feminist scholarship has achieved an undeniable importance and visibility in only a few years. That the academic disciplines—conservative, labyrinthine, and hoary as they may be—have even begun to change is only one aspect of the excitement, upheaval, and delight of feminist scholarship.

Conclusion

This book has sought to analyze the relationship between feminism and scholarship by examining five diverse, broadly representative academic fields and by considering research on selected aspects of oppression and liberation. As our work on this project took shape, so did our understanding of what it means to apply a fundamentally political concept – feminism – to the world of academic research. We noted in the Introduction the difficulty of drawing even rough boundaries between scholarship on women that is feminist and that which is not, and the discussions in the subsequent chapters have continued to explore why and how this is so. Now we return to this issue to elaborate on what we have learned about this indispensable yet fundamentally elusive concept and to venture an answer to the question: What makes scholarship feminist?

Our examination of feminist research has also illuminated the system that structures academic scholarship: the disciplines. By examining feminist research in several fields at once, we have learned something about the relations of the disciplines to one another and the resilience of their power to organize knowledge. Much feminist commentary has taken a defiant stance with respect to the disciplines, insisting on the need to reject their prevailing frameworks and envisioning women's studies as an interdisciplinary field in its own right. Our study has put us in a position to investigate what this call to transcend the disciplines has meant and to ponder the situation of feminist research as it has emerged within and without the disciplines. At the end of this examination of feminist scholarship, therefore, we can make some observations about the way the disciplines function to organize knowledge and to assess the complexities of this particular interdisciplinary effort. The body of scholarship we have been examining in this book can be characterized as both feminist and interdisciplinary. Yet what these claims mean can only be determined as the field develops and grows, and our evaluation of them, even after a decade and a half, necessarily must reflect a field in progress.

The Concept of Feminist Scholarship

Throughout this book we have approached the field of feminist scholarship by examining the kind of research it includes. Now it is time to look at some of the complexities involved in drawing boundaries around the field and the problems involved in defining the feminist ideas at its core. Several factors combine to hinder a precise determination of its boundaries: the varieties of feminism, both political and intellectual; the changing context of scholarship on the subject of women; and the differences among disciplines even as to what is considered to be "about women." These obstacles suggest that it may be futile to define feminist scholarship by patroling its borders or specifying its center. Rather, what gives the field coherence is the relation of the parts to the whole and its link to the more general feminist movement that brought it into being.

One source of problems is that the debates considered central to feminist thinking evolve and change. As one set of questions becomes less intellectually productive and stimulating, others emerge to the fore. In the early years unresolved theoretical issues centered around "reform" versus "revolution" and on the primacy of economic and political structures, as opposed to sexual and psychological ones, to account for women's subordination. More recently feminist debate has shifted its focus to the place of gender in the future we envision for women: Some feminists believe that gender differences are a pernicious product of society and ought to be eliminated; others hold that female characteristics will provide value and strength for women and society in the future. As information on women begins to accumulate, scholars apply varying analytic frameworks to that knowledge to try to make sense of women's condition and to suggest how to change it. Once scholarship on women arrives at the interpretive level, the issue is not which analytic scheme is feminist, but which feminist framework is best, which ideas have the greatest power to explain oppression, to analyze social inequality, and to envision liberation. The existence of competing feminist frameworks is extremely important—the exchange between them is how our thought grows in complexity and power—but it makes it impossible to draw exact lines between feminist and nonfeminist ideas by reference to theoretical content.

At the most we might say that all feminist analyses begin with the concepts of oppression and liberation, but even these basic ideas cannot be used rigidly to distinguish feminist from nonfeminist scholarship. The prior conduct of scholarship itself has been identified as oppressive, and the very act of accumulating knowledge on women has been extremely liberating. Once feminists had criticized the disciplines for denying or distorting information about women, much of their effort concentrated on gathering knowledge to fill the void left by the sexist practices of the disciplines. While we have seen that some of the new research on women explicitly addresses the questions of liberation and oppression, it does not all do so, and it would be counterproductive to use that as a criterion to distinguish feminist from nonfeminist work. However, although we acknowledge that some contemporary feminist scholarship simply studies women and does not explicitly explore the basic concepts of oppression and liberation, this is not to say that the mere accumulation of information on women is the point of the entire field. Over time scholarship "just on women" promises less and less if it is not synthesized and meshed with basic analytic concepts and feminist debates. Research on women becomes part of feminist scholarship by relating itself to the field as a whole and to the dialogue that it encompasses.

Finally, as we have stressed in preceding chapters, research on women must be evaluated in relation to its disciplinary context. What we learn about women through individual disciplines derives from different traditions of learning, making it hard to find common criteria to determine what counts as feminist scholarship across various fields. It is our conclusion that feminism within the world of scholarship is best conceived as a progression of ideas proceeding from certain perspectives, rather than a precisely delimited body of material. At the heart of feminist scholarship in all fields of study is an awareness of the problem of women's oppression and of the ways in which academic inquiry has subtly subsidized it, a sense of the possibilities for liberation, and a commitment to make scholarship work on women's behalf. The critiques that ensue from such a stance act, figuratively, as stones dropped in a pool of water. The waves they produce clear space for a multiplicity of ideas and investigations about women and other relevant, new topics. Not all of the work made possible is itself explicitly feminist in character, in the sense that one can detect in any given article a critique of male bias or a contribution to the literature on oppression. But a good deal of it is congruent with those critiques and analyses and shores them up as evidence of the possibilities for new study that they have awakened. Eddying at the edges of the pool are disparate works about women that have relatively little in common with those central, pathbreaking critiques, but in the context of the whole they can be seen to have a place in the world of feminist scholarship.

The Ideal of Interdisciplinary Study

Since the beginning of the feminist revival in the academy, it has been a goal of many scholars to transcend the inhibiting boundaries that divide disciplines from one another and to achieve a fuller, more integrated approach to the study of women. The pioneer journals that fostered the growth of research on women saw their role, in part, as providing a forum for exchange of ideas from many fields and analytical perspectives. For some time, it was a commonplace that research on women would eventually coalesce into an interdisciplinary field. But more recently feminist scholars have begun to consider the complexities of doing interdisciplinary research and to debate the virtues of integrating work from many disciplines versus conceiving of women's studies as a discipline in itself. As of now, there is no generally accepted understanding of what interdisciplinary research means in women's studies. In our discussion we have, at different points, used the terms "multidisciplinary," "interdisciplinary," and "transdisciplinary" to emphasize different aspects of the effort to integrate scholarship from many fields.[1]

Whatever shape the field of feminist scholarship eventually assumes, it will have been fed from many different disciplines. This book has demonstrated the many points at which research on women from various academic areas overlaps and converges. It also has shown the limitations on disciplinary integration and suggests that the traditional disciplines will continue

1. *Theories of Women's Studies*, ed. Gloria Bowles and Renate Duelli Klein (London: Routledge and Kegan Paul, 1983). See particularly, Gloria Bowles, "Is Women's Studies an Academic Discipline?," 32–45, and Sandra Coyner, "Women's Studies as an Academic Discipline: Why and How to Do It," 46–71.

to play an important role in shaping research on women in the future. Like the preceding discussion of the feminist character of this scholarship, our discussions about the possibilities for interdisciplinary study on women must be provisional, but they also suggest the shape that frameworks for work on women are likely to exhibit for some time.

Let us start with an appreciation for the factors that have enhanced the ability of feminist scholarship to achieve so much toward becoming an interdisciplinary field. Perhaps first and foremost, the connection to the women's liberation movement has provided a foundation for shared perspectives and ideas. From the very beginning the analytic concepts of oppression and liberation have been especially important as organizing principles for the feminist scholar. These are, of course, fundamentally political ideas, imported into the academy from the feminist movement, and they contribute a dimension of intellectual coherence to feminist studies not available to all interdisciplinary efforts. While fields like American or urban studies, for example, amalgamate scholarship from several disciplines around a set of shared topics, it is not just the subject of women that unifies feminist scholarship. Rather, the politics of modern feminism provides women's studies with an additional way to bring together diverse scholarship into a unified endeavor.

Second, many of the central works of feminist scholarship draw from methods of inquiry that do not fit into any one of the standard academic compartments but have flourished outside of the contemporary American university. These perspectives include Marxism, psychoanalysis, and most recently structuralism. While these are all intellectual traditions that precede feminism, have been marked by a decided male bias, and were subject to feminist critiques very much like those directed at the academic traditions, they have contributed to the interdisciplinary character of feminist scholarship because they themselves draw on research from many academic fields: Marxism from history, economics, and political theory; psychoanalysis from psychology, literature, and philosophy; structuralism from linguistics, anthropology, literature, and philosophy. Work by such widely known feminists as Juliet Mitchell, Gayle Rubin, Dorothy Dinnerstein, and Rayna Rapp, to name but a few, draws from one or more of these multidisciplinary intellectual traditions.

Within more standard academic fields certain disciplinary boundaries have proved particularly permeable, as combined research perspectives have generated new ideas and insights. For instance, studies of the social and cultural milieu of nineteenth-century British and American middle-class women have drawn so evenly on the perspectives of history and literature that it makes sense to talk about one body of scholarship spanning both fields. The same may be said of research on the effects of modernization on women in the Third World, because it integrates concepts and methods of economics, anthropology, political science, sociology, and education to the point that an individual researcher's disciplinary orientation is not always immediately apparent. Still, it is worth observing that not all disciplines have proved equally amenable to merger, and feminist scholarship is also notable for likely disciplines that have remained apart, such as history and philosophy. In fact, interdisciplinary trends are striking precisely because so much feminist scholarship retains a strongly disciplinary character. This fact directs our attention to the shape the disciplines impose on scholarship and how deep their continuing imprint is.

Often, especially with respect to a subject like women, the differences between disciplines appear to be those of research focus: literature studies writings by and about women, history investigates women of the past, anthropology studies women in other cultures, and so on. This view would suggest that different disciplines provide information on particular sectors of women's existence that can be brought together into a whole. It is as if knowledge about women were a jigsaw puzzle and the different disciplines were the pieces that would fit together into a complete picture, if only we persevere in their arrangement. The jigsaw model neglects the fact that the deepest distinctions among disciplines are not topical but methodological, which is why the research that comes from them may be both disparate and incommensurable. We have found there is no one picture, no single integration of the disciplines to be discovered in the realities of women's lives. In the writing of this book, for example, an organization employing topics that appear to follow aspects of women's reality, like work, daily life, family, and so forth, did not permit the full incorporation of even our five fields. Far from being exhaustive, such topics import an inevitable analytical construction that in this case consistently underrepresents the contributions of some fields, such as philosophy and literature, and overrepresents others, notably the social sciences.

Our efforts to integrate the research on women from many different fields has not only come up against impervious methodological barriers; it has also demonstrated how much feminists continue to learn from the varieties of traditional discourse. In short, the disciplines are not solely nefarious boundary builders that prevent us from seeing the unitary condition of women. They afford different ways of knowing, and it is this that makes their integration so difficult and their power to shape scholarship so strong.

From the start and to the present, feminist scholars have exhibited a profound conflict over the attitude they adopt toward the disciplines. At one extreme there is the urge to reject them altogether as hopelessly male-biased, establishing in their stead a body of knowledge specific to women and unified by that fact. On the other hand, there is the recognition that knowledge cannot develop without research tools, that one cannot usefully start from scratch to develop new research on women, and that we have all been trained in particular disciplines. There is the desire to be incorporated into the curriculum of the disciplines, as well as the fear of being compromised, absorbed, and diluted. We ourselves have confronted and struggled with this conflict in the writing of this book, alternating between stressing interdisciplinary research on women, movement thinking, and disciplinary work.

To a degree, these conflicts are the product of the real difficulties of embarking on a new scholarly venture, but we are convinced that just as important is the fact that feminist scholarly perspectives are still by and large unwelcome in the academy and in the traditional disciplines especially. As we have seen, sexist bias continues to find a place in the university and even adapts to the mushrooming research on women. This has serious consequences for feminist scholars both in women's studies programs and traditional departments. One still hears complaints that the study of women is not "solid" or important, and feminists still lose their positions for this reason. Therefore, while on an intellectual level feminists must ask, "Where and in what context is our work best conducted?" on a practical level they also confront the question, "Where can we work at all?"

But the answer—"to work where we can"—is only in part practical. Throughout the development of feminist research, questions about the institutional solution to sexism in the academy have persisted. Gloria Bowles and Renata Duelli-Klein contend that "the crucial debate which will shape the development of women's studies throughout the 1980s" will be between the autonomy of women's studies versus its integration into the disciplines.[2] The perspective we have developed throughout this book suggests that there

2. Bowles and Klein, "Introduction: Theories of Women's Studies and the Autonomy/ Integration Debate," ibid., 1.

cannot be an either/or answer to this question. The intellectual tasks of feminist scholarship require us to work both inside traditional disciplines and independent of them. Feminist scholarship has generated a body of knowledge that is rigorous and provocative; it suggests ways of thinking and imagining that promise a new understanding of the world. The entirety has a coherence that cannot be forced into existing disciplinary frameworks. From the beginning, it has required independent sites for development—journals, conferences, and departments—to continue. At the same time feminist scholarship continues to respond to the imperative that knowledge for and about women must not be made into a special interest. This book began with an investigation of the ways in which the disciplines were distorted by what they did not know about women; it ended with a study of the disciplines' minimal response, to date, about all that we have learned about women. The impulse to transform the disciplines is as important to feminist scholarship as its independent development as a field, and this is the most challenging of the goals of integration.

Thus while no longer in its infancy, feminist scholarship continues to consider to what extent one can or even must employ the methods of distinct disciplines to further our understanding of women and to what extent the study of women can be independent of these traditional approaches. Significantly, these questions parallel a continuing tension within the women's movement: How does one preserve feminism's political independence and integrity and yet expand its political base and pragmatic impact? The close links between scholarly feminism and the activist movement make this parallel inevitable and appropriate.

Selected Bibliography

This bibliography is a preliminary guide to the vast literature generated by feminism in recent years, not a comprehensive listing of the many articles, books, and monographs that have appeared. Thousands of works have been published that not only criticize academic inquiry and its assumptions and biases but that also create a new literature on women's lives and on the social systems that shape them. For more than a decade there have been journals devoted exclusively to disseminating this new scholarship—*Signs*, *Feminist Studies*, *Women's Studies*, *International Journal of Women's Studies*, and *Frontiers*, to name a few. Long-established disciplinary journals have begun to publish special issues focusing on feminist-inspired research, and several regularly publish such material. Hundreds of books have seen their way into print as well. A comprehensive guide to this literature is an important task that must be undertaken elsewhere.

Our goals in compiling this bibliography are more modest. We have selected materials that provide: (1) a sampling of key works in feminist studies, regardless of their disciplinary orientation; (2) a representative selection of works in the disciplines covered in this book that critique and challenge male-centered scholarship; and (3) an extensive coverage of review articles on feminist scholarship within the disciplines as well as on topics that have received multidisciplinary treatment.

These references were chosen from surveys of the literature in the disciplines covered in this book, searches through major disciplinary journals and bibliographies in these fields, surveys of feminist studies journals and books, and searches through bibliographic sources like *Women's Studies Abstracts*.

Acker, Sandra. "Feminist Perspectives on the British Sociology of Education." Paper presented at British Sociological Association, Annual Conference, Lancaster, Apr. 8, 1980.

————, et al. *World Yearbook of Education: Women and Education.* New York: Kogan, Page, 1984.

Addelson, Kathryn Pyne. "Words and Lives." *Signs* 7 (1981), 187–99.

Agonito, Rosemary, ed. *History of Ideas on Women.* New York: Putnam, 1977.

Agre, Gene P., and Barbara Finklestein. "Feminism and School Reform: The Last Fifteen Years." *Teachers' College Record* 80 (1978), 307–15.

Albin, Rochelle Sernmel. "Psychological Studies of Rape." *Signs* 3 (1977), 423–35.

Aldrich, Michele L. "Women in Science." *Signs* 4 (1978), 126–35.

Alexander, Karl, and Bruce K. Eckland. "Sex Differences in the Educational Attainment Process." *American Sociology Review* 39 (1974), 668–82.

Almquist, Elizabeth. "Women in the Labor Force." *Signs* 2 (1977), 843–55.

Alper, T. G. "Achievement Motivation in College Women: A Now-You-See-It-Now-You-Don't Phenomenon." *American Psychologist* 29 (1974), 194–203.

Angress, Ruth K. "German Studies: The Woman's Perspective." In Walter F. W. Lohnes and Valters Nollendorf, eds. *German Studies in the United States: Assessment and Outlook*, Monatshefte Occasional, Vol. 1, Madison: University of Wisconsin Press, 1976.

Angrist, Shirley S. "An Overview." *Signs* 1 (1975), 175–83.

Aptheker, Bettina. *Women's Legacy: Essays on Race, Sex, and Class in American History.* Amherst: University of Massachusetts Press, 1982.

Ardener, Shirley, ed. *Perceiving Women.* London: Malaby, 1975.

Armitage, Susan. "Western Women's History: A Review Essay." *Frontiers* 5 (1980), 71–73.

Arthur, Marylin B. "Classics." *Signs* 2 (1976), 382–403.

Atkinson, Jane Monnig. "Anthropology." *Signs* 8 (1982), 236–58.

Auerbach, Nina. *Communities of Women: An Idea in Fiction.* Cambridge, Mass.: Harvard University Press, 1979.

Baker, Robert, and Frederick Elliston, eds. *Philosophy and Sex.* Buffalo: Prometheus Books, 1975.

Baker, Susan W. "Biological Influence on Human Sex and Gender." *Signs* 6 (1980), 80–96.

Ballou, Patricia K. "Bibliographies for Research on Women." *Signs* 3 (1977), 436–50.

Banner, Lois W. "On Writing Women's History." *Journal of Interdisciplinary History* 2 (1971), 347–58.

Barber, Elinor G. "Some International Perspectives on Sex Differences in Education." *Signs* 4 (1979), 584–92.

Barrett, Carol J. "Review Essay: Women in Widowhood." *Signs* 2 (1977), 856–68.

Barroso, Carmen. "Psychology, Development and Women—Do They Have Anything in Common?" *Women's Studies International Forum* 4 (1981), 163–68.

Beard, Mary. *Woman as Force in History: A Study in Tradition and Realities.* New York: Macmillan, 1946.

Berkin, Carol, and Mary Beth Norton. *Women of America: A History.* Boston: Houghton Mifflin, 1979.

Bird, Elizabeth, et al. *Half the Sky: An Introduction to Women's Studies.* London: Virago, 1979.

Birdsall, Nancy. "Women and Population Studies." *Signs* 1 (1976), 699–712.

Bishop, Sharon, and Marjorie Weinzweig, eds. *Philosophy and Women.* Belmont, Calif.: Wadsworth, 1979.

Blanchard, Lydia. "Women and Fiction: The Limits of Criticism." *Studies in the Novel* 9 (1977), 339–54.

Blaska, Betty. "College Women's Career and Marriage Aspirations: A Review of the Literature." *Journal of College Student Personnel* 19 (1978), 302–5.

Blau, Francine D. "On the Role of Values in Feminist Scholarship." *Signs* 6 (1981), 538–40.

———, and Carol L. Jusenius. "Economists' Approaches to Sex Segregation in the Labor Market: An Appraisal." *Signs* 1 (1976), 181–99.

Bleek, Catherine, et al. *Feminist Literary Criticism: A Symposium.* San Jose, Calif.: Diotima Press, 1974.

Boals, Kay. "Political Science." *Signs* 1 (1975), 161–74.

Booth, Wayne C. "Freedom of Interpretation: Bakhtin and the Challenge of Feminist Criticism." *Critical Inquiry* 9 (1982), 45–76.

Boring, P. Z. *Sex Role Stereotyping in the Schools.* Washington, D.C.: National Education Association, 1973.

Boserup, Ester. *Women's Role in Economic Development.* New York: St. Martin's Press, 1970.

Bowles, Gloria, and Renate Duelli Klein, eds. *Theories of Women's Studies.* London: Routledge and Kegan Paul, 1983.

Boxer, Marilyn J. "For and about Women: The Theory and Practice of Women's Studies in the United States." *Signs* 7 (1982), 661–97.

Branca, Patricia. "Women's History: Comments on Yesterday, Today and Tomorrow." *Journal of Social History* 11 (1978), 575–79.

Breines, Wini, Margaret Cerullo, and Judith Stacey. "Social Biology, Family Studies and Anti-Feminist Backlash." *Feminist Studies* 4 (1978), 43–68.

———, and Linda Gordon. "The New Scholarship on Family Violence." *Signs* 8 (1983), 490–531.

Bridenthal, Renate, and Claudia Koonz, eds. *Becoming Visible: Women in European History.* Boston: Houghton Mifflin, 1977.

Broverman, Inge K., et al. "Sex Role Stereotypes: A Current Appraisal." *Journal of Social Issues* 28 (1972), 59–78.

Brown, Linda K. "Women and Business Management." *Signs* 5 (1979), 266–87.

Brugh, Anne E., and Benjamin R. Beede. "American Librarianship." *Signs* 1 (1976), 943–56.

Caplan, Ann Patricia. "Indian Women: Model and Reality. A Review of Recent Books, 1975–1979." *Women's Studies International Quarterly* 2 (1978), 461–80.

Carroll, Berenice A. "Political Science Part I: American Politics and Political Behavior." *Signs* 5 (1979), 289–306.

———. "Political Science Part II: International Politics, Comparative Politics, and Feminist Radicals." *Signs* 5 (1980), 449–58.

———, ed. *Liberating Women's History: Theoretical and Critical Essays*. Urbana: University of Illinois Press, 1976.

Chapman, Jane Roberts. "Economics." *Signs* (1975), 139–46.

Chaukin, Wendy. "Occupational Hazards to Reproduction: A Review Essay and Annotated Bibliography." *Feminist Studies* 5 (1979), 310–25.

Chodorow, Nancy. *The Reproduction of Mothering*. Berkeley: University of California Press, 1978.

Christian, Barbara. *Black Women Novelists: The Development of a Tradition, 1892–1976*. Westport, Conn.: Greenwood Press, 1980.

Cott, Nancy F. *The Bonds of Womanhood: "Woman's Sphere" in New England, 1780–1835*. New Haven: Yale University Press, 1977.

———, and Elizabeth H. Pleck, eds. *A Heritage of Her Own: Toward A New Social History of American Women*. New York: Simon and Schuster, 1979.

Crocker, Phyllis L. "Annotated Bibliography of Sexual Harassment in Education," *Women's Rights Law Reporter* 7 (1982), 91–106.

Cruikshank, Margaret, ed. *Lesbian Studies*. Old Westbury: Feminist Press, 1982.

Cunningham, Stuart. "Some Problems of Feminist Literary Criticism." *Journal of Women's Studies in Literature* 1 (1979), 159–78.

Dale, Roger, et al. *Education and the State: Politics, Patriarchy and Practice*. Lewes, England: Falmer, 1981.

David, Miriam E. *The State, the Family and Education*. London: Routledge and Kegan Paul, 1980.

Davis, Natalie. "Women's History in Transition: The European Case." *Feminist Studies* 3 (1976), 83–103.

Deckard, Barbara S. *The Women's Movement: Political, Socioeconomic and Psychological Issues*. New York: Harper and Row, 1975.

Degler, Carl. *At Odds: Women and the Family in America from the Revolution to the Present*. New York: Oxford University Press, 1980.

Depner, Charlene E., and Virginia E. O'Leary. "Understanding Female Careerism: Fear of Success and New Directions." *Sex Roles* 2 (1976), 259–68.

De Rios, Marlene Dobkin. "Why Women Don't Hunt: An Anthropologist Looks at the Origin of the Sexual Division of Labor in Society." *Women's Studies* 5 (1978), 241–47.

Deseran, Forrest A., and William W. Falk. "Women as Generalized Other and Self-Theory: A Strategy for Empirical Research." *Sex Roles* (1982), 283–98.

Dinnerstein, Dorothy. *The Mermaid and the Minotaur.* New York: Harper and Row, 1976.

Dodge, Norton T. "Women in Economic Development: A Review Essay." *International Review of Education* 19 (1973), 161–66.

Donovan, Josephine. "Feminism and Aesthetics." *Critical Inquiry* 3 (1977), 605–8.

_____, ed. *Feminist Literary Criticism: Explorations in Theory.* Lexington: University of Kentucky Press, 1975.

Driver, Anne. "Religion." *Signs* 2 (1976), 434–42.

DuBois, Ellen, "Beyond the Victorian Syndrome: Feminist Interpretations of the History of Sexuality." *Radical America* 16 (1982), 149–54.

_____, et al. "Politics and Culture in Women's History: A Symposium." *Feminist Studies* 6 (1980), 26–64.

Eichler, Margrit. *The Double Standard: A Feminist Critique of Feminist Social Science.* London: Croom Helm, 1980.

_____. "Sociology of Feminist Research in Canada." *Signs* 3 (1977); 409–22.

Ellmann, Mary. *Thinking about Women.* New York: Harcourt, Brace, Jovanovich, 1968.

English, Jane. "Philosophy." *Signs* 3 (1978), 823–31.

_____, ed. *Sex Equality.* Englewood Cliffs, N.J.: Prentice-Hall, 1977.

Evans, Mary. "In Praise of Theory: The Case for Women's Studies." *Feminist Review* 10 (1982), 61–74.

_____. "Women's Studies Research in the United States: A Review and Discussion." *Women's Studies International Quarterly* 4 (1981), 221–24.

Faderman, Lillian. *Surpassing the Love of Men: Romantic Friendship and Love between Women from the Renaissance to the Present.* New York: Morrow, 1981.

Farwell, Marilyn R. "Adrienne Rich and an Organic Feminist Criticism." *College English* 39 (1977), 191–203.

_____, and Michael Wallace. "The History and Politics of Birth Control: A Review Essay." *Feminist Studies* 5 (1979), 201–15.

Ferber, Marianne A. "Women and Work: Issues of the 1980's." *Signs* 8 (1982), 273–95.

Fetterley, Judith. *The Resisting Reader: A Feminist Approach to American Fiction.* Bloomington: Indiana University Press, 1978.

Finn, Jeremy D. "Sex Differences in Educational Outcomes: A Cross-National Study." *Sex Roles* 6 (1980), 9–26.

———, Loretta Dulberg, and Janet Reis. "Sex Differences in Educational Attainment." *Harvard Educational Review* 49 (1979), 477–503.

———, Janet Reis, and Loretta Dulberg. "Sex Differences in Educational Attainment: The Process." *Comparative Education Review* 24 (1980), S33–S52.

Fitzpatrick, M. Louise. "Nursing." *Signs* 2 (1977), 818–34.

Flexner, Eleanor. *Century of Struggle: The Women's Rights Movement in the United States.* Cambridge, Mass.: The Belknap Press, 1959.

Frazier, Nancy, and Myra Sadker. *Sexism in School and Society.* New York: Harper and Row, 1973.

Freedman, Estelle B. "Sexuality in Nineteenth-Century America: Behavior, Ideology, and Politics." *Reviews in American History* 10 (1982), 196–215.

Freimuth, M. J., and G. A. Hornstein. "A Critical Examination of the Concept of Gender." *Sex Roles* 8 (1982), 515–32.

Friedl, Ernestine. *Women and Men: An Anthropologist's View.* New York: Holt, Rinehart and Winston, 1975.

Frye, Marilyn. *The Politics of Reality: Essays in Feminist Theory.* Trumansburg, N.Y.: Crossing Press, 1983.

Galloway, Sue. "Women, the New Feminism: Its Periodicals." *Wilson Library Journal* (1972), 150–52.

Gardiner, Judith Kegan. "Psychoanalytic Criticism and the Female Reader." *Literature and Psychology* 26 (1978), 100–107.

Gerstenberger, Donna, and Carolyn Allen. "Women Studies / American Studies, 1970–1975." *American Quarterly* 29 (1977), 263–79.

Gilbert, Sandra M. "Life Studies, or Speech after Long Silence: Feminist Critics Today," *College English* 40 (1979), 849–63.

———, and Susan Gubar. *The Madwoman in the Attic: The Woman Writer and the Nineteenth-Century Literary Imagination.* New Haven: Yale University Press, 1979.

Gilligan, Carol. *In a Different Voice: Psychological Theory and Women's Development.* Cambridge: Harvard University Press, 1982.

———. "In a Different Voice: Women's Conception of the Self and of Morality." *Harvard Educational Review* 47 (1977), 481–517.

———. "Woman's Place in a Man's Life Cycle." *Harvard Educational Review* 49 (1979), 431–46.

Glazer, Nona, and Helen Youngelson Waehrer, eds. *Woman in a Man-Made World: A Socioeconomic Handbook*, 2nd ed. Chicago: Rand McNally, 1977.

Glazer-Malbin, Nona. "Housework." *Signs* 1 (1976), 905–22.

Gordon, Ann D., et al. *Women in American Society: An Historical Contribution.* Boston: New England Free Press, n.d.

Gordon, Linda. "A Socialist View of Women's Studies: A Reply to the Editorial." *Signs* 1 (1975), 559–66.

_____. "What Should Women's Historians Do? Politics, Social Theory and Women's History." *Marxist Perspectives* 1 (1978), 128–36.

_____. *Woman's Body, Woman's Right: A Social History of Birth Control in America*. New York: Grossman, 1976.

_____, et al. "A Review of Sexism in American Historical Writing." *Women's Studies* 1 (1972), 133–58.

Gornick, Vivian, and Barbara K. Moran, eds. *Woman in Sexist Society*. New York: Basic Books, 1971.

Gould, Carol, ed. *Beyond Domination: New Perspectives on Women and Philosophy*. Totowa, N.J.: Rowman and Allanheld, 1983.

_____, and Marx Wartofsky, eds. *Women and Philosophy: Toward a Theory of Liberation*. New York: G. P. Putnam, 1976.

Gould, Meredith. "The New Sociology." *Signs* 5 (1980), 459–67.

Grahl, Christine, et al. "Women's Studies: A Case in Point." *Feminist Studies* 1 (1972), 109–20.

Green, Rayna. "Native American Women." *Signs* 6 (1980), 248–67.

Haber, Barbara, ed. *The Woman's Annual: 1980 Year in Review*. Boston: G. K. Hall, 1981.

_____. *Women in America: A Guide to Books, 1963–1975. With an Appendix on Books Published 1976–1979*. Urbana: University of Illinois Press, 1981.

Harding, Sandra, and Merill B. Hintikka, eds. *Discovering Reality: Feminist Perspectives on Epistemology, Metaphysics, Methodology, and Philosopohy of Science*. Boston: D. Reidel, 1983.

Harris, Barbara J. "Recent Work on the History of the Family: A Review Article." *Feminist Studies* 3 (1976), 159–72.

Harrison, James B. "Men's Roles and Men's Lives." *Signs* 4 (1978), 324–36.

Hartsock, N. "The Barracks Community in Western Political Thought—Prologomena to a Feminist Critique of War and Politics." *Women's Studies International Forum* 5 (1982), 283–86.

Hayler, Barbara. "Abortion." *Signs* 5 (1979), 307–23.

Heckman, James J. "A Partial Survey of Recent Research on the Labor Supply of Women." *American Economic Review* 68 (1978), 200–207.

Hein, Hilde. "Women and Science: Fitting Men to Think about Nature." *International Journal of Women's Studies* 4 (1981), 369–77.

Hernes, Helga Maria. "Social Research on Women in Norway: Emphasis on Power, Welfare, and Change." *Women's Studies International Quarterly* 2 (1982), 4–7.

Hirsch, Marianne. "Mothers and Daughters." *Signs* 7 (1981), 200–22.

Hochschild, Arlie. "A Review of Sex-Role Research." *American Journal of Sociology* 78 (1973), 1011–29.

Hoffman, Rita M. "Language and Sex Textbooks: A Review." *Women's Studies International Quarterly* 3 (1980), 313–18.

Hollis, Patricia. "Working Women." *History* 62 (1977), 439–45.

Holzberg, Carol S. "Anthropology: The Science of Man?" *International Journal of Women's Studies* 1 (1978), 438–44.

Howe, Florence. "The New Scholarship on Women: The Extent of the Revolution." *Women's Studies Quarterly* 10 (1982), 27–29.

Hubbard, Ruth, et al., eds. *Women Look at Biology Looking at Women.* Cambridge, Mass.: Schenkman Publishing, 1979.

Huber, Joan. "Sociology." *Signs* 1 (1976), 685–98.

————, ed. *Changing Women in a Changing Society.* Chicago: University of Chicago Press, 1973.

Hughes, Helen MacGill. "Women in Academic Sociology, 1925–1975." *Sociological Focus* 8 (1975), 215–22.

Hull, Gloria P., Patricia Bell-Scott, and Barbara Smith, eds. *All the Women Are White, All the Blacks Are Men, But Some of Us Are Brave: Black Women's Studies.* Old Westbury: Feminist Press, 1982.

Huntington, Suellen. "Issues in Woman's Role in Economic Development: Critique and Alternatives." *Journal of Marriage and the Family* 37 (1975), 1001–12.

Iglitzin, Lynne B., and Ruth Ross, eds. *Women in the World: A Comparative Study.* Santa Barbara: Clio Press, 1976.

Jacobus, Mary. "Is There a Woman in This Text?" *New Literary History*, 14 (1982), 117–41.

————, ed. *Women Writing and Writing about Women.* New York: Barnes and Noble, 1979.

Jaggar, Alison M. *Feminist Politics and Human Nature.* Totowa, N.J.: Rowman and Allanheld, 1983.

————, and Paula Rothenberg Struhl. *Feminist Frameworks: Alternative Theoretical Accounts of the Relations between Women and Men.* New York: McGraw-Hill, 1978.

Jaquette, Jane S. "Political Science." *Signs* 2 (1976), 147–64.

————, ed. *Women in Politics.* New York: John Wiley and Sons, 1974.

Jay, Nancy. "Gender and Dichotomy." *Feminist Studies* 7 (1981), 38–56.

Jehlen, Myra. "Archimedes and the Paradox of Feminist Criticism." *Signs* 6 (1981), 575–601.

Juhasz, Suzanne. "The Critic as Feminist: Reflections on Women's Poetry, Feminism, and the Art of Criticism." *Women's Studies* 5 (1977), 113–27.

————. "The Feminine Mode in Literature and Criticism." *Frontiers* 2 (1977), 96.

Jusenius, Carol L. "Economics." *Signs* 2 (1976), 177–89.

Kahne, Hilda. "Economic Research on Women and Families." *Signs* 3 (1978), 652–65.

————, and Andrew I. Kohen. "Economic Perspectives on the Roles of Women in the American Economy." *Journal of Economic Literature* 13 (1975), 1249–92.

Kanter, Rosabeth Moss. *Work and Family in the United States: A Critical Review and Agenda for Research and Policy.* New York: Russell Sage, 1977.

Kaplan, Sydney J. "Literary Criticism." *Signs* 4 (1979), 514–27.

Keller, Evelyn Fox. "Feminism and Science." *Signs* 7 (1982), 589–602.

————. "Women and Science: Two Cultures or One?" *International Journal of Women's Studies* 4 (1981), 414–19.

Kelly, Gail Paradise. "Research on the Education of Women in the Third World: Problems and Perspectives." *Women's Studies International Quarterly* 1 (1978), 365–73.

————, and Carolyn M. Elliott, eds. *Women's Education in the Third World: Comparative Perspectives.* Albany: SUNY Press, 1982.

Kelly, Joan. "The Doubled Vision of Feminist Theory: A Postscript to the 'Women and Power' Conference." *Feminist Studies* 5 (1979), 216–27.

Kelly-Gadol, Joan. "The Social Relation of the Sexes: Methodological Implications of Women's History." *Signs* 1 (1976), 809–24.

Keohane, Nannerl O. "Feminist Scholarship and Human Nature." *Ethics* 93 (1982), 102–13.

Kerber, Linda K., and Jane D. Mathew, eds. *Women's America: Refocusing the Past.* New York: Oxford University Press, 1982.

Kessler-Harris, Alice. *Out to Work: A History of the Wage-Earning Women in the United States.* New York: Oxford University Press, 1982.

Kilson, Marion. "Women and African Literature." *Journal of African Studies* 4 (1977), 161–66.

Kimball, Meredith M. "Women and Science: A Critique of Biological Theories." *International Journal of Women's Studies* 4 (1981), 318–38.

Knaster, Meri. "Women in Latin America: The State of Research." *Latin American Research Review* 11 (1976), 3–74.

Kolodny, Annette. "Dancing through the Minefield: Some Observations on the Theory, Practice, and Politics of a Feminist Literary Criticism." *Feminist Studies* 6 (1980), 1–25.

————. "The Feminist as Literary Critic." *Critical Inquiry* 2 (1976), 821–32.

————. "Literary Criticism." *Signs* 2 (1976), 382–403.

————. "A Map for Rereading: Or, Gender and the Interpretation of Literary Texts." *New Literary History* 11 (1980), 451–65.

————. "Some Notes on Defining a Feminist Literary Criticism." *Critical Inquiry* 2 (1975–76), 75–92.

Kopp, C. B., ed. *Becoming Female: Perspectives on Development*. New York: Plenum, 1979.

Kramer, Cheris, et al. "Perspectives on Language and Communication." *Signs* 3 (1978), 638–51.

Krieger, Susan. "Lesbian Identity and Community: Recent Social Science Literature." *Signs* 8 (1982), 91–108.

Kuhn, Annette, and AnnMarie Wolpe, eds. *Feminism and Materialism: Women and Modes of Production*. Boston: Routledge and Kegan Paul, 1978.

Ladner, Joyce. *Tomorrow's Tomorrow: The Black Woman*. Garden City, N.Y.: Doubleday, 1972.

Lakoff, Robin. *Language and Women's Place*. New York: Harper and Row, 1975.

Lamb, Margaret. "Feminist Criticism." *The Drama Review* 63 (1974), 46–50.

Lamphere, Louise. "Review Essay: Anthropology." *Signs* 2 (1977), 612–27.

Lange, L., and L. M. G. Clark, eds. *The Sexism of Social and Political Theory*. Toronto: University of Toronto Press, 1979.

Langland, Elizabeth, and Walter Gove, eds. *A Feminist Perspective in the Academy: The Difference It Makes*. Chicago: University of Chicago Press, 1983.

Lavrin, Asuncion. "Latin American Women's History." *Latin American Research Review* 13 (1978), 314–18.

Leacock, Eleanor. "Women's Status in Egalitarian Society: Implications for Social Evolution." *Current Anthropology* 19 (1978), 247–55.

⸺, and Mona Etienne. *Women and Colonization: Anthropological Perspectives*. New York: Praeger, 1980.

Leeson, Joyce, and Judith Gray. *Women and Medicine*. London: Tavistock, 1978.

Leibowitz, Lila. *Females, Males and Families: A Biosocial Approach*. North Scituate, Mass.: Duxbury Press, 1978.

Leifer, Myra. "Pregnancy." *Signs* 5 (1980), 754–65.

Leonard, K. "Women in India: Some Recent Perspectives." *Pacific Affairs* 52 (1979), 95–107.

Lerner, Gerda. *The Majority Finds Its Past: Placing Women in History* New York: Oxford University Press, 1979.

Levy, Betty. "The Schools' Role in the Sex Stereotyping of Girls: A Feminist Review of the Literature." *Feminist Studies* 1 (1972), 5–24.

Lewin, Ellen, and Virginia Olesen. "Lateralness in Women's Work: New Views on Success." *Sex Roles* 6 (1980), 619–30.

Lewis, Diane K. "A Response to Inequality: Black Women, Racism and Sexism." *Signs* 3 (1977), 339–61.

Lipman-Blumen, Jean. "Changing Sex Roles in American Culture: Future Directions for Research." *Archives of Sexual Behavior* 4 (1976), 433–46.

Lloyd, Cynthia, ed. *Sex Discrimination and the Division of Labor*. New York: Columbia University Press, 1975.

Longres, John F., and Robert H. Bailey. "Men's Issues and Sexism: A Journal Review." *Social Work* 24 (1979), 26–32.

Lopata, Helena. "Sociology." *Signs* 2 (1976), 165–76.

Lougee, Carolyn. "Modern European History." *Signs* 2 (1977), 628–54.

Maccoby, Eleanor E., and Carolyn N. Jacklin. *The Psychology of Sex Differences.* Stanford: Stanford University Press, 1974.

McConnell-Ginet, Sally, Ruth Borker, and Nelly Furman. *Women and Language in Literature and Society.* New York: Praeger, 1980.

MacCormack, Carol P., and Marilyn Strathern, eds. *Nature, Culture and Gender.* Cambridge: Cambridge University Press, 1981.

McDowell, Deborah E. "New Directions for Black Feminist Criticism." *Black American Literature Forum* 14 (1980), 153–59.

McFeeley, Mary Drake. *Women's Work in Britain and America from the Nineties to World War I: An Annotated Bibliography.* Boston: G. K. Hall & Co., 1982.

McGaw, Judith A. "Women and the History of American Technology." *Signs* 7 (1982), 798–828.

McIntosh, Peggy. "Warning: The New Scholarship on Women May Be Hazardous to Your Ego." *Women's Studies Quarterly* 10 (1982), 29–31.

McRobbie, Angela. "The Politics of Feminist Research: Between Talking, Text and Action." *Feminist Review* 12 (1982), 46–57.

Mahowold, Mary B., ed. *Philosophy of Woman: Classical to Current Concepts.* Indianapolis: Hackett, 1978.

Mandlebaum, Dorothy R. "Women in Medicine." *Signs* 4 (1978), 136–45.

Marcus, Jane. "Art and Womanhood: From the Female Imagination to Feminine Consciousness." *Women's Studies* 5 (1977), 101–5.

————. "Storming the Toolshed," *Signs* 8 (1982), 622–40.

Marks, Elaine. "Women and Literature in France." *Signs* 3 (1978), 832–43.

Martin, J. R. "Excluding Women from the Educational Realm." *Harvard Educational Review* 52 (1982), 133–48.

Martin, Wendy, and Mary Louise Briscoe. "Women's Studies: Problems in Research." *Women's Studies* 2 (1974), 249–59.

Martin-Leff, Ann. "Women's History—Is That Real History?" *New Directions For Women* 7 (1978–79), 4.

Maxfield, Margaret W. "The Proper Study of Womankind." *International Journal of Women's Studies* 2 (1979), 593–95.

May, Elaine Tyler. "Expanding the Past: Recent Scholarship on Women in Politics and Work." *Reviews in American History* 10 (1982), 216–33.

Mayes, Sharon S. "Sociology, Women and Fiction." *International Journal of Women's Studies* 2 (1979), 203–20.

Merchant, Carolyn. *The Death of Nature: Women, Ecology and the Scientific Revolution.* San Francisco: Harper and Row, 1980.

Milkman, Ruth. "Organizing the Sexual Division of Labor: Historical Perspectives on 'Woman's Work' and the American Labor Movement." *Socialist Review* 10 (1980), 1–19.

Miller, Roberta Balstad. "Women and American History." *Women's Studies* 2 (1974), 105–13.

Millett, Kate. *Sexual Politics*. Garden City, N.Y.: Doubleday, 1970.

Millman, Marcia, and Rosabeth Moss Kanter, eds. *Another Voice: Feminist Perspectives on Social Life and Social Science*. Garden City, N.Y.: Doubleday, 1975.

Mitchell, Juliet. *Psychoanalysis and Feminism*. New York: Vintage–Random House, 1975.

————. *Woman's Estate*. New York: Pantheon, 1971.

Mohantz, Chandra Talpade. "On Difference: The Politics of Black Women's Studies." *Women's Studies International Forum* 6 (1983), 243–47.

Morgan, Robin, ed. *Sisterhood Is Powerful*. New York: Random House, 1970.

Moulton, Janice. "Philosophy." *Signs* 2 (1976), 422–33.

Narvarro, Marysa. "Research on Latin American Women." *Signs* 5 (1979), 111–20.

Nash, June, and Helen Safa. *Sex and Class in Latin America*. New York: Praeger, 1975.

————, and María Patricia Fernández-Kelly, eds. *Women, Men and the International Division of Labor*. Albany: SUNY Press, 1983.

Norton, Mary Beth. "American History." *Signs* 5 (1979), 324–37.

Ochs, Carol. *Women and Spirituality*. Totowa, N.J.: Rowman and Allanheld, 1984.

Okin, Susan Moller. *Women in Western Political Thought*. Princeton: Princeton University Press, 1979.

Olsen, T., and V. Willemsen. "Fear of Success: Fact or Artifact?" *Journal of Psychology* 98 (1978), 65–70.

Ortner, Sherry, and Harriet Whitehead. *Sexual Meanings: The Cultural Construction of Gender*. Cambridge: Cambridge University Press, 1981.

Osborne, Martha L., ed. *Women in Western Thought*. New York: Random House, 1979.

O'Sullivan, Katherine. "Feminism and Political Philosophy." *Feminist Studies* 8 (1982), 179–94.

Parker, Rosika, and Griselda Pollock. *Old Mistresses: Women, Art and Ideology* New York: Pantheon–Random House, 1982.

Parlee, Mary Brown. "Psychology." *Signs* 1 (1975), 119–38.

————. "Psychology and Women." *Signs* 5 (1979), 121–33.

Patai, Daphne. "Beyond Defensiveness: Feminist Research Strategies." *Women's Studies International Forum* 6 (1983), 177–89.

Phillips, Susan. "Sex Differences and Language." *Annual Review of Anthropology* 9 (1980), 523–44.

Pierce, Christine. "Philosophy." *Signs* 1 (1975), 487–503.

Pottker, J., and A. Fishel, eds. *Sex Bias in the Schools.* Teaneck, N.J.: Fairleigh Dickinson University Press, 1977.

Quazzaz, al-, A. "Current Status of Research on Women in the Arab World." *Middle Eastern Studies* 14 (1978), 372–80.

Quinn, Naomi. "Anthropological Studies on Women's Status." *Annual Review of Anthropology* 6 (1977), 181–222.

Rabine, Leslie. "Feminist Writers in French Romanticism." *Studies in Romanticism* 4 (1977), 491–507.

Ram, Rati. "Sex Differences in the Labor Market Outcomes of Education." *Comparative Education Review* 24 (1980), S53–S77.

Rapp, Rayna [see also Reiter, Rayna]. "Anthropology." *Signs* 4 (1979), 497–513.

_____. "Family and Class in Contemporary America: Notes toward an Understanding of Ideology." *Science and Society* 42 (1978), 278–300.

_____, Ellen Ross, and Renate Bridenthal. "Examining Family History." *Feminist Studies* 5 (1979), 174–200.

Register, Cheri. "Literary Criticism." *Signs* 6 (1980), 268–82.

_____. "In Defiance of the Evidence: Notes on Feminist Scholarship." *Women's Studies International Quarterly* 1 (1978), 215–18.

Reiter, Rayna. *Toward an Anthropology of Women.* New York: Monthly Review Press, 1975.

Reuben, Elaine. "Can a Young Girl from a Small Mining Town Find Happiness Writing Criticism for the *New York Review of Books?*" *College English* 34 (1972), 39–47.

Rich, Adrienne. *Lies, Secrets and Silence: Selected Prose, 1966–1978.* New York: Norton, 1979.

_____. *Of Women Born: Motherhood as Experience and Institution.* New York: Norton, 1976.

Richter, Linda. "The Ephemeral Female: Women in Urban Histories." *International Journal of Women's Studies* 5 (1982), 312–28.

Roberts, Helen, ed. *Doing Feminist Research.* London: Routledge and Kegan Paul, 1981.

Roberts, Joan, ed. *Beyond Intellectual Sexism: A New Woman, a New Reality.* New York: David McKay, 1976.

Robinson, Lillian S. *Sex, Class, and Culture.* Bloomington: Indiana University Press, 1978.

_____. "Treason Our Text: Feminist Challenges to the Literary Canon." *Tulsa Studies in Women's Literature* 2 (1983), 83–98.

_____. *Women and Fictions.* London: Methuen, 1985, in press.

Rogers, Susan Carol. "Woman's Place: A Critical Review of Anthropological Theory." *Comparative Studies in Society and History* 20 (1978), 123–62.

Rohrlich-Leavitt, Ruby. *Women Cross-Culturally: Change and Challenge.* The Hague: Mouton, 1975.

Rosaldo, Michelle Zimbalist. "The Use and Abuse of Anthropology: Reflections on Feminism and Cross-Cultural Understanding." *Signs* 5 (1980), 389–417.

———, and Lamphere, L. *Woman, Culture and Society.* Stanford: Stanford University Press, 1974.

Rosen, Ruth. "Sexism in History, or Writing Women's History Is a Tricky Business." *Journal of Marriage and the Family* 33 (1971), 541–44.

Rosenberg, Rosalind. *Beyond Separate Spheres: Intellectual Roots of Modern Feminism.* New Haven: Yale University Press, 1982.

Rosenthal, Peggy. "Feminist Criticism: What Difference Does It Make?" In *Women's Language and Style,* ed. Douglas Butturff and Edmund L. Epstein. Akron: L and S Books, 1978.

Ruth, Sheila. *Issues in Feminism: A First Course in Women's Studies.* Boston: Houghton Mifflin, 1980.

———. "Methodocracy, Misogyny, and Bad Faith: Sexism in the Philosophical Establishment." *Metaphilosophy* 10 (1979), 48–61.

Ryan, Mary P. "The Explosion of Family History." *Reviews in American History* 10 (1982), 181–95.

———. *Womanhood in America: From Colonial Times to the Present.* New York: New Viewpoints, 1975.

Sachs, Albie, and Joan Hoff-Wilson. *Sexism and the Law.* London: Martin Robertson, 1978.

Sacks, Karen. *Sisters and Wives: The Past and Future of Sexual Equality.* Westport, Conn.: Greenwood Press, 1979. Rpt., Urbana: University of Illinois Press, 1982.

Salili, F. "Determinants of Achievement Motivation for Women in Developing Countries." *Journal of Vocational Behavior* 14 (1979), 297–305.

Sanday, Peggy Reeves. *Female Power and Male Dominance: On the Origins of Sexual Inequality.* Cambridge: Cambridge University Press, 1981.

Sargent, Lydia, ed. *Women and Revolution.* Boston: South End Press, 1981.

Sassen, Georgia. "Success Anxiety in Women: A Constructive Interpretation of Its Source and Significance." *Harvard Educational Review* 50 (1980), 13–24.

Sayers, Janet. "Biological Determinism, Psychology and the Division of Labour by Sex." *International Journal of Women's Studies* 3 (1980), 241–60.

Scharf, Betty R. "Sexual Stratification and Social Stratification." *British Journal of Sociology* 28 (1977), 450–66.

Schlegel, Alice, ed. *Sexual Stratification: A Cross Cultural View.* New York: Columbia University Press, 1977.

Schuman, Pat, and Gay Detlefsen. "Sisterhood Is Serious: An Annotated Bibliography." *Library Journal* 96 (1971), 2587–90.

Shanley, Mary. "The History of the Family in Modern England." *Signs* 4 (1979), 740–50.

Sherman, J. A. *On the Psychology of Women: A Survey of Empirical Studies.* Springfield, Ill.: Charles C. Thomas, 1971.

Sherman, Julia A., and Evelyn Torton Beck, eds. *The Prism of Sex.* Madison: University of Wisconsin Press, 1977.

Shöpp-Shilling, Hanna-Beate. "Women's Studies, Women's Research and Women's Research Centres: Recent Developments in the U.S.A. and in the F.R.G." *Women's Studies International Quarterly* 2 (1978), 103–16.

Showalter, Elaine. *A Literature of Their Own: British Women Novelists from Brontë to Lessing.* Princeton: Princeton University Press, 1977.

_____. "Literary Criticism." *Signs* 1 (1975), 435–60.

_____. "Women in the Literary Curriculum." *College English* 32 (1971), 855–62.

Sicherman, Barbara. "American History." *Signs* 1 (1975), 461–86.

Silverstone, Rosalie. "Office Work for Women: An Historical Review." *Business History* 18 (1976), 98–110.

Simmons, John, and Leigh Alexander. "The Determinants of School Achievement in Developing Countries: A Review of the Research." *Economic Development and Cultural Change* 26 (1978), 341–57.

Simons, Margaret A. "Racism and Feminism: A Schism in the Sisterhood." *Feminist Studies* 5 (1979), 384–401.

Singh, A. M. "The Impact of Migration on Women and the Family: Research, Policy and Programme Issues in Developing Countries." *Social Action* 30 (1980), 181–200.

Smith, Barbara. "Toward a Black Feminist Criticism." *Women's Studies International Quarterly* 2 (1978), 183–94.

Smith, Dorothy. "A Peculiar Eclipsing: Women's Exclusion from Man's Culture." *Women's Studies International Quarterly* 1 (1978), 281–96.

_____. "Women's Perspective as a Radical Critique of Sociology." *Sociological Inquiry* 44 (1974), 7–13.

Smith, D. E., and S. J. David, eds. *Women Look at Psychiatry.* Vancouver: Press Gang Publishers, 1975.

Smith-Rosenberg, Carroll. "The Female World of Love and Ritual: Relations between Women in Nineteenth-Century America." *Signs* 1 (1975), 1–30.

_____. "The New Women and the New History." *Feminist Studies* 3 (1975), 185–98.

Speizer, Jeanne J. "Role Models, Mentors, and Sponsors: The Elusive Concepts." *Signs* 6 (1981), 692–712.

Spender, Dale. *Women of Ideas and What Men Have Done to Them from Aphra Behn to Adrienne Rich.* London: Routledge and Kegan Paul, 1982.

————, ed. *Men's Studies Modified: The Impact of Feminism on the Academic Disciplines.* Oxford: Pergamon Press, 1981.

Stack, Carol, et al. "Anthropology." *Signs* 1 (1975), 147–60.

Stacey, Judith, et al., eds. *And Jill Came Tumbling After.* New York: Dell, 1974.

Stanley, Julia Penelope, and Susan J. Wolfe. "Toward a Feminist Aesthetic." *Chrysalis* 6 (1978), 57–71.

Stanley, Liz, and Sue Wise. *Breaking Out: Feminist Consciousness and Feminist Research.* London: Routledge and Kegan Paul, 1983.

Steady, Filomina Chioma, ed. *The Black Woman Cross-Culturally.* Cambridge, Mass.: Schenkman, 1981.

Stein, Sondra. "Diving into the Wreck: A History of Our Own." *Feminist Studies* 4 (1978), 127–39.

Stewart, Abigail J., and Marjorie B. Platt. "Studying Women in a Changing World." *Journal of Social Issues* 38 (1982), 1–19.

Stimpson, Catharine R. "Ad/d Feminam: Women, Literature, and Society." In *Literature and Society*, ed. Edward W. Said. Baltimore: Johns Hopkins University Press, 1980.

————, and Ethel S. Person. *Women, Sex and Sexuality.* Chicago: University of Chicago Press, 1982.

Strobel, Margaret. "African Women." *Signs* 8 (1982), 109–31.

Strober, Myra H., and David Tyack. "Why Do Women Teach and Men Manage? A Report on Research on Schools." *Signs* 5 (1980), 494–503.

Tanner, Nancy Makepeace. *On Becoming Human.* Cambridge: Cambridge University Press, 1981.

Tapper, Nancy. "Mysteries of the Harem? An Anthropological Perspective on Recent Studies of Women of the Muslim Middle East." *Women's Studies International Quarterly* 2 (1978), 481–88.

Terborg-Penn, Rosalyn, and Sharon Harley, eds. *The Afro-American Woman: Struggles and Images.* Port Washington, N.Y.: Kennikat Press, 1978.

Thorne, Barrie, and Nancy Henley. *Language and Sex: Difference and Dominance.* Rowley, Mass.: Newbury House, 1975.

————, with Marilyn Yalom, ed. *Rethinking the Family: Some Feminist Questions.* New York: Longman, 1982.

Tidball, M. Elizabeth. "Of Men and Research: the Dominant Themes in American Higher Education Include Neither Teaching Nor Women." *Journal of Higher Education* 47 (1976), 373–89.

Tiffany, Sharon W. "Models and the Social Anthropology of Women: A Preliminary Assessment." *Man* 13 (1978), 34–51.

————. "Women in Cross-Cultural Perspective: A Guide to Recent Anthropological Literature." *Women's Studies International Forum* 5 (1982), 497–502.

_____. "Women, Power, and the Anthropology of Politics: A Review," *International Journal of Women's Studies* 2 (1979), 430–42.

Tilly, Louise A. "The Social Sciences and the Study of Women: A Review Article." *Comparative Studies in Society and History* 20 (1978), 163–73.

_____, and Joan W. Scott. *Women, Work and Family*. New York: Holt, Rinehart Winston, 1978.

Tobias, Sheila. "The Study of Women." *Choice* 8 (1971), 1295–1301.

_____. "Women's Studies: Its Origins, Its Organizations and Its Prospects." *Women's Studies International Quarterly* 1 (1978), 85–98.

_____, and Carol Weissbrod. "Anxiety and Mathematics: An Up-Date." *Harvard Education Review* 50 (1980), 63–70.

Tolchin, S., and M. Tolchin. *Clout: Women, Power, and Politics*. New York: Coward, McCann and Geoghegan, 1974.

Trebilcot, Joyce, ed. *Mothering: Essays in Feminist Theory*. Totowa, N.J.: Rowman and Allanheld, 1983.

Tressmer, D. "The Cumulative Record of Research on Fear of Success." *Sex Roles* 2 (1976), 217–36.

_____. *Fear of Success*. New York: Plenum Publishers, 1977.

Van Allen, Judith. "Modernization Means More Dependency," *The Center Magazine* 7 (1974), 60–67.

Vance, Carol S. "Gender Systems, Ideology, and Sex Research: An Anthropological Analysis." *Feminist Studies* 6 (1980), 129–43.

Vaughter, Reesa M. "Psychology." *Signs* 2 (1976), 120–46.

Verbrugge, Martha H. "Woman and Medicine in Nineteenth Century America." *Signs* 1 (1976), 957–72.

Vetter, Betty M. "Women in Natural Sciences." *Signs* 1 (1976), 713–20.

Vetterling-Braggin, Mary, ed. *"Femininity," "Masculinity," and Androgyny": A Modern Philosophical Discussion*. Totowa, N.J.: Rowman and Littlefield, Adams, 1982.

_____. *Sexist Language: A Modern Philosophical Analysis*. Totowa, N.J.: Littlefield, Adams, 1981.

_____, Frederick Elliston, and Jane English, eds. *Feminism and Philosophy*. Totowa, N.J.: Littlefield and Adams, 1977.

Vicinus, Martha. "Sexuality and Power: A Review of Current Work in the History of Sexuality." *Feminist Studies* 8 (1982), 133–56.

Villemez, Wayne J. "Male Economic Gain from Female Subordination: A Caveat and Reanalysis." *Social Forces* 56 (1977), 626–36.

Vogel, Lise. "Fine Arts and Feminism: The Awakening Consciousness." *Feminist Studies* 2 (1974), 3–37.

Walker, Beverly M. "Review of *Sex Roles* and *Psychology of Women Quarterly*." *Women's Studies International Forum* 4 (1981), 229–34.

Walsh, Mary Roth. *Doctors Wanted: No Women Need Apply*. New Haven: Yale University, 1977.

Warren, Mary Anne. *The Nature of Woman: An Encyclopedia and Guide to the Literature*. Pt. Reyes, Calif.: Edge Press, 1980.

Watson, Barbara Bellow. *Women's Studies: The Social Realities*. New York: Harper and Row, 1976.

Weinbaum, Batya. *The Curious Courtship of Women's Liberation and Socialism*. Boston: South End Press, 1978.

Wekerle, Gerda R. "Women in the Urban Environment." *Signs* 5 (1980), S188–S214.

Wertz, Dorothy C. "Social Science Attitudes toward Women Workers, 1870–1970." *International Journal of Women's Studies* 5 (1982), 161–71.

Westkott, Marcia. "Feminist Criticism of the Social Sciences." *Harvard Educational Review* 49 (1979), 422–30.

Whitbeck, Caroline. "Women and Medicine: An Introduction." *Journal of Medical Philosophy* 7 (1982), 119–34.

Wolff, Janet. "Women's Studies and Sociology." *Sociology* 2 (1977), 155–61.

Wood, Elizabeth. "Women in Music." *Signs* 6 (1980), 283–97.

Woodhall, Maureen. "Investment in Women: A Reappraisal of the Concept of Human Capital." *International Review of Education* 19 (1973), 9–29.

Yanagisako, Sylvia Junko. "Family and Household: The Analysis of Domestic Groups." *Annual Review of Anthropology* 8 (1979), 161–205.

Young, Kate, Carol Wolkowitz, and Roslyn McCullagh. *Of Marriage and the Market*. London: CSE Books, 1981.

Zimmerman, Bonnie. "What Has Never Been: An Overview of Lesbian Feminist Literary Criticism." *Feminist Studies* 7 (1981), 451–76.

Zinn, Maxine Baca. "Mexican-American Women in the Social Sciences." *Signs* 8 (1982), 259–72.

Index

Abortion, 8, 32, 68, 76–79, 150, 164, 170, 177
Activity of women. *See* Agency of women
Addams, Jane, 20, 55
Affirmative action, 32, 72, 132–34, 164, 170, 177, 187, 189
Africa, 24, 42, 47, 89, 137, 138, 142, 143
Agency of women, 17, 22–23, 34, 39–67, 68, 70, 86; in anthropology, 40–48, 65–66; in history, 48–58; in literature, 58–66; in educational studies, 74–75. *See also* Oppression vs. agency of women as focus of feminist scholarship
Anderson, Sherwood, 107
Androgyny, 129, 178
Anthropology, 6, 8, 16, 21–25, 36, 40–48, 58, 65–66, 67, 68, 76, 91, 92–101, 109, 115, 122, 161, 170, 178–79*n*, 179, 181–83, 185–89, 192, 195, 200
Antifeminism, 9, 127, 129
Anyon, Jean, 74
Appel, Michael, 74
Aristotle, 30

Arnot, Madeline MacDonald, 74
Auerbach, Nina, 57, 65
Austen, Jane, 58, 65, 66, 162

Bartky, Sandra, 108
Beard, Mary, 17, 49–50
Bengelsdorf, Carollee, 150–51
Benston, Margaret, 116–17
Berkshire Conference of Women Historians, 4*n*
Bernikow, Louise, 61–62
Biological determinateness, 24, 26, 27, 80, 97–100, 103, 109, 122, 127–28
Biraimah, Karen, 74
Birth control, 98, 141, 161, 163, 188
Birthing practices, 8, 42, 162
Black, Cyril, 89
Black family, 44, 51, 121–24. *See also* Black women; Race; Slavery
Black women, 44, 57, 60–61, 63–64, 74, 123–24. *See also* Black family; Race; slavery
Boserup, Ester, 137
Bowles, Gloria, 202
Bridges, Amy, 122

Estler, Suzanne, 72
Ethics, 29–30, 32, 76, 159, 170, 188,
  190–91, 193
Ethnocentrism, 24, 43, 94, 144. *See also*
  Racism
Etienne, Mona, 93
Europe, 49, 136, 140, 144, 184, 189

Faderman, Lillian, 58
Family, 15, 19–21, 41–42, 44, 46, 47,
  57, 59, 69–70, 73, 76, 109–10,
  113–24, 128–29, 136–53, 161, 163,
  178*n*, 182–83, 186, 188. *See also* Black
  family; Domesticity; Kinship; Public /
  private, distinction between
Fanon, Frantz, 89–90
Faulkner, William, 107
Femininity, 20, 55, 73, 75, 103–4,
  108–9, 113, 123, 129, 132, 161, 179
Feminist scholarship, 2–10, 195–203;
  interdisciplinary, 4–5, 10, 44, 86–87,
  99, 126, 195–96, 198–202; and the
  women's liberation movement, 5–6,
  9–10, 35, 58, 86, 89, 94, 105,
  116–19, 121, 126–27, 175, 179–80,
  184, 196, 199. *See also* Disciplines; Op-
  pression vs. agency of women as focus
  of feminist scholarship; Women's
  studies; *and particular disciplines such as*
  Anthropology; Educational studies;
  History; Literature; Philosophy
Ferguson, Ann, 119
Fetterley, Judith, 107–8
Figes, Eva, 35
Firestone, Shulamith, 35, 92, 96
Fitzgerald, F. Scott, 107
Fitzpatrick, Blanche, 130–31
Flax, Jane, 151
Flexner, Eleanor, 17
Foucault, Michel, 99*n*
Frazier, Nancy, 27, 70
Freud, Sigmund, 99. *See also*
  Psychoanalysis
Fuller, Mary, 74
Freeman, Mary Wilkins, 60
Fried, Marlene Gerber, 133
Frye, Marilyn, 112–13, 134

Gardside, Christine, 30

Gender, 24–28, 36, 46–48, 72, 92, 100,
  103, 109, 111, 128–29, 137, 143, 145,
  153, 161–64, 176, 179, 181–83,
  186–91, 192, 196. *See also* Sex-gender
  system
Genet, Jean, 90
Gibbs, Lois, 120
Gilbert, Sandra, 63
Gilligan, Carol, 69, 79*n*
Glaspell, Susan, 60
Goldman, Emma, 100*n*
Gordon, Linda, 98
Gould, Carol, C., 31
Greer, Germaine, 35, 58
Grim, Patrick, 103
Gubar, Susan, 63

Hageman, Alice, 150–51
Harding, Sandra, 111
Hawthorne, Nathaniel, 107
Heilbrun, Carolyn, 35
Hemenway, Robert, 60
Hemingway, Ernest, 107
Heterosexuality, critique of, 35, 64,
  99–100, 111–12, 162
Hines, Darlene, 50
History, 4*n*, 6, 19–21, 39, 48–58,
  66–67, 68, 76, 91, 98, 100, 101,
  109*n*, 115, 144, 162–64, 176, 181–85,
  186, 188–89, 192, 200. *See also* Social
  history
Hochschild, Arlie, 28
Homosexuality. *See* Lesbianism
Homosociality, 57–58. *See also* Lesbianism;
  Women, relations between
Hooks, Belle, 123
Horner, Matina, 27, 133
Housework. *See* Domestic labor; Work, in
  the home
Howe, Florence, 4*n*, 16
Human nature, 31, 76, 81–82, 102
Hunting and gathering societies, 22, 92–94
Hurston, Zora Neale, 60

Ideology, 15–16, 36, 41, 46–47, 67, 73,
  76, 79–83, 101–13, 122, 128. *See
  also* Inferiority of women, myth of;
  Oppression

Moers, Ellen, 62
Montgomery, Judith, H., 107
Moral reasoning, 69, 78–79, 80, 101
Morgan, Kathryn, 129
Morgan, Lewis Henry, 92
Morgan, Robin, 90
Morris, WIlliam, 190
Morton, Peggy, 117
Motherhood, 22, 32, 42, 68, 78, 90,
   97–98, 104, 109–12, 115, 119,
   124, 129, 138, 140, 143–44, 146–50,
   153, 162. See also Birthing practices;
   Reproduction
Moynihan, Daniel P., 44, 124n

Nash, June, 137
National Women's Studies Association, 5
Nature, 102–3, 104, 114, 128; vs. cul-
   ture, 46. See also Biological determinate-
   ness; Human nature
Newton, Judith, 66
Nicholson, Linda, 114

Okin, Susan Moller, 81
Olsen, Tillie, 59, 61
Oppression, 9–10, 16, 32, 36, 46, 56, 58,
   70, 76, 82, 86–125, 128, 133, 135–37,
   141, 143, 145, 162, 164, 195–99; vs.
   agency of women as focus of feminist
   scholarship, 39–40, 45, 48–49, 66–68;
   psychology of, 72–74, 89–90, 108–11;
   origins of, 87, 91–101, 110, 113, 124,
   145, 152. See also Family; Ideology; Inferiority of women, myth of; Lesbianism; Male bias; Public/private,
   distinction between; Racism; Sex-gender
   system; Women's work
Ortner, Sherry, 46, 96–97, 99

Parsons, Katherine Pyne, 79–80
Parsons, Talcott, 96, 136, 144
Patriarchy. See Oppression
Paulme, Denise, 24
Phelps, Elizabeth Stuart, 59
Philosophy, 6, 7, 8, 28–32, 36, 39,
   67–68, 75–83, 91, 100, 101–6, 111,
   113, 127, 132, 163–64, 170, 175, 178,

183, 186, 188–91, 193, 200–201. See
   also Ethics; Political theory
Pierce, Christine, 102
Political role of women, 20, 41–42, 47,
   68, 95, 120, 151–52, 189
Political science, 39, 44, 68, 200
Political theory, 32, 68, 76, 80–82, 114,
   127, 193, 200
Pornography, 32, 105
Prostitution, 138, 140, 164, 178n
Psychoanalysis, 100, 109–11, 199. See also
   Freud, Sigmund
Psychology, 6, 27, 200. See also Ideology;
   Oppression; Psychoanalysis
Public/private, distinction between, 19,
   46, 80–82, 87, 96–98, 113–24, 126,
   141, 180

Race, 24, 28, 29, 48, 62, 79, 88–89,
   145, 186–87. See also Black family;
   Black women; Racism; Slavery
Racism, 122–24. See also Slavery
Radical feminism, 87, 89, 135
Rape, 32, 76, 90, 105, 164, 178n
Rationality, 30, 31n, 80, 101–2, 111
Rapp, Rayna, 24, 95, 122, 200
Reiter, Rayna. See Rapp, Rayna
Reproduction, 20, 34, 43, 45, 80–81,
   92, 96–100, 110, 112, 113–16, 128,
   138, 143, 145, 149, 153, 163. See also
   Birth control; Motherhood
Rich, Adrienne, 90, 111–12
Rogers, Barbara, 141
Rohrlich-Leavitt, Ruby, 24–25, 93–95
Roosevelt, Eleanor, 20
Rosaldo, Michelle Zimbalist, 95–99,
   110, 145
Ross, Ellen, 21
Rubin, Gayle, 91, 98–100, 145, 200
Rubin, Lillian, 122

Sacks, Karen, 93–94, 97
Sadker, Myra, 27, 70
Safa, Helen, 137
Sanday, Peggy, 96
Schmidt, Dolores Barracano, 107
Schmink, Marianne, 139

A Note on the Authors

ELLEN CAROL DUBOIS is an associate professor of history and American studies at the State University of New York–Buffalo and the coordinator of women's studies there. She is the author of *Feminism and Suffrage: The Emergence of an Independent Women's Movement in America 1848–1869* (1978), and the editor of *Elizabeth Cady Stanton, Susan B. Anthony: Correspondence, Writings, Speeches* (1981).

GAIL PARADISE KELLY is a professor in the faculty of educational studies at the State University of New York–Buffalo. She is coauthor of *Women's Education in the Third World: Comparative Perspectives* (1982), *Comparative Education* (1982), and *Colonialism and Education* (1978).

ELIZABETH LAPOVSKY KENNEDY is an associate professor of American studies/women's studies at the State University of New York–Buffalo. She has a doctorate in anthropology from Cambridge University. She is currently completing, with Madeline Davis, *Survival and Resistance: The History of a Lesbian Community*.

CAROLYN W. KORSMEYER is associate professor of philosophy at the State University of New York–Buffalo. In addition to her interest in feminist theory, she has written extensively in the field of aesthetics.

LILLIAN S. ROBINSON, whose background is in English and comparative literature, is an affiliated scholar at the Stanford University Center for Research on Women and currently holds a chair as visiting professor of humanities at Albright College in Reading, Pennsylvania. She is the author of *Sex, Class and Culture* (1978) and *Monstrous Regiment: The Lady Knight in Sixteenth Century Epic* (1985). As a poet, she was the 1983 D. H. Lawrence Fellow in Creative Writing and has won the Pablo Neruda Poetry prize.